# THE WELSH CRIMINAL JUSTICE SYSTEM

# THE WELSH CRIMINAL JUSTICE SYSTEM
## ON THE JAGGED EDGE

*Robert Jones and Richard Wyn Jones*

UNIVERSITY OF WALES PRESS
2022

© Robert Jones and Richard Wyn Jones, 2022

Reprinted 2022

All rights reserved. No part of this book may be reproduced in any material form (including photocopying or storing it in any medium by electronic means and whether or not transiently or incidentally to some other use of this publication) without the written permission of the copyright owner except in accordance with the provisions of the Copyright, Designs and Patents Act 1988. Applications for the copyright owner's written permission to reproduce any part of this publication should be addressed to the University of Wales Press, University Registry, King Edward VII Avenue, Cardiff CF10 3NS

*www.uwp.co.uk*

*British Library Cataloguing-in-Publication Data*

A catalogue record for this book is available from the British Library.

ISBN 978-1-78683-943-5
e-ISBN 978-1-78683-944-2

The rights of Robert Jones and Richard Wyn Jones to be identified as authors of this work have been asserted in accordance with sections 77 and 79 of the Copyright, Designs and Patents Act 1988.

Typeset by Chris Bell, cbdesign
Printed by CPI Antony Rowe, Melksham

*Er cof am ddau Daid a dwy Nain*
*Iris a Bob Jones, Trefnant*
*ac*
*Alice a Thomas Lloyd Hughes, Betws yn Rhos*

Power does not always corrupt... But what power always does is reveal.
*Robert Caro (2019: 206)*


Responsibility without power is the most dangerous of all situations for a political party with progressive pretensions.
*Aneurin Bevan (1952: 26)*

# CONTENTS

List of figures, tables and maps ... ix

Acknowledgements ... xi

**Chapter 1** Introduction: a Welsh criminal justice system? ... 1

**Chapter 2** Outcomes in the Welsh criminal justice system ... 19

**Chapter 3** Whitehall and the Welsh criminal justice system: what power reveals ... 55

**Chapter 4** The Welsh Government and criminal justice: responsibility without power ... 83

**Chapter 5** On policy-making and policy taking: two case studies ... 115

**Chapter 6** Scrutiny and accountability across the jagged edge ... 141

**Chapter 7** The future of the Welsh criminal justice system ... 167

Appendix: list of research participants ... 189

Notes ... 191

Bibliography ... 211

Index ... 281

# LIST OF FIGURES, TABLES AND MAPS

FIGURES

| | | |
|---|---|---|
| Figure 2.1 | The rate of police recorded crime (excluding fraud) in England and Wales per 1,000 population, 2015 to 2019 | 23 |
| Figure 2.2 | The number of police officers per 100,000 people in England and Wales, 2010 to 2020 | 27 |
| Figure 2.3 | The number of police community support officers (PCSOs) per 100,000 people in England and Wales, 2010 to 2020 | 28 |
| Figure 2.4 | Arrest rate per 1,000 population in England and Wales, 2015/16 to 2019/20 | 29 |
| Figure 2.5 | Conviction rates in England and Wales, 2013 to 2019 (%) | 31 |
| Figure 2.6 | Immediate custodial sentences handed out at courts in Wales and the average Welsh prison population (based on home address), 2013 to 2019 | 33 |
| Figure 2.7 | Average prison population rate per 100,000 in western Europe, 1999 to 2018 | 34 |
| Figure 2.8 | Prison population rates per 100,000 in England and Wales using home address, 2013 to 2019 | 35 |
| Figure 2.9 | Rates of imprisonment and probation supervision per 10,000 people by ethnic group in Wales in 2019 | 36 |
| Figure 2.10 | The use of community sentences in Wales, 2010 to 2019 | 42 |

| | | |
|---|---|---|
| Figure 2.11 | Probation rates per 100,000 in England and Wales, 2014 to 2019 | 43 |
| Figure 2.12 | Imprisonment rate per 100,000 women in prison in England and Wales (based on home address prior to entering custody), 2013 to 2019 | 45 |
| Figure 2.13 | Children (under 18s) in custody per 100,000 children in England and Wales (based on region of youth offending team), 2002 to 2020 | 49 |
| Figure 2.14 | Rate of assaults by children on children at young offender institutions in England and Wales per 100, 2017 to 2019 | 50 |

## TABLES

| | | |
|---|---|---|
| Table 2.1 | Proportion of adults and children who were victims of crime and anti-social behaviour, year ending March 2020 (%) | 24 |
| Table 2.2 | The percentage of cases where a person was charged or summonsed by police forces in Wales by offence group, 2017 to 2020 (%) | 26 |
| Table 2.3 | The prison estate in Wales, 2019 | 37 |
| Table 3.1 | Departments, agencies and public bodies (reserved) with responsibility for criminal justice in Wales, 2020 | 59 |
| Table 4.1 | The location of criminal justice functions in the Welsh Government, 2021 | 98 |
| Table 6.1 | Senedd committee reports on inquiries with criminal justice-relevant focus (fifth Senedd only) | 154 |

## MAPS

| | | |
|---|---|---|
| Map 2.1 | Crown and magistrates' courts in Wales, 2010 to 2019 | 31 |
| Map 2.2 | The prison estate in England and Wales | 39 |
| Map 2.3 | Youth offending team areas in Wales and the secure estate | 51 |

# ACKNOWLEDGEMENTS

This book could not have been written without the support of others, and we are delighted – and not a little relieved – to finally be in a position to thank those who have helped us along the way.

First and foremost, we owe a debt of gratitude to our interviewees who gave so freely of their time and insights. While they must remain anonymous, they will know who they are! Thank you one and all. We are also grateful to the Economic and Social Research Council and Welsh Government who jointly funded the 'Justice and Jurisdiction' project in Cardiff University's Wales Governance Centre between September 2018 and November 2020. It was this award (ES/S008454/1) that allowed Rob to undertake the research that underpins much of this book. We are similarly grateful to all of those involved in the work of the Commission on Justice in Wales, and in particular its chair, (Lord) John Thomas, for the opportunity to input our preliminary findings into their deliberations. Their stimulus and – on occasion – challenge was important in forcing us to dig deeper for evidence as well as clarify our own thinking. We remain confident that their report will ultimately be regarded as a key inflection point in the modern history of Wales. It certainly deserves to be.

Our colleagues in the Wales Governance Centre provided essential support throughout. Guto Ifan's pathbreaking research into the funding arrangements for the Welsh criminal justice system was not only a vital resource but an inspiration. We were also fortunate in being able to conduct joint research with Luke Nicholas and Huw Pritchard which has fed into this book. More generally Huw has provided a vital sounding board over many years, with his own pioneering work in the field (Pritchard 2016) opening many doors for this project. The sage advice of Lucy Hammond and Dan Wincott helped us navigate more than one bureaucracy, while the consistent interest and enthusiasm of Richard Caddell, Nye Davies and Jac Larner helped sustain us through the most intensive writing period. Rachel Minto was kind enough to arrange an informal seminar based on part of the book which, helpfully, forced the pace in terms of putting words on pages. During that seminar Laura McAllister made a number of very useful suggestions which we were then able to follow up and include in subsequent drafts. Cian Siôn generously gave much of his time and expertise to produce the tables and figures that play such a central role in Chapter 2. More latterly, Greg Davies (now at Liverpool University), Adam Evans (now at the Houses of Parliament), Emyr Lewis (now at Aberystwyth) and Hugh Rawlings (an honorary professor at Cardiff attached to the Centre) all provided detailed comments on the penultimate draft of the book. We are particularly grateful to our friend and colleague Ed Gareth Poole, who was ready to devote more of his time than we could have reasonably expected in order to cast his careful eye over the text. Finally, Lucy Hammond (again) provided invaluable assistance with the cover. We are fortunate indeed to have been able to rely on such an outstandingly able and collegiate group. *Diolch o galon!*

Also owed a debt of gratitude are the following friends and colleagues who have all assisted in various ways as we have developed the arguments set out here: Alan Cogbill, Jonathan Evans, Chris Harding, Michael Harrison, Trevor Jones, Dusty Kennedy, Michael Levi, Iolo Madoc-Jones, Paul Morris, Sarah Nason, Richard Rawlings and Cerith Thomas. A special mention to another Cardiff colleague, Kirsty Hudson, who was involved in countless conversations with the two of us about criminal justice in Wales, long before we thought there might be a book in it. Her influence permeates the following pages.

We are deeply conscious of how fortunate we are in being able to work with and rely upon such an engaged and supportive community of collaborators. This makes it even more important than usual to stress that none of them is to be blamed for any mistakes or mis-steps that remain. They are solely our responsibility.

The University of Wales Press remains one of the jewels in the crown of scholarship in Wales. We are grateful for the professionalism, patience and

# ACKNOWLEDGEMENTS

support provided by its staff and, in particular, Adam Burns, Dafydd Jones, Llion Wigley and Elin Williams.

Finally on a more personal note, we would like to thank the following: Luke Jamieson, Dave Jones, Sue Jones, Eirig Wyn Jones, Owain Wyn Jones, Siôn Parry, Gail Peek, Kenneth Radcliffe, Sarah Richards, Kevin Rush and Eli Stamnes. Not all have taken an interest in the book; indeed, some may have given the impression that they were actively disinterested in it! Yet it would not have been completed without their support. The book is dedicated to the memory of two sets of much missed grandparents. *Ehed amser, erys cof.*

# 1
## INTRODUCTION
## A Welsh criminal justice system?

WE ARE LONG familiar with the idea that Welsh politics or Welsh sport represent distinctive spheres with their own institutional structures and characteristics. Over the last two decades of devolution, we have become accustomed to the existence of a Welsh National Health Service and school curriculum. While the jury may still be out on the extent to which it is conceptually accurate, let alone useful, discussion of the Welsh economy is also commonplace. It remains the case, however, that talk of a Welsh criminal justice system retains a very unfamiliar ring.

To be clear, no one could or would seek to deny that criminal justice institutions exist *in* Wales. In our own cases, we recall all too well the impact of childhood visits to the sites of our local pre-modern jails – Ruthin and Beaumaris, respectively – and the gruesome fascination of the exhibitions on display. Meanwhile, it is hard to imagine that anyone brought up in Cardiff, Swansea or their immediate environs will be unaware of the brooding presence of their Victorian city-centre prisons. For better or worse, they have for several generations formed an indelible, unavoidable part of their urban landscapes. Moreover, even if very few now retain their original purpose, court buildings remain a (usually notable) feature of the architectural heritage of smaller towns right across the country. The same is true (including the history of wholesale closures) of police stations as well.

The point at issue, rather, is the extent to which there is anything distinctively Welsh about the systems and practices given physical manifestation in contemporary versions of these buildings, be it prisons, courts, police stations or probation offices. Anything, that is, beyond their geographical location. As far as the twentieth-century history of Wales is concerned, the answer to that question was a relatively simple one. No, there was not.[1] Wales was part, and a relatively peripheral part at that, of a single England and Wales criminal justice system. Any Welsh distinctiveness was confined to limited adaptation to the fact that a (decreasing) proportion of the country's population remained culturally distinct from what was clearly an English norm. For example, Welsh-language Bibles in witness boxes and flexibility (usually informal) from court officers when faced with the functionally monoglot. From the 1960s onwards, following sustained pressure from language activists, including civil disobedience, this gradually morphed into a more positive attitude towards the Welsh language.[2] Nonetheless, these adjustments aside, it was fundamentally the same criminal justice system from Holyhead to Harwich and from Milford Haven to Middlesbrough. In such a context, to posit the existence of a distinctive contemporary Welsh criminal justice system would have seemed merely fanciful, in both academic and popular discourse alike.

The academic discipline of criminology is now a well-established presence in most Welsh universities, and criminologists based in Wales have made internationally significant contributions to it. Fiona Brookman, Martina Feilzer, Katy Holloway, Roy King, Michael Levi, Michael Maguire and Peter Raynor are only some of the most obvious names with which to conjure in this regard. The operation of criminal justice institutions in Wales has often provided vital data for criminological research for academics based in Wales or, indeed, elsewhere. But it is almost invariably the case that 'England and Wales' has provided the largely taken-for-granted systemic context for both research and teaching in the various departments and research institutes concerned (exceptions are highlighted elsewhere in this book). Largely because it was assumed that there was no distinctive Welsh criminal justice space to analyse and explain.

That was then. The central contention of this book is things have now changed. As an unintentional if unavoidable consequence of the devolution process, it no longer makes sense to think of an undifferentiated England and Wales system. Rather we now see emerging within what is still, formally, a single England and Wales legal jurisdiction, a distinct – cf. separate – Welsh criminal justice system. In the pages that follow, we will seek, for the first time in an academic context, to map, explore and explain this system. We argue that the unplanned and haphazard nature of its emergence – 'unintentional if unavoidable' – in large part explains its key characteristics, namely its byzantine complexity and lack of political accountability. These characteristics, we further argue, make it very difficult to see how the system as it is currently organised can hope to ameliorate, let alone successfully transform, the very poor outcomes that also characterise Wales's distinct criminal justice system. Which is precisely why we conclude our discussion with a consideration of possible futures for this system; in particular in the wake of the publication of the report of the Commission on Justice in Wales – the Thomas Commission – in October 2019 (Thomas Commission 2019).

But before we can proceed to describe the structure of the book and set out its key arguments in more detail, it is first necessary to embark on a brief constitutional excursus. This because it is impossible to understand what makes Wales's criminal justice system distinct without first understanding the particular and highly anomalous form that devolution has taken in Wales. As this is something to which we will return time and again and, indeed, shapes the entire discussion, clarifying at the outset the sheer oddity (in comparative constitutional terms) of the governmental structures that underpin the Welsh criminal justice system is a prerequisite for all that follows.

## WELSH DEVOLUTION AS CONSTITUTIONAL EXPERIMENTATION

It is almost certainly no exaggeration to say that the United Kingdom (UK) has more experience of implanting and nurturing systems of government across the globe than any other state in history. The extraordinary resilience and influence of the 'Westminster model' of government has been much commented upon (see, inter alia, de Smith 1961; Lijphart 1984, 1999; Mackintosh 1970; Rhodes et al. 2009; for a useful critical overview Russell and Serban 2021). These accounts vary as to its essential characteristics, not least because examples would now seem to come in all shapes and sizes.[3] But one of the most fundamental features – so fundamental that it is often overlooked – is particularly pertinent when we consider the case of Wales.

That is that the 'Westminster model' system of government is built on a triumvirate of institutional branches that are all intimately interlinked yet remain separate; an executive, a legislature and a judiciary. This *trias politica* provide the fundamental constitutional building blocks. Indeed, given that Montesquieu was effectively generalising on the basis of the English case when he developed his doctrine of the separation of powers, it is plausible to argue that this most fundamental characteristic of the Westminster model has become the institutional yardstick by which all modern constitutional polities are measured (Montesquieu [1748] (1989): 156–66).

It is not only new states that Westminster has created in its own image on the basis of this tripartite division between legislature, executive and judiciary. The same is currently true of devolved Northern Ireland and Scotland where devolved legislatures and executives operate within separate Scottish and Northern Irish legal jurisdictions and justice systems.[4] This was previously the case in Northern Ireland between 1921 and 1972. It remains true for the various Crown Dependencies that circulate within the UK's wider orbit. It is also true for the sub-state levels of government that exist within a significant number of independent 'Westminster family' states, be they formally federal or not. In short, at both state or sub-state levels, Westminster model polities are constructed as a 'three-legged stool', where executive, legislature and judiciary combine to support the political system as a whole.

Considered against this background, since the establishment of what is now the Senedd or Welsh Parliament in 1999, Welsh devolution can be conceived of as a series of constitutional experiments that have attempted to diverge from – or, more pejoratively, offend against – the fundamentals of this form of government.[5]

The initial devolution settlement was highly unorthodox both in terms of the powers and the structure of devolved government. As our primary concern here is with the latter, we need not linger long over the former, except to note that the then National Assembly for Wales was initially endowed with executive powers drawn from a whole host of different Acts of the Parliament dating back all the way to 1841 (see The National Assembly for Wales (Transfer of Functions) Order 1999). None of this legislation had been drafted envisaging a situation in which the executive powers they created would ever be wielded outside the Whitehall system of collective cabinet responsibility, let alone by a Welsh legislature enjoying its own democratic mandate seeking to pursue a distinctive policy agenda. Yet with no primary law-making powers, the Assembly was confined to passing secondary legislation which fell within this labyrinthine and incoherent web of competencies.

It's hard to think of any historical precedent for this form of government. Hard also not to conclude that the lack of precedent should have served as a warning that there were very good reasons to avoid this convoluted and largely ineffectual form of devolved empowerment. Eighteen years later, with the enactment of the Wales Act 2017 and following a tortuous journey featuring other (failed) experiments in constitutional design, Welsh devolution was finally constituted as a reserved powers model of legislative devolution (for an overview of the rise and fall of the original model of devolution see, respectively, Wyn Jones and Scully 2012: 26–56 and Rawlings 2018). In comparative terms, Wales had taken a long detour only to arrive at a decidedly orthodox arrangement for devolved empowerment.

As with powers so with structure. Welsh devolution was initially constructed as a one-legged stool. Every undergraduate student of devolution will be aware that, for the first eight years of its existence, there existed no formal separation between the executive and the legislature in the National Assembly. It was rather constituted as a single 'body corporate' with a cabinet grafted onto it. A misshapen piece of constitutional architecture that soon proved unworkable to the extent that devolved politicians were forced to try to mark out a de facto division of powers between the legislature and what we now know as the Welsh Government. This division was formalised by way of the Government of Wales Act 2006. Since that legislation came into full force and effect in 2007, in terms of both their structures and internal practices, the Welsh Government and Senedd – again – look much more like orthodox 'Westminster model' institutions (cf. Mitchell 2010). The legacy of this initial period, however, lives on in the confusion about roles and responsibilities, which remains such a depressingly common feature of public discourse in and about Wales.

Yet even after cleaving to the 'Westminster model' in terms of the organisation of and relationship between legislature and executive, in constitutional terms Welsh devolution remains – in essence – a two-legged stool. That is because there is no juridical equivalent of the devolved Welsh executive and legislature. Rather, as we have already noted, Wales remains part of the single England and Wales legal jurisdiction with justice functions specifically reserved to Westminster and Whitehall.[6] Not only that, but Westminster and Whitehall control of these functions is jealously guarded by an approach to legislative drafting that moves well beyond the 'belt and braces' to the positively constrictive.[7]

The Wales Act 2017, which created a reserved powers model of devolution, was not (as many had hoped) a comprehensive, consolidated piece of legislation, but rather proceeded by way of amending the Government of Wales Act 2006, largely through inserting new sections and schedules. Justice and jurisdiction-related reservations on the legislative competence of the Senedd are set out in a new Schedule 7A of the 2006 Act. The Schedule sets out those matters 'in relation to' which the Senedd may not legislate, by reason of a new section 108A(2)(c) (with certain exceptions). This formulation ('in relation to') has a far greater impact in terms of limiting legislative competence, because of the extensive and detailed list of reservations, than it has in the corresponding provision in the Scotland Act 1998.[8] In addition, a new section 110A of the 2006 Act requires that any new Welsh legislation be accompanied by a 'justice impact assessment', explaining its impact on the 'justice system in England and Wales'. It goes without saying that there is no reciprocal requirement for the UK Parliament, acting in its 'England and Wales' guise, to provide an assessment of the impact of any legislative changes that it makes on devolved services in Wales. Little wonder, therefore, that this provision has been described as 'petty' and 'squarely at odds with the proper constitutional acceptance of internal institutional autonomy' (Rawlings 2018: 68).

In recent years academic commentators on politics and public policy in Scotland have tended to adopt terminology familiar to the study of federal polities distinguishing between 'self-rule' and 'shared rule' (Elazar 1987). Self-rule refers to the extent that a given sub-state body is able to act autonomously in implementing policies, passing laws, allocating funding, and so on; shared rule to the extent that sub-state level can influence the policies being pursued by the central state itself. Transposing this typology to the current context, the provisions introduced by the Wales Act 2017 suggest that the UK Government does not regard control over the justice system in Wales as being 'shared' with Wales's devolved institutions. Rather, at least at the formal, constitutional level, the Home Office and the Ministry of Justice, the bodies responsible for policing and justice in Wales, treat these functions as – in essence – *theirs*. Any intrusion by Wales's devolved institutions is to be carefully corralled and controlled.

At which point, with Welsh devolution constituted as a two-legged stool, and with the UK Government apparently strongly committed to keeping Wales within a single England and Wales legal and justice system that it controls, readers may be forgiven for concluding that all talk of an actually existing Welsh criminal justice system remains fanciful. In the field of justice is it still not a case of 'for Wales, see England' or, more diplomatically, 'for Wales, see 'England and Wales'? The short answer is no. This is because of the way in which criminal justice functions reserved to Westminster and Whitehall inevitably intersect and interact with – indeed, rely on – services and functions that are controlled by Wales's devolved institutions. Thus creating a wider criminal justice system that spans both reserved (non-devolved) and devolved competencies and responsibilities.

## JUSTICE AND THE 'JAGGED EDGE'

As we have seen, the legislation that underpins the current Welsh devolution dispensation makes clear that criminal justice functions are reserved to Westminster and Whitehall. Not only metaphorically speaking, the 'keep out' signs proliferate; and where Welsh devolved incursion is unavoidable, it is permitted only along clearly demarcated (and closely monitored) footpaths. Nonetheless, the criminal justice system in Wales is distinct. This reflects the fact that those institutions responsible for criminal justice simply *cannot* operate in isolation from broader frameworks and institutions of social policy, which in Wales are now almost all devolved.[9] In other words, the wider criminal justice system in Wales includes not only the prison, police, youth justice and probation services as well as the judiciary and courts services (all non-devolved), but also encompasses mental health and drug rehabilitation services, housing, social services, and the education system.[10] The latter are not only the responsibility of Wales' devolved institutions but also, to an ever-increasing degree, operate differently from those found in England. This means that in post-devolution Wales, even absent a separate justice system, those charged with responsibility for conceiving and operationalising criminal justice policy are almost invariably operating across the line between devolved and reserved responsibilities.

'Line' is, moreover, a misnomer. Rather, as will be illustrated in much more detail in the chapters that follow, the division between reserved and devolved functions in the area of criminal justice is far from straightforward or easily delineated.[11] It is rather a policy space best characterised as being constituted across a 'jagged edge' of intersecting competences and responsibilities shared between two governments with different political priorities and accountable through different electoral mandates.[12] All of which serves to make the criminal justice system in Wales different. Different from Scotland and Northern Ireland where devolved executives and legislatures align with separate legal jurisdictions and justice systems. But also different from England where UK Government and Westminster control over England and Wales criminal justice institutions aligns with their de facto roles as England's executive and legislature. By contrast, whereas in England, Scotland and Northern Ireland (constitutional) competences and responsibilities align across the wider criminal justice system, it is precisely a *lack of alignment* that defines the situation in Wales.

Given the degree of inter-dependence between the justice system and the wider realm of public policy, even whilst core criminal justice institutions continue as England and Wales bodies, the past two decades has witnessed substantial institutional adaptation in the criminal justice system in Wales. This reflects the fact that both sides of the constitutional divide have strong incentives to find ways of working together across the jagged edge of devolved and non-devolved competences. The resulting institutional web – in effect, a system of de facto and incomplete administrative devolution – will be mapped in Chapters 3 and 4, and the experience of those working within it illustrated in Chapter 5. But before proceeding, it is important to note the obvious potential problems that arise when choosing to defy usual 'Westminster family' practice by replacing the third leg of the *trias politica* with what might well be regarded as the constitutional equivalent of a piece of balsa wood.

In 1998, writing in anticipation of the establishment of the National Assembly for Wales, the doyen of Welsh constitutional law, Professor Richard Rawlings, published a far-sighted and indeed prophetic critique of the then UK Government's plans for 'The New Model Wales' (Rawlings 1998).[13] His essay sounded a cautionary note against those who at the time had sought to make a virtue of the 'innovative' (cf. experimental) nature of the first Welsh devolution dispensation.[14] Whilst others foresaw a new kind of constitutional arrangement underpinning a new kind of politics – 'new politics' was very much in vogue – Rawlings warned that the price of ignoring basic constitutional principles in the construction of Wales's devolved institutions would likely be confusion and frustration. In particular, the following coda has continued to resonate: 'Insufficient attention has been paid to constitutional values in the design of the architecture ... with not enough weight given to the constitutional demand for separation of powers' (Rawlings 1998: 509). Whether or not the author would recognise it as such, his was – in effect – a Burkean call to respect the wisdom of past constitutional knowledge. It did not take long for Rawlings to be completely vindicated. As has already been noted, in very short order the limitations of the one-legged stool model of devolution had become clearly apparent and the source of considerable exasperation. As a result, broad cross-party agreement was secured to carve out a more orthodox division between executive and the legislature; albeit de facto in the first instance. A process that would subsequently be mapped in Rawlings's 2003 magnum opus, *Delineating Wales*.

The continuation of the England and Wales legal system was the assumed context for Rawlings's 1998 analysis, while the wider justice system featured not at all. This is entirely unsurprising given that, at the time, even a move to fully fledged legislative devolution appeared a relatively distant prospect. Nonetheless, the *method* that is deployed to such devastating effect in Rawlings's essay remains applicable. It is therefore worth considering the 'in principle' problems that might arise from the unique way in which the Welsh criminal justice system is structured, and in particular the way that normal Westminster-family rules for constitutional construction do not apply. Not least because doing so provides a yardstick for measuring the success (or otherwise) of the web of institutions that has emerged, largely haphazardly, to span the jagged edge of reserved and devolved control.

There are three obvious potential problems arising from the failure to follow the normal Westminster model of organisation with regards the Welsh criminal justice system. The first are the costs – not only financial but also the wider opportunity costs – likely to arise from the additional complexities that will inevitably characterise a criminal justice system organised in this highly unorthodox way. Secondly is the ability of such a system to deliver 'joined-up' policy solutions when neither level of government has control over all of the policy levers necessary to effect change;

this in a policy area notorious for its often seemingly intractable difficulties. Thirdly and relatedly, is the accountability of a system in which responsibility is divided between different levels elected on very different bases (UK vs Wales) and even electoral systems. There are therefore good 'in principle' reasons to be concerned about the extent to which the constitutional underpinnings of Wales's distinct criminal justice system allows it to deliver a cost-efficient, effective and properly accountable service to the country's citizens.

The 2004 report of the Richard Commission provided a devastating indictment of the original model of devolution and was a key moment in the transition to a more orthodox separation between Wales's devolved legislature and executive, and – less directly – to full-fledged legislative devolution (Richard Commission 2004; Wyn Jones and Scully 2012: 42–53; also, McAllister 2005). Even if the names of the institutions concerned have changed, the commissioners' vision for a mature Welsh democracy retains the character of a pole star: a guiding light in what has proven to be consistently turbulent constitutional weather.

> The Assembly is the democratically representative body for the whole of Wales. The Welsh Assembly Government should be able to formulate policies within clearly defined fields, and should have the power to implement all the stages for delivery, in partnership with the UK Government and other stakeholders. The Assembly Government should be able to set its own priorities and timetables for action. It should be accountable to the people of Wales for its policies and their implementation. (Richard Commission 2004: 241)

It is probably fair to say that this vision overstates the degree of constitutional neatness obtainable in any multi-level system. Nonetheless, the continued survival of a single England and Wales legal jurisdiction, as well as the jagged edge of competences and responsibilities that defines the Welsh criminal justice system, means that, even after the advent of legislative devolution, Wales continues to fall far short of the Richard Commission's ideal. As far as its various responsibilities in the area of justice are concerned, the Welsh Government is clearly not in a position to formulate and implement policies across all stages of delivery. Decisions by the UK Government acting in its England and Wales guise in the context of the criminal justice system can also serve to undermine the ability of the Welsh Government to implement effective policy, even in areas of clear devolved competence (as will be illustrated in more detail below). But in addition, even if it is clearly the 'dominant partner' in both the jurisdiction and in justice policy, to the extent that it is seriously interested in addressing the problems of the criminal justice system in Wales, then the UK Government is similarly unable to formulate and implement policies across all stages of delivery because it cannot act independently of Welsh devolved institutions.[15] As a result of which, neither is accountability a straightforward issue in this field for either the UK or Welsh parliaments.

Yet the question remains: what, if anything, do these various anomalies mean in practice? It is one thing to point to 'in principle' deviations from what is usually considered good – indeed, normal – constitutional practice. We may even aver that there are almost certainly good reasons for this practice having developed and having been reproduced so widely. But the extent to which the Welsh justice system's divergence from the constitutional norms of the Westminster model causes actual difficulties 'on the ground' is an important question meriting empirical investigation. We should not simply assume, a priori, that any problems resulting from the Welsh system's divergence from orthodoxy are serious, let alone insurmountable. After all, and as will be discussed in the final chapter, the UK Government, as well as many Welsh Labour MPs, remain strongly committed to the continuation of the status quo, arguing that Wales benefits substantially from the four and a half centuries of accumulated experience embodied in the England and Wales legal and justice systems (see Bryant 2020; Evans 2020; Jones 2013; cf. Lewis 2019). Nor, until very recently, has the Welsh Government disagreed with this view (e.g. Welsh Government 2008a).

We have already noted the way that Rawlings's 1998 critique of the model of devolution embodied in the same year's Government of Wales Act proved almost eerily prescient. Almost as soon as the National Assembly for Wales began meeting, the deficiencies of Wales's new devolved constitution became so obvious as to become impossible to ignore. By contrast, it is only very recently that the potential problems of the post-devolution criminal justice system in Wales have been the subject of wider political or public debate. One possible explanation of this state of affairs could be that, whatever constitutional purists might want to argue, the current system works pretty well. In the best traditions of the British civil service, those involved in the operation of the criminal justice system in Wales have found a way to 'muddle through'. But of course, there are alternative explanations.

It is certainly plausible to argue that the constitutional churn that has characterised Welsh devolution since 1999, as a result of the failure of the original, experimental dispensation, has meant that there has been little capacity to engage with the possibility of devolving further large areas of policy. Even if this were not the case, it may be that the intractable and politically toxic nature of the public policy challenges that characterise criminal justice would in any case have served to suppress the appetite for change: 'OK, this might well be an anomaly, but do we really want or need *this* responsibility?' Meanwhile, the lack of attention to Wales as a unit of analysis in the academic discipline of criminology has meant that the kind of external voices that might otherwise have started a debate have been more or less silent (Jones 2017). So perhaps the criminal justice system in Wales has been made to function smoothly despite the constitutional anomaly that it undoubtedly represents? Or perhaps it has not, but that has been occluded by other factors that mean that it is only now that this matter is beginning to receive serious attention? In what follows we endeavour to provide an empirical basis that will allow judgement to be rendered.

## METHODOLOGY AND DATA

This book draws on several different sources in addition to the usual range of extant academic work and official reports. First, we draw on previous research conducted by one of the present authors, Robert Jones. Rob's doctoral research into imprisonment in and for Wales was based on multiple interviews with the family members of prisoners, staff in various agencies involved in resettlement services focused on prisoners in or from Wales, and with former prisoners themselves (Jones 2017). All of this has provided invaluable background for the present study. In addition, Rob has continued with the practice that he began during his doctoral studies by rooting out disaggregated official data to better understand criminal justice outcomes in Wales (much of which has now been published in Jones 2018a, 2018b, 2019a, 2019b, 2020a, 2020b). Given the Ministry of Justice's (continuing) reluctance to publish Welsh-only data itself, these efforts have had to rely heavily on Freedom of Information requests. We will return to these data at various points below.

Secondly, this book adds to this already wide base of research by drawing on twenty-nine in-depth interviews that were conducted especially for it. The interviewees are all individuals who play various leadership roles across the criminal justice and social policy landscape in Wales (see Appendix). Interviews were conducted between June and December 2018 and were organised on a semi-structured basis; the latter allowing us to develop our understanding iteratively throughout the various conversations rather than attempting to follow some pre-ordained path. In addition, one focus group discussion was conducted for this study and is also drawn upon below. It included five participants involved in the scrutiny of policing and other criminal justice institutions within Wales. Given the political sensitivities involved as well as the sector's dependence on partnership and joint working, all of these data were collected on the basis of anonymity. Thus, following what has been described as the 'ubiquitous' practice in the field, all interviewees are referred to by pseudonyms (Lahman et al. 2015: 445). Furthermore, we have lightly edited their comments so as to remove any identifying features that might allow interviewees to be recognised by other means.

Thirdly, the Commission on Justice in Wales – the Thomas Commission – was another centrally important source of data and information. In part this is because the commission's establishment prompted our colleagues and ourselves in Cardiff University's Wales Governance Centre to produce five reports into the workings of the justice system (Ifan 2019a, 2019b, 2019c; Jones et al. 2019; Jones and Wyn Jones 2019), all of which were submitted as evidence to the commission. We draw heavily on these analyses in the following pages but, in particular, this book can be seen as a substantial elaboration of the arguments first sketched in our March 2019 report, *Justice at the Jagged Edge in Wales* (Jones and Wyn Jones 2019).

In addition to prompting work in the Governance Centre, the commission's call for evidence elicited a wide range of responses from various other stakeholders, amounting to almost two hundred written submissions. The commission also arranged over forty oral evidence sessions. Together this forms a veritable treasure trove: the most comprehensive insight into the workings of the justice system in Wales ever assembled.[16] Given that the conventional academic literature is scant in its coverage of Wales, we have been fortunate indeed to be able to draw on this resource as well as the commission's own analysis whilst producing this study.

Since this book has been written during an unprecedented global pandemic, our data collection stops at an enforced if logical break point at the outset of the March 2020 lockdown. It will be for future research to investigate the impact of the pandemic (in the interim see Criminal Justice Joint Inspection 2021a; House of Commons Justice Committee 2020a, 2020b; Jones 2020a). That said, whatever the other longer-term consequences of the pandemic, because we argue that the conditions and constraints that define the Welsh criminal justice system are fundamentally structural in nature, they will undoubtedly re-emerge as the system moves on from fire-fighting the immediate challenges posed by COVID-19.

## ORGANISATION

This book is organised into seven chapters. Following on from this introduction, Chapter 2 – 'Outcomes in the Welsh criminal justice system' – starkly illuminates what emerges when Wales is taken seriously as unit of analysis, namely a series of strikingly poor outcomes. On many key measures the Welsh criminal justice system performs even worse than that of England, a country with a well-deserved reputation as among the worst performers in western Europe.

Chapters 3 and 4 are inter-linked and together map the Welsh criminal justice system. They do so by focusing in turn on either side of the jagged edge of competencies and responsibilities that we argue not only runs through but defines it. As its title suggests, 'Whitehall and the Welsh criminal justice system: what power reveals', Chapter 3 focuses on the senior partner in the system. Drawing on Robert Caro's dictum cited in the frontispiece – 'what power *always* does is reveal' – we discuss what Whitehall's stewardship of the Welsh criminal justice system reveals not only about the wider 'England and Wales' justice system but also about its attitudes to Wales. It is a story of UK Government ministries and a flanking network of highly centralised England and Wales institutions in which almost all policy-making capacity is based in London. Adaptation to the reality of Welsh devolution – even institutional recognition of Wales's very existence

– is minimal. Where adaptations have been made to try to bridge to the devolved level, we find that the best efforts of the staff involved are undermined by another structural characteristic of criminal justice policy at the England and Wales level, namely a tendency to almost constant upheaval and churn to bolster the performative claims of successive UK governments.

The succeeding Chapter 4 ('The Welsh Government and criminal justice: responsibility without power') focuses on the role of the devolved level in the operation of the Welsh criminal justice system. It shows how the Welsh Government's responsibilities extend right into the heart of prisons, the courts and the probation system, with the devolved responsibilities – and funding commitments – particularly extensive in relation to policing. These functions are additional to the more obvious (and extensive) role played by Welsh Government in buttressing criminal justice institutions through its responsibilities for housing, health and social services, education, and so forth. The chapter also begins to explore the difficulties that the Welsh Government experiences when seeking to carry out these responsibilities, and in particular the ways that the current arrangements for the Welsh criminal justice system serve to undermine its attempts at coherent, evidence-based policy-making. Aneurin Bevan's warning of the danger of responsibility without power also cited in the frontispiece could hardly be more apposite.

Chapter 5 is entitled 'On policy-making and policy taking: two case studies'. Here we explore the operation of the Welsh criminal justice system through the prism of two case studies. The first of these focuses on housing provision for those being released from prisons, while the second shifts its attention to the apparently arcane question of how Wales's police forces are funded. Between them, the case studies illustrate the ways in which two of the three 'in principle' problems that we identified as being the likely result of the constitutional underpinnings of the Welsh criminal justice system serve to shape the daily experience of those charged with operating it. For these men and women, the opportunity costs incurred as a result of additional complexity generated by the current arrangements, as well as the formidable barriers to joined-up policy-making that they represent, are a source of deep and abiding frustration.

Similarly, Chapter 6, 'Scrutiny and accountability across the jagged edge', shows how the 'in principle' obstacles to scrutiny and accountability across the constitutional jagged edge of intersecting competences and responsibilities shape the lived reality of the Welsh criminal justice system. Despite the very poor outcomes detailed in Chapter 2, and the resulting suffering and hardship experienced by individuals, families and communities, the very structure of that system precludes serious scrutiny or accountability at either the England-and-Wales or devolved Welsh levels.

Having drawn on multiple different sources to illustrate and explore the current operation of the Welsh criminal justice system, our concluding chapter looks to the future. We first interrogate the arguments put forward by those who would see the current constitutional arrangements maintained. Following from this, we discuss the increasing calls for full devolution, in particular the recent policy stance adopted by the Welsh Government and the recommendations of the Thomas Commission. Finally, we consider how the academic field of criminology and wider civil society might contribute to the development of a different kind of Welsh criminal justice system: one that is better at protecting the most vulnerable members of society, more effective and more humane.

\* \* \*

Until only a few years ago, to the very limited extent that there was any discussion about the future of the justice system in Wales, it was as a by-product of a debate about whether or not a Welsh legal jurisdiction was required for Wales to arrive at a sustainable devolution *settlement* that was truly worthy of that name (see, inter alia, Jones 2008; Jones and Williams 2004; National Assembly for Wales Constitutional and Legislative Affairs Committee 2012; Silk Commission 2014; Percival 2017; Pritchard 2019; Rawlings 2018, 2019; Wales Office 2013; Wales Governance Centre and Constitution Unit 2015, 2016; Welsh Government 2012a, 2016a).[17] The *possibility* of a Welsh jurisdiction loomed far larger than the *reality* of a Welsh criminal justice system that was already distinct from that of England as a result of the establishment and continued development after 1999 of democratic devolution. Political, public and academic discourse alike all appear to have struggled to even register the existence of the latter.

Since the passage of the Wales Act 2017, however, this prioritisation would seem to have shifted, and to have done so decisively. This shift is symbolised by the Thomas Commission's decision to treat the question of establishing a Welsh legal jurisdiction as a means to an end: with that end being improving the operation and performance of the justice system in Wales. Relatedly, there is a growing realisation that, even though justice remains a formally reserved matter to the UK level, it (and especially the criminal justice system) nonetheless operates differently in Wales. In Cardiff, at least, political representatives now appear to be increasingly willing to ask searching questions about the operation of this system across the jagged edge of devolved and non-devolved competences (for recent examples see Hutt 2019; Welsh Government 2018a; 2022a). As a result, establishing a Welsh jurisdiction is now increasingly regarded as a necessary by-product of – rather than a precursor to – the devolution of some or all of the wider justice system.

But even as political awareness and debate has evolved, academia continues to lag behind. Notwithstanding the work of scholars in youth justice (Deering and Evans 2021; Field 2015; Haines 2009; Haines and Case 2015; Thomas 2015a) and, most recently, Roxanna Dehaghani and Daniel Newman (2021) in 'bringing in Wales into discussions of England and Wales', this book represents the first systematic exploration of the operation of Welsh criminal justice system in the unique context of Wales's post-devolution constitutional arrangements. Even if it does no more than inspire others to continue with that exploration, we will be more than satisfied. In inviting others to continue with this work it should be stressed that we do not claim that this book represents the final word on the Welsh criminal justice system as it has evolved over the past decades. Quite the opposite: it is a starting point. But in providing an overview of the extant sources as well as some of the conceptual vocabulary necessary to make sense of the terrain, it should – we hope – provide at least a few signposts across what remains, in scholarly terms, *terra incognita*.

That said, perhaps optimistically, our ambitions extend beyond the academy. This is also a book aimed at those policy makers responsible for the Welsh criminal justice system and for everyone interested in the future of the country. Our belief is that any serious assessment of the structural problems and contradictions that are inherent in the Welsh criminal justice system as currently ordered – as well, of course, as their resulting pathologies – renders the case for serious reform irrefutable. It also underlines the fact that in this case, serious reform means far-reaching *constitutional* change: namely the devolution of the justice system as a whole.

There is no doubt a considerable irony here. For while any call for the full devolution of the Welsh criminal justice system may appear radical to some, in the context of the Westminster model of government it is merely the restatement of the most elemental basic principle: it is nothing more or less than a demand for 'British' constitutional orthodoxy. Writing in the early 1960s about the global influence of the Westminster model, S. A. de Smith noted its grip on what we might term the constitutional imaginary of those who were otherwise struggling to rid themselves of the yoke of Empire. In somewhat condescending terms, he posited that 'The last voice to incant the slogan "British is best" [in constitutional terms] is likely to be that of a colonial nationalist on an obscure and remote island' (de Smith 1961: 2). As it transpires, that obscure and remote island is in fact the island of Britain – *ynys Prydain* – and those voices speak with a variety of Welsh accents. But as the following pages make abundantly clear, the case for constitutional reform is not based on principle alone, it is also because devolution is a necessary prerequisite for the far-reaching policy changes that are so obviously required in the Welsh criminal justice system. Until that occurs, it is individuals and communities across Wales that will continue to pay a very heavy price for the failures of the current dispensation.

# 2
# OUTCOMES IN THE WELSH CRIMINAL JUSTICE SYSTEM

WE INTRODUCED this book by remarking on just how unaccustomed we all are to considering Wales as a distinct unit in relation to the delivery of criminal justice. Although a criminal justice system clearly exists across the territory of Wales, the idea that there might be anything distinctly or distinctively Welsh about that system remains, even now, an unfamiliar one. To the extent that Wales is considered at all it is as part of a single England and Wales legal jurisdiction and justice system. But even this characterisation might be considered somewhat euphemistic; elevating the place of Wales beyond what is justifiable. In truth, even the limited recognition that is embodied in the 'and Wales' addendum is of strikingly recent pedigree.

Until 1998, successive holders of the post of Lord Chief Justice appear to have been more than content to be regarded as the Lord Chief Justice of England.[1] It was only in that year that 'and Wales' was added to the title even if the title-holder's writ had already run to Wales for four hundred years and more before that.[2] Even now, almost a quarter of a century after both that name change and the introduction of devolution, mention of the law of England and Wales rather than English law, the England and Wales rather than the English legal system, or even the England and Wales rather than English prison system, brings with it a sense of the interloper; or a modish political correctness. Under it all, the essence remains the same and – of course – essentially English.

Generations of scholars have certainly been in no doubt that they have been commenting on an 'English' prison system (McConville 1981; Playfair 1971; Zellick 1975), 'English' penal policy (Hall-Williams 1970; Rutherford 1988; Walker and Giller 1977), 'English' probation system (McWilliams 1986; Nellis 2004), 'English' parole scheme (Hood 1974), the 'English model' of sentencing (Ashworth and Roberts 2013; Cross and Ashworth 1981) and 'English' policing practices (Emsley 1991, 2007; Loader and Mulcahy 2003). Yet each of these contributions analysed a system or set of practices that extended over the territory of England and Wales. Wales was similarly absent when Phil Scraton and colleagues produced their *Prisons Under Protest*, an excoriating study of the crisis that engulfed 'English penal establishments' in 1990 – this moniker neglecting the fact that rioting also took place in a prison located in Wales's capital city (1991: ix).[3]

Indeed, scholars have regularly called 'Englishness' in aid as they have sought to understand the nature of criminal justice policy across the jurisdiction. Historical accounts of policing, for example, have repeatedly deployed the notion of 'English values' while exploring the emergence of a distinct set of policing practices. Mark Finnane (2016: 461) juxtaposes the 'sharp oppositions' between policing practices on either side of the English Channel in the early nineteenth century; differences that many regarded as reflecting a distinctly 'English resistance' to the policy reforms emerging at the time in continental Europe. Leon Radzinowicz and Roger Hood's *The Emergence of Penal Policy* traces a series of 'English reactions' that led to the rejection of positivist criminological ideas at the start of the twentieth century (1986: 3). In analysing the rejection of controversial plans unveiled in 1846 to introduce indeterminate sentencing for repeat offenders, the same authors draw on contemporaneous extracts from *The Times* to demonstrate how notions of 'Englishness' were central to the dismissal of any proposed changes to the trajectory of penal policy.

These examples are not used to single out individual authors: they were drawn from a potentially unlimited pool of cases. The common theme is simply that the taken-for-granted territorial frame for the understanding of criminal justice matters is 'England', even while the geographical extent of the actual institutions and policies being analysed encompasses both England *and* Wales. In no case does it seem that Wales was consciously excluded or slighted by the various authors we have cited. Rather, as part of a single England and Wales system, Wales was rendered quite literally invisible.[4]

Nor does it seem that appending 'and Wales' to the official designations of various criminal justice institutions has changed this situation in any meaningful way. This is undeniably true in the field of scholarship.[5] With the exception of a few relatively small-scale studies, to which we will refer throughout our subsequent discussion, there remains very little engagement with the ways in which Welsh devolution has impacted on the operation of the criminal justice system in Wales, let alone any attempt at providing a synthetic overview such as one attempted in the following pages (but for more limited treatments, see Haines 2009; Jones 2020c; Evans et al. 2021). Indeed, at the time of writing, we are aware of only one module – a Welsh-medium module taught at Aberystwyth – that focuses explicitly on the operation of the Welsh criminal justice system, this across all eight universities in Wales that currently provide undergraduate or postgraduate criminology programmes.[6] While some other academic criminologists will be incorporating Wales into their teaching, to cite the infamous 1888 *Encyclopaedia Britannica* entry, for most it is still a case of 'for Wales, see England'.

In the remainder of this book we seek to render Wales visible as a distinct space for the delivery of criminal justice; a space whose very distinctiveness is defined by the way it straddles the jagged edge between devolved and non-devolved competences and responsibilities. But before we can explore this terrain in any detail, we need first to provide a broad overview of its general contours. This is because, as we have already mentioned, it remains almost wholly unfamiliar territory, even to those otherwise deeply interested in the state of contemporary Wales.

Yet in seeking to provide only basic, top-line data, we encounter an immediate problem, namely the paucity of easily accessible data. Indeed, we might posit that one of the reasons that the operation of the Welsh criminal justice system remains so unfamiliar is that finding out about it requires substantial – even inordinate – effort, including extensive utilisation of the rights afforded to putative researchers by Freedom of Information legislation.[7] Even now, those Whitehall ministers and officials responsible for 'England and Wales' seem to be deeply resistant to the notion that it is their job to proactively assist those who would take the 'and Wales' addendum seriously.[8] While 'England' may have become 'England and Wales', here is an early indication that the previous mindset remains largely intact and undisturbed.

The structure of the remainder of this chapter delineates what might be termed the arc of criminal justice policy, from crime to arrest (hence policing) and prosecution, and then onto sentencing, imprisonment and probation. We have also included sections on women and youth justice, both of which are customarily treated separately. Throughout we seek to disaggregate Welsh from English (or English and Welsh) data to ensure that the situation in Wales itself can stand revealed. Note that we have not sought to provide disaggregated data for England's 'official' regions. This for the simple reason that the failure of New Labour's plans for regional devolution means that there is no English regional equivalent of Wales's devolved parliament and government, meaning that the policy context is very different (for an overview, see Henderson and Wyn Jones 2021: 167–94). Indeed, to the extent to which more recent UK governments have been intent on 'devolving' justice powers within England (though not to Wales – see Chapter 7), it is to altogether different territorial units. Nor have we, with one notable exception (with regards to imprisonment rates), made any attempt to draw statistical comparisons with other jurisdictions. The latter would undoubtedly be a most worthwhile exercise, but to go down that route would entail producing a very different kind of book. Our objective here is more limited if still ambitious: it is to provide a basic overview of the performance and outcomes of the Welsh criminal justice system, rendering what has been largely unseen at least a little more familiar.

CRIME

We begin with levels of crime. There are two standard means of measurement: the first relies on police records (that is, on crimes formally registered by the police) while the second builds up an aggregate picture of crime based on the experiences of respondents to various surveys. Figure 2.1 compares crime in Wales and England as recorded by police forces in both countries. As is clear, on this measure since 2015 police recorded crime levels in Wales are consistently lower than those found in England.[9] When broken down by offence category, however, the picture becomes distinctly less rosy (from a Welsh perspective). Wales records a higher rate (per 1,000 population) of violent offences, sexual offences, drug offences, public order offences, criminal damage and arson offences, and miscellaneous crimes against society

(Office for National Statistics 2020a). Even more concerning is that while offences involving violence against the person represented just over a quarter (26.5 per cent) of police recorded crime in Wales in 2015, this figure had increased to more than a third (37.6 per cent) of police-recorded crime by 2019 (Office for National Statistics 2020b).

**Figure 2.1** The rate of police recorded crime (excluding fraud) in England and Wales per 1,000 population, 2015 to 2019[10]

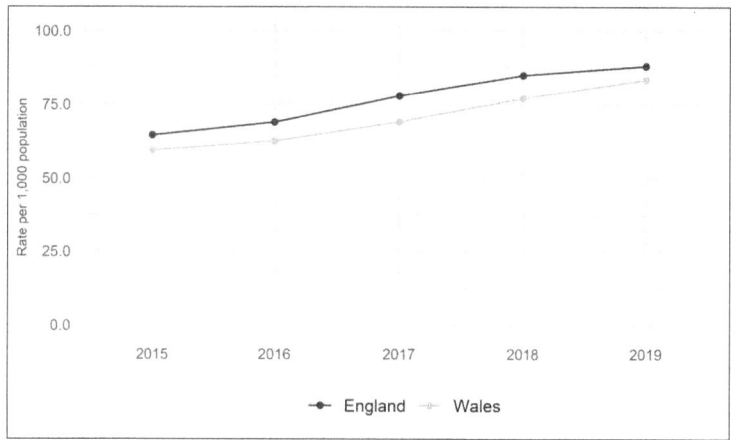

*Source:* Office for National Statistics (2020a)

There is, however, an extensive literature on the limitations of crime data based on official police records, and a pervasive sense that they do not adequately convey the true extent of crime (e.g. Boivin and Cordeau 2011; Buil-Gil et al. 2021; Burrows et al. 2000; Goudriaan et al. 2006; Skogan 1977). In an attempt to address this problem, national crime surveys have been devised and refined since 1982 in order to try to provide governments with a more accurate picture of crime and victimisation.[11] Originally called the British Crime Survey, the annual Crime Survey of England and Wales (CSEW) (as it has been known since 2012) offers a detailed overview of the prevalence of crime and anti-social behaviour, including a breakdown of those who are victims by age, ethnic identity, sexual orientation, gender identity, religious identity, household status, relationship status, employment status, income and lifestyle.

Until 2019, this detailed overview treated England and Wales as a single unit.[12] Since then the Office for National Statistics has begun to publish *some* CSEW data that can allow us to disaggregate Wales as a unit. The survey for the year ending March 2020 shows that levels of adult victimisation in Wales were lower than the England and Wales total (see Table 2.1). In the year ending March 2020, 14.4 per cent of adults in Wales had been a victim of crime compared with 19.2 per cent of adults across England and Wales (Office for National Statistics 2020d).[13] The same survey showed slightly fewer respondents in Wales (38 per cent) reporting that they had been victims of anti-social behaviour compared with the proportion across England and Wales combined (40 per cent) (Office for National Statistics 2020e). CSEW data also allow us to compare the experiences of crime across different communities. Predictably, it confirms that those adults living in Wales' most deprived areas had experienced more crime than those living in those areas that are least deprived (16 per cent vs 13.6 per cent, respectively) (Office for National Statistics 2020d).[14] Similarly, those living in the most deprived communities were much more likely to have experienced anti-social behaviour in their local area than those living in the least deprived communities (50 per cent vs 32 per cent) (Office for National Statistics 2020e).

**Table 2.1** Proportion of adults and children who were victims of crime and anti-social behaviour, year ending March 2020 (%)[15]

|  |  | per cent | | |
| --- | --- | --- | --- | --- |
|  | Deprivation (area) | England | Wales | England and Wales |
| Crime (adults) | 20% most deprived | 19.5 | 16.0 | |
|  | 20% least deprived | 18.6 | 13.6 | |
|  | All communities |  | 14.4 | 19.3 |
| Anti-social behaviour (adults) | 20% most deprived | 48 | 50 | |
|  | 20% least deprived | 33 | 32 | |
|  | All communities |  | 38 | 40 |
| Crime (children) | All communities |  | 11.0 | 6.6 |

*Source:* Office for National Statistics (2020d, 2020e, 2020f)

It was not until January 2009 that children aged 10 to 15 years were first included in the Crime Survey of England and Wales. Although many children's services in Wales are devolved to the Welsh Government (see youth justice, below), Wales-only data on children's experiences of victimisation was first published only in 2019. In contrast to the experiences reported by adults, in the year ending March 2020 a higher proportion of children in Wales (11 per cent) reported experiencing crime or anti-social behaviour victimisation than at the England and Wales level (6.6 per cent). Across the same period the proportion of children surveyed who reported being a victim of violence was almost twice as high in Wales (5.1 per cent) than across England and Wales as a whole (2.6 per cent) (Office for National Statistics 2020f).

While the rate of police-recorded crime has increased over recent years (Figure 2.1), the rate at which crimes are being solved has steadily fallen. An inquiry by the House of Commons Home Affairs Committee found that there were 65,000 fewer charges brought in the three years to 2017 across England and Wales, despite a 21 per cent increase in recorded crime (House of Commons Home Affairs Committee 2018b).[16] Speaking in 2019, the then Metropolitan Police commissioner, Cressida Dick, described the police detection rate for some offences across England and Wales as 'woefully low' (Dick 2019). This can be illustrated clearly by Table 2.2, which indicates that the proportion of police-recorded crimes in Wales where a person was charged or summonsed has fallen across every offence group since 2017. Comparing Wales to England we also find another concerning trend. In England between 2017 and 2020 charges or summonses fell by a quarter (26 per cent), while police-recorded crime rose by 15 per cent. In Wales over the same period, charges or summonses fell by 21 per cent, while police-recorded crime increased by 27 per cent (Home Office 2020a; Office for National Statistics 2020b). In other words, the gap between crime and (potential) resolution seems to be growing at a more rapid rate in Wales than is the case over the border.

Explanations for the decline in 'clear-up' rates tend to focus on the impact of the sharp falls in police budgets seen in the wake of austerity, as well as the increase in the number of complex and serious cases requiring additional police resources (House of Commons Home Affairs Committee 2018b). Financial pressures have undoubtedly encouraged some forces, most notably the Metropolitan Police, to formally prioritise the

**Table 2.2** The percentage of cases where a person was charged or summonsed by police forces in Wales by offence group, 2017 to 2020 (%)

|  | % per cent | | | |
| --- | --- | --- | --- | --- |
|  | 2017 | 2018 | 2019 | 2020 |
| Violence against the person | 19.2 | 14.8 | 12.2 | 9.9 |
| Sexual offences | 13.3 | 9.9 | 9.9 | 5.7 |
| Robbery | 33.8 | 26.6 | 22.5 | 16.5 |
| Theft offences | 13.3 | 11.6 | 10.9 | 8.5 |
| Criminal damage and arson | 8.7 | 7.3 | 7.3 | 6.3 |
| Drug offences | 44.3 | 42.8 | 39.7 | 33.3 |
| Possession of weapons | 59.2 | 53.9 | 51.0 | 46.2 |
| Public order | 20.0 | 14.8 | 10.4 | 9.2 |
| Miscellaneous crimes against society | 27.4 | 22.1 | 18.5 | 16.6 |
| All police-recorded crime | 16.7 | 13.8 | 12.3 | 10.1 |

*Source:* Home Office (2020a)

investigation of certain offences while deprioritising others (BBC News 2017a; Hales and Higgins 2016). The Welsh Government's attempts to shield the country's police forces from some of the impact of austerity (Lowe et al. 2015) may potentially help explain why the proportion of cases leading to charges or summonses has declined somewhat less precipitately in Wales (21 per cent) than it has in England (26 per cent). This might also help to explain why recorded crime has increased more rapidly in Wales (27 per cent) than in England (15 per cent).[17]

POLICE

The four police forces responsible for territorial policing in Wales are Dyfed-Powys, Gwent, North Wales and South Wales. A range of other agencies also play a role in policing in Wales, namely the British Transport Police, the Civil Nuclear Constabulary, the National Crime Agency and the Ministry of Defence Police. The British Transport Police (2021) has eight police stations in Wales as well a station in England (Shrewsbury Railway Station) that is included within its Wales sub-division. Beyond that, however, the Ministry of Defence Police (2017) has only one officer based in Wales while both the National Crime Agency (which focuses on serious and organised crime) and the Civil Nuclear Constabulary (2021) currently appear to have no permanent staff presence in the country.[18]

Significant cuts to police funding in England and Wales as a result of the austerity policies of successive UK governments resulted in a decline in the number of police officers in post. After a steady fall between 2010 and 2016, police officer numbers in Wales have since recovered somewhat, albeit the total number remains lower than the one recorded in 2010 (see Figure 2.2). Overall, the number of police officers per 100,000 people in Wales has fallen from 242 in 2010 to 221 in 2020 – the latter amounting to 6,998 police officers (Home Office 2020b). Comparing Wales with England, while in 2010 the number of police officers per 100,000 people in Wales (242) was lower than England's (259), by 2020 the number in Wales (221) was marginally higher than that in England (216).

Police community support officers (PCSOs) also provide a visible police presence in Wales. Introduced by the Police Reform Act 2002, PCSOs aid police officers in addressing low-level offences and have played a central role in the Welsh Government's efforts to promote and improve community safety. Since the Home Office announced cuts to PCSO fund-

**Figure 2.2** The number of police officers per 100,000 people in England and Wales, 2010 to 2020

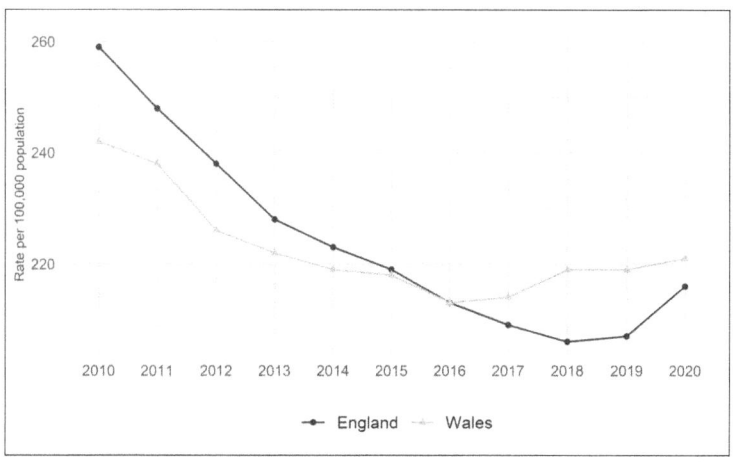

Home Office (2020b); Office for National Statistics (2020g, 2020h)

ing in 2011, the Welsh Government has provided additional funding for PCSOs across Wales (Lowe et al. 2015). As shown in Figure 2.3, this has meant that while the number of PCSOs per 100,000 people in England more than halved between 2010 and 2020, the number in Wales actually increased slightly (albeit from a lower starting point). In absolute terms, this means that in March 2020 there were 807 PCSOs. Given the combination of police officer and PCSO numbers, it is perhaps not surprising that the CSEW in the year ending March 2020 found that one in five (21 per cent) people reported that police and PCSO foot patrols were highly visible in Wales, as compared to 15 per cent across England and Wales (Office for National Statistics 2020i).

**Figure 2.3** The number of police community support officers (PCSOs) per 100,000 people in England and Wales, 2010 to 2020

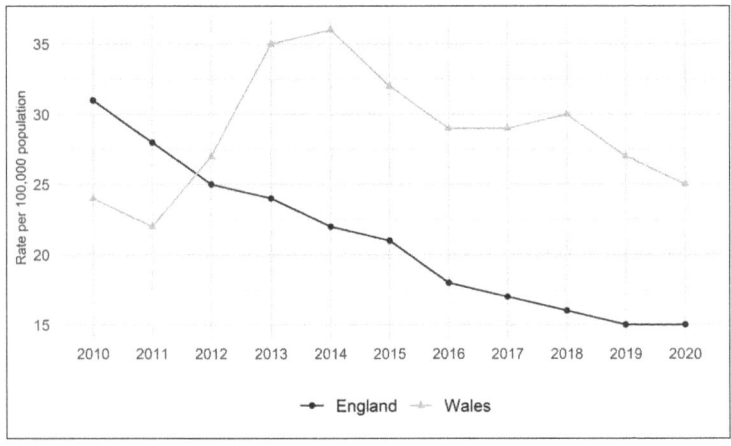

*Source:* Home Office (2020c); Office for National Statistics (2020g; 2020h)

Official police data is only one of a number of different ways of measuring police performance and effectiveness (as acknowledged by Her Majesty's Inspectorate of Constabulary and Fire and Rescue Services (2021)). Nonetheless, as is clear from Figure 2.4, official data on the number of police arrests paints a striking picture. Arrests for notifiable offences in Wales have fallen by nearly a quarter (23 per cent) since 2015 (from 59,865 in 2015 to

46,082 in 2020) (Home Office 2020d).[19] In absolute terms, in the year ending March 2020 this means that there were 13,783 fewer arrests for notifiable offences in Wales than in 2014/15. Despite this, police data also show that individuals are consistently more likely to be arrested in Wales than in England (even though Wales has, of course, a lower overall crime rate).

**Figure 2.4** Arrest rate per 1,000 population in England and Wales, 2015/16 to 2019/20

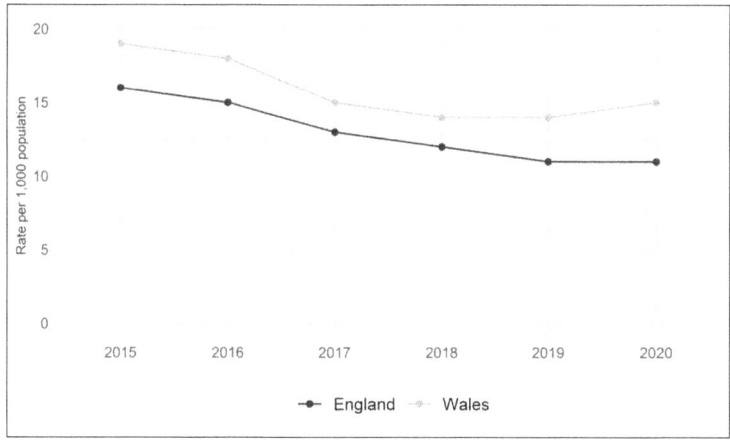

*Source:* Home Office (2020d)

As the overall number of arrests declines, however, police use of controversial stop and search powers is increasing (Home Office 2020e). Between 2017/18 and 2019/20, the total number of stops and searches in Wales has increased by 116 per cent from 11,576 to 24,964; the latter representing an average of sixty-eight every day (Home Office 2020e).[20] A longstanding concern across England and Wales is that these powers are used disproportionately against individuals from a Black, Asian and minority ethnic (BAME) background (Lammy 2017; Macpherson 1999; Reid 2009; Waddington et al. 2004). In Wales, data from 2019/20 shows that there were 7 stop and searches per 1,000 White people. The comparable numbers for individuals from other ethnic backgrounds were 47 per 1,000 Black people, 15 per 1,000 individuals from a mixed ethnic group, and 14 per 1,000 Asian people (Home Office 2020f).[21] Similarly, members of BAME groups are over-represented among those members of the public against whom Welsh police used force in the course of their duties. Specifically, while 4.4 per cent of the Welsh population are classified as BAME (according to the 2011 census), in 2019/20, 9.9 per cent of all recorded incidents in which police used restraints in encounters with the public involved individuals from a BAME background. Similarly, one in ten (10.2 per cent) incidents in which Welsh forces used Conducted Energy Device (i.e. a TASER) was against someone from a BAME group, while 15.8 per cent of all incidents where a police dog was used involved individuals from a BAME background (Home Office 2020g).[22] These data add to longstanding concerns about the ways in which ethnic minority communities have been and are policed in Wales – concerns focused in particular on a number of high-profile cases (Jackson 2018a; Williams 2021).

Unfortunately, while CSEW does gather information on public confidence in and perceptions of the police broken down by sex, age and ethnicity, these data are only available on an all-England and Wales basis. What we do know is that, overall, the CSEW found in 2019/20 that 72 per cent of adults in Wales were confident that local police were doing a good job compared with 74 per cent across England and Wales (Office for National Statistics 2020j). This fell to 68 per cent for those living within the 20 per cent most deprived communities in Wales.

## PROSECUTIONS

The Crown Prosecution Service (CPS) prosecutes all criminal cases in Wales. CPS Cymru-Wales is one of fourteen distinct areas that form part of a wider England and Wales body led by the director of public prosecutions. Each area has its own Chief Crown Prosecutor who is responsible for prosecutions, maintaining professional standards and contributing to national (*sic*) policy and strategy (Crown Prosecution Service 2021a). In line with trends across England and Wales as a whole, the number of prosecutions in Wales has fallen in recent years. In 2019, 97,458 defendants were proceeded against in Wales, a 7 per cent decline on the number recorded in 2013 (Ministry of Justice 2020a). But as the number of prosecutions fall, the conviction rate in Wales continues to rise. As is clear from Figure 2.5, since 2013 the proportion of cases resulting in a conviction has been higher in Wales than in England for six of the previous seven years.

OUTCOMES IN THE WELSH CRIMINAL JUSTICE SYSTEM    31

**Figure 2.5**   Conviction rates in England and Wales, 2013 to 2019 (%)

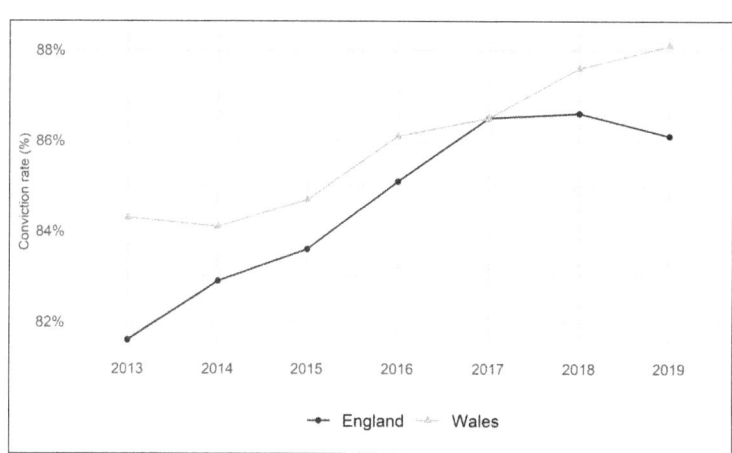

*Source:* Ministry of Justice (2020a)

**Map 2.1**   Crown and magistrates' courts in Wales, 2010 to 2019

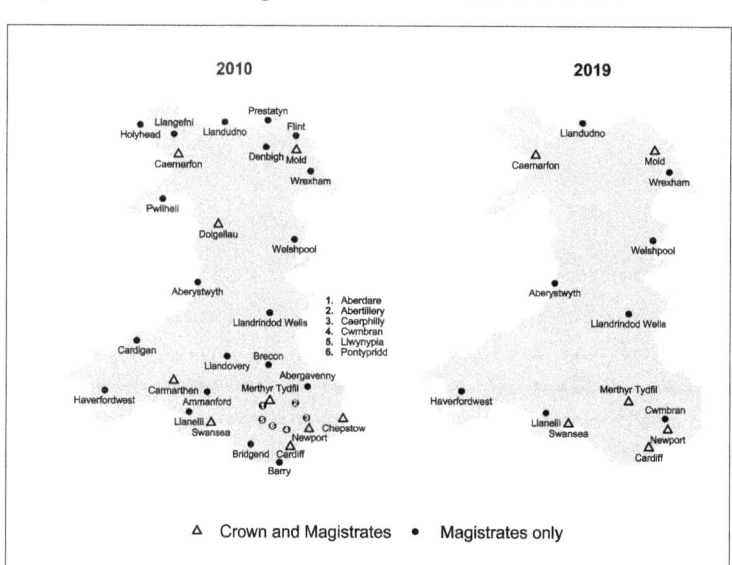

## COURTS

Criminal cases in Wales are heard across the country's six Crown courts and fourteen magistrates' courts, all of which are operated by HM Courts and Tribunals Service Wales. They are the survivors of a very significant programme of closures that followed cuts to the Ministry of Justice's budget. No less than twenty-three Crown and magistrates' courts have closed in Wales since 2010 (Thomas Commission 2019).[23] This in turn has led to growing concerns about the considerable 'hardship and stress' facing court users in Wales who are now expected to travel long distances to reach alternative court settings in a country where public transport links are often poor (Newman 2019: 4). So concerned was the Thomas Commission (2019: 361) about the impact of these closures that it called for a moratorium on further closures unless or until a Wales-wide courts strategy has been put in place (the closures of the past decade having taken place in the absence of such a strategy).

Concerns over access to justice in Wales – both literal and figurative – have been further compounded by drastic cuts to the legal aid budget since 2011 (Thomas Commission 2019).[24] As the population of Wales is, on average, poorer than that of England and legal aid is means tested, these cuts have inevitably had a disproportionate effect in Wales. The equally inevitable consequence of these cuts is that more of those coming into contact with the criminal justice system are doing so without adequate advice or representation (Bowcott 2019; Cohen-Ennis 2021; Newman and Dehaghani 2022), an outcome that puts a different gloss on the aforementioned increase in Wales's conviction rates.

## PRISONERS, PRISONS AND THE USE OF IMMEDIATE CUSTODY

As illustrated by Figure 2.6, in 2019, 5,777 custodial sentences were handed out by courts in Wales, 5,228 to men and 510 to women (on imprisonment in Wales, see House of Commons Welsh Affairs Committee 2007; Jones 2018a, 2019b, 2020b).[25] Those jailed joined a prison population that has increased significantly since the 1990s, a result not simply of year-on-year increases in the number of those handed immediate custodial sentences, but also of increases in sentence length reflecting the desire of successive UK governments to 'get tough' on crime (House of Commons Justice Committee 2008; Hough et al. 2003; Millie et al. 2003; Roberts and Ashworth 2016). This has been manifested in numerous legislative and policy changes including the introduction of indeterminate sentences for public protection and their subsequent replacement with extended determinate sentences in 2012; changes in the minimum terms for offences such as murder, and increases in the sentencing severity for offences such as the possession of weapons, sex offences and motoring offences (Sentencing Council for England and Wales 2018). In Wales, this has meant that the proportion of offenders who are serving sentences of four years or more has increased from 34 per cent of Welsh prisoners (based on home address) in 2017 to 40 per cent in 2019 (Ministry of Justice 2020b).[26] Following the enactment of the Ministry of Justice's latest plans to increase sentence lengths for a host of offences across England and Wales (Ministry of Justice 2020c; Home Office and Ministry of Justice 2021), this trend looks set to continue.

The end result of this constant ratcheting-up is that, since 1999, England and Wales as a whole has consistently recorded a higher average imprisonment rate than any other country in western Europe (see Figure 2.7). Even more remarkably, Ministry of Justice data reveal that, since 2013 (the first year for which disaggregated data are available), Wales has recorded a higher rate of imprisonment than England (see Figure 2.8); despite total

**Figure 2.6** Immediate custodial sentences handed out at courts in Wales and the average Welsh prison population (based on home address), 2013 to 2019[27]

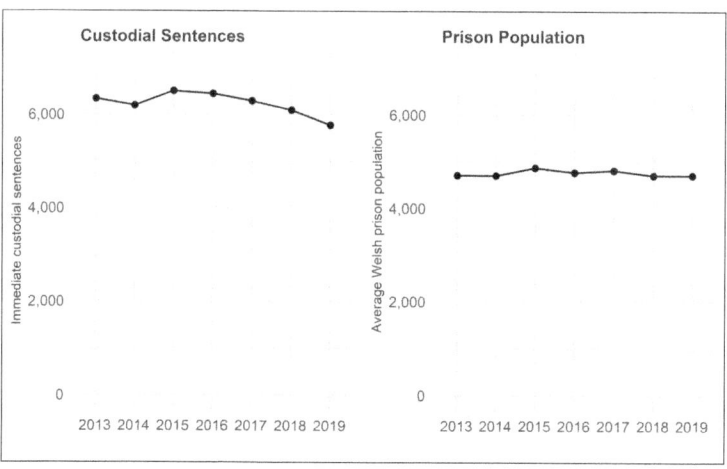

*Source:* Ministry of Justice (2020a, 2020d)

police-recorded crime having been lower in Wales than across the border in every year throughout this period. Our understanding of why Wales is not only an outlier in the context of England and Wales but also in the wider context of western Europe as a whole is distinctly limited. Some have pointed to the declining use of community sentences (National Assembly for Wales Debate, 22 January 2019), in the overall context of higher average custody rates at magistrates' and Crown courts in Wales compared with those same courts in England (Jones 2019a, 2020b).[28] If true, this begs the question of why courts in Wales, using the same sentencing guidelines as those used in England, appear to produce consistently harsher outcomes. We are not aware of any academic research that might explain this trend in Wales. Meanwhile, as discussed further in the final chapter of this book, the Ministry of Justice itself has shown a complete lack of interest in the matter. Worse, it has sought to trivialise the whole issue.

In the previous section we highlighted a disparity in the treatment of different ethnic groups in the context of policing in Wales. The same is true of the courts. A review carried out by David Lammy MP in 2017 found that while BAME men and women comprise just 12 per cent of the population of England and Wales, they made up 25 per cent of its prison population

**Figure 2.7**  Average prison population rate per 100,000 in western Europe, 1999 to 2018[29]

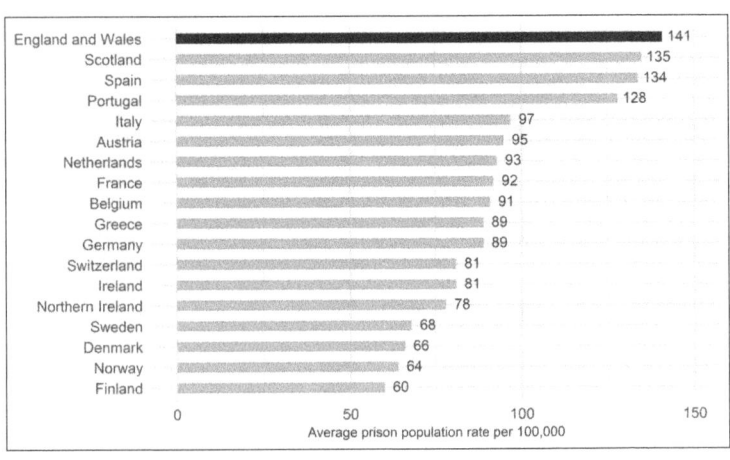

*Source:* Jones (2019a)

**Figure 2.8** Prison population rates per 100,000 in England and Wales using home address, 2013 to 2019

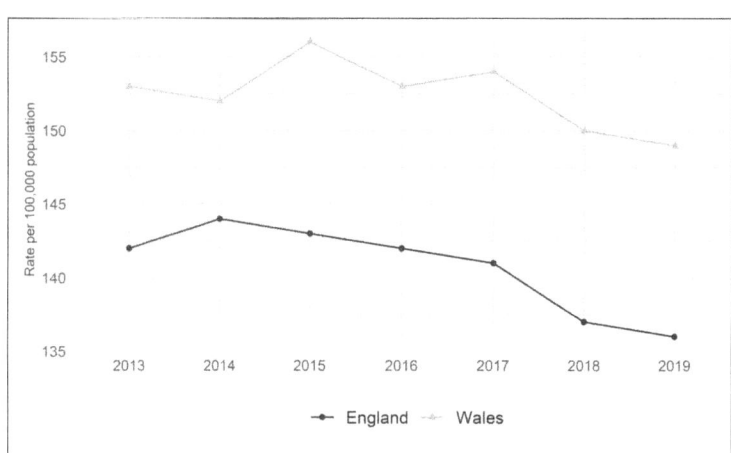

*Source:* Ministry of Justice (2020d, 2020e); Office for National Statistics (2020g; 2020h)

(Lammy 2017). Research carried out on the behalf of the Ministry of Justice concluded that BAME individuals are 'more likely' to be sentenced to immediate custody than White offenders 'under similar criminal circumstances' (Hopkins et al. 2016: 7). The ministry's most recent review of *Statistics on Ethnicity and the Criminal Justice System* shows that across England and Wales, White offenders 'consistently' record a lower average custodial sentence length (ACSL) than other ethnic groups (Ministry of Justice 2021: 5).

Until recently, at least, the debate on racially disproportionate treatment by the criminal justice system has focused almost exclusively on the England and Wales level. For example, although the Lammy review team visited facilities in Wales as part of its inquiry,[30] the final report pays scant attention to the distinct legislative and policy framework in place to tackle inequality and promote fairness in Wales (e.g. The Equality Act 2010 (Statutory Duties) (Wales) Regulations 2011).[31] Meanwhile, the Ministry of Justice's (2021) most recent report on ethnicity and criminal justice fails to provide a disaggregated picture for Wales. Other research is, however, beginning to bring the situation in Wales into clearer focus (see Jones 2019b, 2020b). Unfortunately, the picture that emerges is – once again – a disturbing one.

As a proportion of Wales's overall population (as recorded in the 2011 census), Black prisoners (based on home address) are over-represented in the country's prison population by a factor of six; the comparable figures for prisoners recorded as being from a mixed ethnic background is 2.7 times and for Asian prisoners 1.9 times the White prison population (Ministry of Justice 2020f). As illustrated by Figure 2.9, for every 10,000 Black people living in Wales in 2019, 91 were in prison. This imprisonment rate compared with just 14 White people in every 10,000, 28 Asian people and 41 people from a mixed ethnic background (Jones, 2020b). Moreover, between 2013 and 2019, the average custodial sentence length in Wales was almost 10 months longer for Black prisoners (at 26.2 months) when compared with individuals from a White background (16.4 months) (Ministry of Justice 2020a). Data obtained through the Freedom of Information Act also show that prisoners from a BAME background are more likely to serve a higher proportion of their sentences in prison.[32] Between 2015 and 2018, Ministry of Justice data show that mixed ethnic prisoners from Wales served a higher proportion of their determinate sentences in prison (63 per cent) followed by Black (61 per cent), White (57 per cent) and Asian (57 per cent) prisoners (Ministry of Justice 2020g). While more

**Figure 2.9** Rates of imprisonment and probation supervision per 10,000 people by ethnic group in Wales in 2019

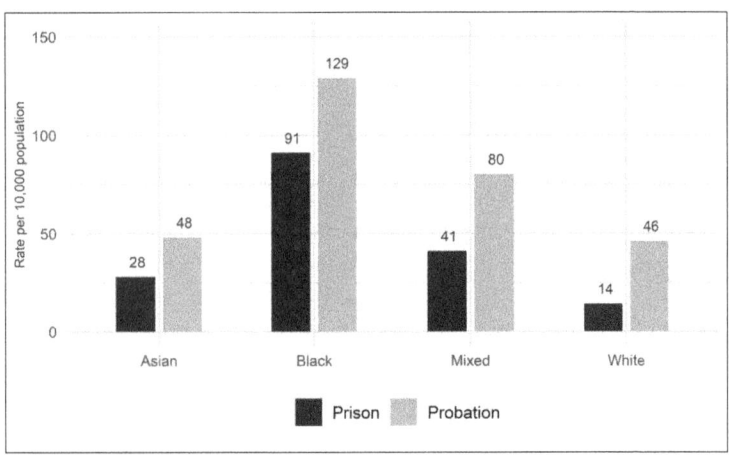

*Source:* Ministry of Justice (2020f); Office for National Statistics (2020g)

research is required before definite judgement can be rendered, the situation in Wales would appear to be at least as bad as that found in England.[33]

The location and the conditions under which Welsh prisoners are held is also a source of serious concern.

The prison estate in Wales itself is comprised of five male prisons that holds a mixture of convicted, unconvicted, sentenced and unsentenced prisoners (see Table 2.3). HMP Berwyn, HMP Cardiff, HMP Swansea and HMP Usk & Prescoed are operated and run by HM Prison and Probation Service (HMPPS) in Wales. HMP Parc in Bridgend is Wales's only private prison and is currently operated by G4S Care and Justice Ltd. The newest of the five, HMP Berwyn in Wrexham opened in February 2017. With a certified normal accommodation of 2,106 prisoners, it is intended to become the largest prison in England and Wales and the second largest in western Europe (Jones 2018a). There is no female prison in Wales, a point to which we will return later.

**Table 2.3** The prison estate in Wales, 2019

| Establishment | Population (2019) | Description |
| --- | --- | --- |
| HMP Berwyn | 1,448 | The prison holds sentenced category C adult males and category B adult males on remand. |
| HMP Cardiff | 717 | A category B local resettlement prison that holds adult males served by courts in the local area. The prison holds a mixture of remanded, unsentenced, sentenced and recalled prisoners. |
| HMP & YOI Parc | 1,642 | This is a category B local prison that holds convicted adult men, young adults (18–20) and young people (16–17) remanded and convicted. |
| HMP Swansea | 417 | A category B local resettlement prison for adult males that holds a mixture of remanded, unsentenced, sentenced and recalled prisoners. |
| HMP Usk & Prescoed | 523 | HMP Prescoed is an adult male open prison that manages category D prisoners. HMP Usk operates as a small category C training prison which largely deals with offenders convicted of offences under the Sex Offenders Act 1997. |

*Source*: Jones (2018a); Ministry of Justice (2020i)

As a consequence of the opening of Berwyn and the recent expansion of Parc, the capacity of the prison estate in Wales now exceeds the total number of prisoners from Wales. Yet the operational realities of an England and Wales prison system mean that Welsh prisoners are very widely dispersed across both countries. In 2019, for example, 34 per cent of all Welsh people in prison were being held in no fewer than, on average, 105 different prisons in England at any given time (Jones 2020b). The corollary is that there are significant numbers of English prisoners (defined here as having an address in England prior to entering custody) held in the Welsh prison estate. In particular, despite having initially been presented as a local prison for north Wales, at the end of December 2019, 70 per cent of all prisoners at HMP Berwyn were from England (Jones 2020b: 23). If and when the prison ever reaches full capacity – its problems have been well-canvassed (e.g. Jones 2020b; O'Connor and O'Murchu 2019) – we may expect that proportion to be even higher.

There have been longstanding concerns about the impact of holding prisoners in establishments many miles away from home. In 2007, the House of Commons Welsh Affairs Committee (2007: 5) concluded that the 'rehabilitation and resettlement' of Welsh prisoners was being 'hampered' by the distances separating outside support services from Welsh prisoners. Research has found that the distances facing Welsh prisoners held in England means that they often receive few family visits, to the point of serving entire sentences without receiving a single visit (Jones 2017). This is particularly problematic given that family members can provide an invaluable source of resettlement support to prisoners upon their release (Brunton-Smith and Hopkins 2013; Codd 2008; Mears et al. 2012; Niven and Stewart 2005).

Concern has also been expressed about the treatment of Welsh prisoners held in prisons outside Wales. Drawing on wider research into the sociology of imprisonment (e.g. Goffman 1961; Sykes 1958), Jones (2017) found that Welsh prisoners often experience a distinct set of 'pains of imprisonment' when held in English institutions. This includes experiencing abusive behaviour from non-Welsh prisoners and derisive treatment from staff (Jones 2017). These 'pains' are particularly acute for Welsh-speaking prisoners. In 2007, the Welsh Language Board found that Welsh prisoners had been prevented from speaking in Welsh at HMP Altcourse in Liverpool after staff demonstrated 'negative attitudes' towards the language (Jones and Eaves 2007: 89). Welsh speakers also experienced 'abuse and deri-

**Map 2.2** The prison estate in England and Wales

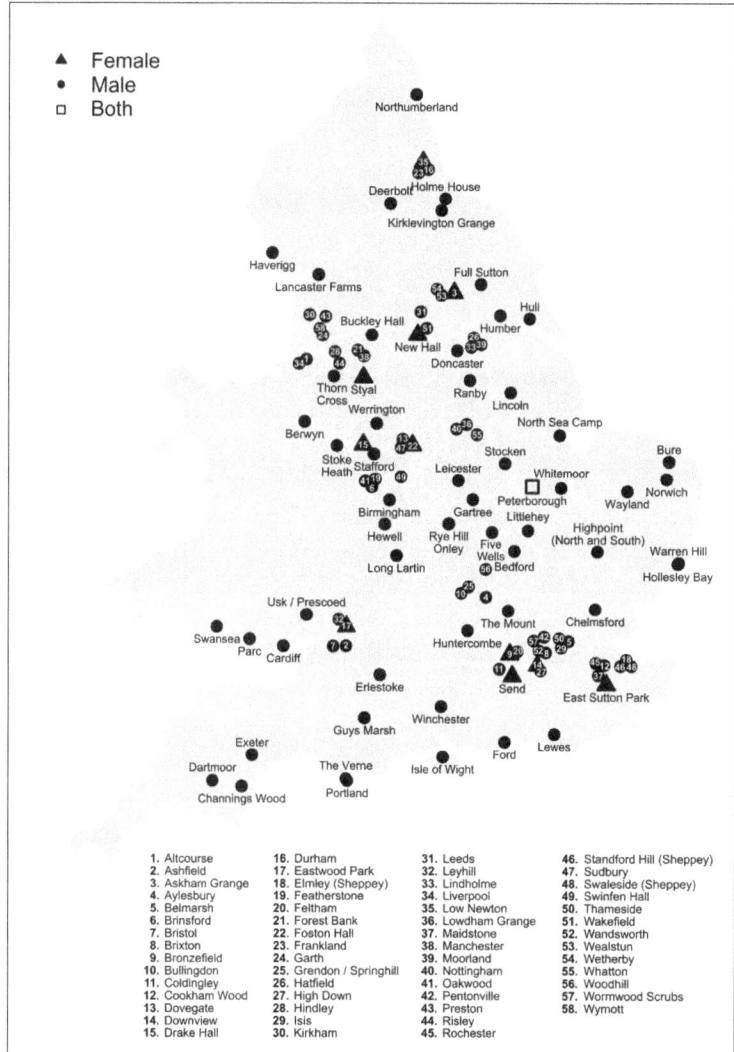

sion' from other prisoners based upon their linguistic identity (Jones and Eaves 2007: 89). In 2014, appearing before the Welsh Affairs Committee, Nick Hardwick, then Chief Inspector of Prisons, acknowledged that 'not nearly enough' was being done by prison officials in England to provide opportunities to Welsh-speaking prisoners (House of Commons Welsh Affairs Committee 2015: Q35). As if to confirm the point, during an inspection of HMP Stoke Heath in September 2015, then a designated Welsh resettlement prison, HM Inspectorate of Prisons (2015a) were told that there were no prisoners who spoke Welsh as a first language. Given that at the time the prison held 436 Welsh prisoners, statistically speaking this is highly unlikely to have been the case (Jones, 2018a).[34]

It should be noted that even in Welsh prisons, provision for Welsh-speaking prisoners is notoriously poor.[35] Despite the claims in 2013 of the then Welsh Secretary, David Jones MP, that establishing a prison in north Wales would give Welsh-speaking prisoners 'more opportunity to speak the language in an environment where its cultural significance is understood' (Ministry of Justice 2013a), Welsh-language provision at HMP Berwyn has regularly been found wanting. This is perhaps not surprising when we consider that the Welsh Language Commissioner reported in 2017 that Welsh-language skills had not been 'identified as an essential or desirable component' for any of the staff positions advertised by the National Offender Management Service at the prison (Independent Monitoring Board 2020; Welsh Language Commissioner 2017: 4). Across the south Wales estate, HM Inspectorate of Prisons has raised repeated concerns about the standard of Welsh-language provision. In its most recent scrutiny visit of HMP Swansea, for example, the inspectors observed that its 'statutory obligation to provide written and spoken materials in the Welsh language on request was largely unmet' while inspectors 'found no evidence of official forms available in Welsh' (HMI Prisons 2020a: 21).[36]

Another more generalised cause for concern is the 'rapid deterioration' in prison safety across the England and Wales estate (House of Commons Justice Committee, 2016: 3). Since 2016, Welsh prisons have born witness to a record number of self-inflicted deaths, prisoner-on-prisoner assaults, self-harm incidents and assaults on prison staff (Jones 2018a, 2019b). The number of drug and alcohol finds, weapon discoveries and prison disturbances in the Welsh prison estate also reached record levels in 2019 (Jones 2020b). Indicative of the deep, systemic malaise engulfing the entire system is that, following the most recent round of prison inspections undertaken by HM Inspectorate of Prisons, inspectors reported that just 46 per cent of its previous recommendations on prison safety in Wales had been fully implemented (Jones 2020b).

## PROBATION AND REOFFENDING

The probation service plays a crucial role in the criminal justice system. Pre-sentencing, it prepares reports to advise courts on the most appropriate sentences for those found guilty. Post-sentencing, the service supervises those sentenced to non-custodial 'community' sentences, as well as those released from prison on licence having served a portion of their custodial sentence behind bars. Since the middle of the previous decade, the service's ability to carry out these tasks effectively has been significantly compromised because of catastrophic mismanagement by the UK Government. A partial-privatisation of the service under the guise of 'Transforming Rehabilitation' – a reform enacted in February 2015 at the behest of then justice secretary, Chris Grayling – proved an unmitigated disaster (Annison 2019; National Audit Office 2019; Walker et al. 2019). So disastrous, in fact, that in June 2020 the government was forced to reverse course and announce the full renationalisation of the service. We return to this particular episode in much more detail in a subsequent chapter.

The number of community sentences handed out at courts in England and Wales has steadily declined in the decade since 2010. As shown in Figure 2.10, in Wales the total fell from 11,489 in 2010 to 5,596 in 2019 (Ministry of Justice 2020j). Although other contributing factors are likely (note the fall between 2011 and 2014), both the House of Commons Justice Committee (2018) and HM Inspectorate of Probation (2019a: 5) attribute some of this decline to a 'lack of judicial confidence' in the probation service resulting from the chaos that followed Transforming Rehabilitation. According to the Centre for Justice Innovation, the decline in the number of community sentences across England and Wales is 'strongly linked' to the fall in the number of cases where a pre-sentence report is used (2018: 1). It found that cases with a pre-sentence report were ten times more likely to receive a community sentence than those without. Ministry of Justice data unearthed via Freedom of Information requests show that the total number of pre-sentence reports prepared in Wales has fallen by 25 per cent since 2014 (Ministry of Justice 2020k). Comparison of England and Wales data reveals some interesting differences between both countries in the context of pre-sentence reports. In 2019, 9 per cent of all such reports prepared in Wales recommended a custodial sentence compared to 6 per cent of reports in England (Ministry of Justice 2020l, 2020m). Not only that, but data from the same year show that courts operating in Wales were

**Figure 2.10**   The use of community sentences in Wales, 2010 to 2019

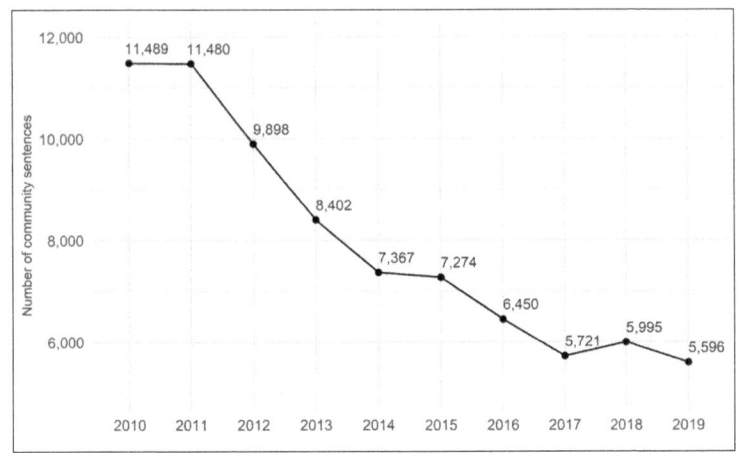

*Source:* Ministry of Justice (2020j)

even more likely to follow that recommendation than English courts. In Wales, 93 per cent of cases in which imprisonment had been recommended in pre-sentencing reports resulted in custodial sentences; the equivalent number in England was 88 per cent (Ministry of Justice 2020l, 2020m).

More generally, not only does Wales consistently have more prisoners per head of population than England, but it also has a larger proportion of its population subject to community sentences. In other words, both its prison and probation population are higher (see Figure 2.11). In 2019, for example, 222 per 100,000 of the Welsh population were subject to a court order, compared with 183 per 100,000 inhabitants in England. Put differently, in the same year 1 in 203 people in Wales were subject to some form of probation supervision, compared with 1 in 238 people in England. Once again, we are aware of no explanation for why this might be the case.

Finally, it is also worth considering reoffending rates. Reducing reoffending has been a stated aim of prison and probation services in England and Wales since 2004.[37] Despite this, almost two decades later, rates of reoffending remain stubbornly high. In 2018, the overall proven reoffending rate in England and Wales was 28.1 per cent. More than a third (35.7 per cent) of adults leaving prison went on to reoffend, including fully 61 per cent of those serving short-term custodial sentences of less than 12 months

**Figure 2.11** Probation rates per 100,000 in England and Wales, 2014 to 2019

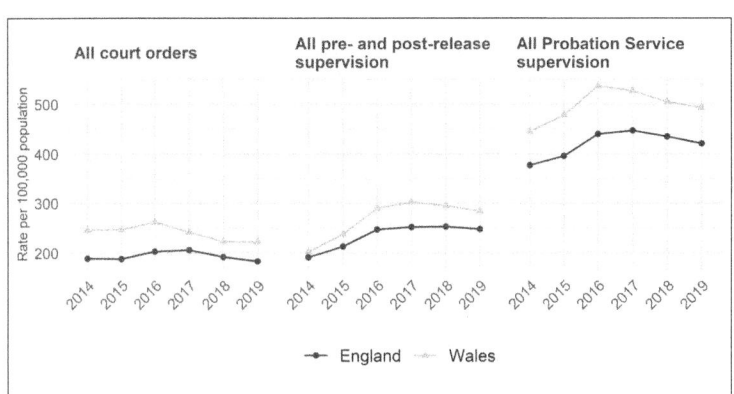

*Source:* Ministry of Justice (2020n) and Office for National Statistics (2020g; 2020h)

(Ministry of Justice 2020o). Once again, disaggregated data show that the situation in Wales is worse than the England and Wales average. Between 2016 and 2018 the average overall reoffending rate was 31.6 per cent in Wales, and 29.1 per cent across both England and Wales. In Wales, 55 per cent of those convicted of theft offences, 43 per cent of those convicted of public order offences and 37 per cent of those convicted of possession of weapon offences went on to commit a further offence (Ministry of Justice 2020p).

## WOMEN IN THE CRIMINAL JUSTICE SYSTEM

We turn now to consider women in the criminal justice system, and in particular the prison system. As with comparable systems across the world, women constitute a small proportion of those who come into contact with the Welsh criminal justice system. Women comprise just over half (50.7 per cent) of the Welsh population (StatsWales 2020a), but only 16 per cent of those arrested by police, 27 per cent of those prosecuted, 28 per cent of those convicted, 19 per cent of those given community sentences (19 per cent), and 9 per cent of those sentenced to immediate custody (Home Office 2020d; Ministry of Justice 2020a). In 2019, women comprised only 6 per cent of the Welsh prison population and 12 per cent of the total caseload managed by Welsh probation services (Ministry of Justice 2020q, 2020r). Here, the situation in Wales is broadly comparable to patterns found across almost all international jurisdictions. This in turn has contributed to a situation in which women's needs and experiences have tended to be overlooked and marginalised by policy makers and researchers alike (Belknap 2020; Bosworth 2000; Chesney-Lind and Pasko 2004; Corston 2007).

Even if they are in the minority, thousands of women in Wales are nonetheless in daily contact with the criminal justice system. Numerous studies also demonstrate that women often face (even) more severe challenges than men. Surveys conducted on an England and Wales basis show that female prisoners are more likely to have experienced emotional, physical or sexual abuse; to have been taken into care as a child; or to have observed violence in the home (Williams et al. 2012a). Women in prison are more likely than men to suffer from a range of mental health problems; to have previously attempted suicide; to have used class A drugs prior to entering prison; to be unemployed in the four weeks prior to entering custody; or to have committed an offence to help support the drug use of someone else (Light et al. 2013). Women are also more likely than men to have no prior criminal convictions before being sentenced to prison; to be sentenced to prison for non-violent offences; and to be sentenced to serve short-term custodial sentences (Prison Reform Trust 2017). Indeed, in 2019, almost 1 in 5 women (19 per cent) sentenced to immediate custody in Wales were handed sentences of one month or less (Jones 2020b; Ministry of Justice 2020a).[38] It is also the case that employment outcomes for women sentenced to short sentences are three times worse than that for men (Coates 2016: 34).[39]

In 2019, based on home address prior to entering custody, there were 261 Welsh women in prison (Ministry of Justice 2020p). As is clear from Figure 2.12, this represents an imprisonment rate that is, once again, consistently higher in Wales than it is in England.[40] A particular problem faced by female prisoners, their families and, indeed, anyone who cares about their well-being and future resettlement, arises from the nature of the prison estate on which they are held. As there are no women's prisons in Wales, all Welsh female prisoners are imprisoned in England. Indeed, in September 2019, while the majority were held either at HMP Eastwood Park in Gloucestershire (51 per cent) or HMP Styal in Cheshire (15 per

**Figure 2.12** Imprisonment rate per 100,000 women in prison in England and Wales (based on home address prior to entering custody), 2013 to 2019

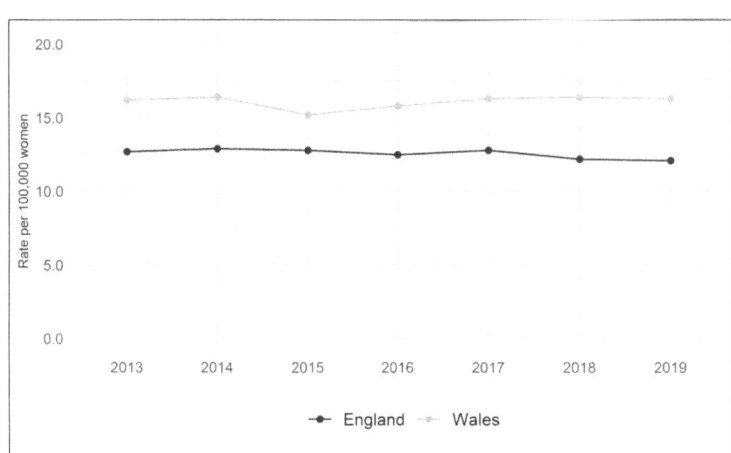

*Source:* Ministry of Justice (2020q, 2020s) and Office for National Statistics (2020g, 2020h)

cent), others were dispersed right across the prison estate from HMP Low Newton in County Durham to HMP Peterborough in Cambridgeshire and HMP Send in Surrey, with Welsh women held in all twelve of England's female prisons (Ministry of Justice 2020q). As a result, most if not all Welsh female prisoners experience the 'distance problems' described earlier in this chapter (see also House of Commons Welsh Affairs Committee 2007; Jones 2018a; Prison Reform Trust 2015; Thomas Commission 2019).

These distance problems serve to compound the distinct and particularly serious challenges faced by female prisoners; challenges that have become more widely recognised over the past 15 years or so, in part due to the much higher average growth rate in the prisoner population for women (5.2 per cent) compared to men (3.5 per cent) between 1993 and 2012 (Ministry of Justice 2020t). This exponential growth resulted in a doubling of the female prison population in England and Wales in just two decades (Prison Reform Trust 2017).[41] As the overall number of female prisoners has increased, so too have concerns over the safety and well-being of these often particularly vulnerable individuals.

The death of six women at HMP Styal between 2002 and 2003 led to the preparation of a landmark report by Baroness Jean Corston (2007; see also House of Commons Justice Committee 2013). Corston noted that despite the similarities in the circumstances surrounding these self-inflicted deaths, there was 'little indication' that lessons were being learnt to help prevent these incidents from happening again in the future (Corston 2007: 5).[42] Although the number of self-inflicted deaths in the female prison estate fell in the years immediately following the report's publication, levels of self-inflicted death and self-harm among prisoners remain frighteningly high (e.g. Hawton et al. 2014; INQUEST 2014). Ministry of Justice figures show that there were 3,130 incidents of self-harm for every 1,000 female prisoners in 2019, compared with 650 incidents per 1,000 male prisoners in England and Wales (Ministry of Justice 2020u).[43]

One of the major issues affecting the mental health and well-being of female prisoners is the separation of mothers from their children. Corston (2007: 30) reports being told by imprisoned mothers that being separated from their children was a form of 'mental torture'. Across England and Wales, a staggering 18,000 children a year are separated from their mothers by imprisonment.[44] A report by the UK Government's Social Exclusion Unit (2002) found that only half of women who had been in contact with their children prior to their imprisonment received a visit after entering prison. It need hardly be underscored how imprisoning women at substantial distances from their children will only exacerbate the damage (on both sides) caused by such separation.[45]

Since its publication in 2007, the Corston report has become *the* starting point for debates about female imprisonment and plans for reform (though see Elfleet 2017 for a critical account of its impact and legacy). Its publication catalysed government investment in community-based alternatives which, by 2013, had led to the development of more than thirty community support projects for women (House of Commons Justice Committee 2013). In Wales, what is recognised as the 'distinct set of issues' facing Welsh female prisoners led to the establishment of a number of programmes and initiatives (House of Commons Welsh Affairs Committee 2007: 19; Rees et al. 2017). A Women's Turnaround Project was established to provide Welsh female offenders and those deemed to be at risk of victimisation with a community-based service aimed at addressing their needs (Holloway and Brookman 2010). In 2013, the Integrated Offender Management (IOM) Cymru Women's Pathfinder project was established to attempt to reduce the number of female arrests in Wales and to divert women from custody by improving community provision (Holloway et al. 2017). In 2019, the Welsh Government and Ministry of Justice (2019a) published a joint blueprint to improve services for females in Wales who have offended, which commits both governments to deliver services that are 'distinct to Wales', and to reduce the number of Welsh women in prison (Welsh Government and Ministry of Justice 2019a: 1). Even more recently, in May 2020, the then minister of state for prisons and probation, Lucy Frazer QC, announced that the very first women's residential centre for female offenders would be sited in Wales, offering an alternative to imprisonment for women convicted of low-level offences (Ministry of Justice 2020w).

While there is hope that at least some of the problems that we have highlighted in this discussion might be addressed by these new developments, it would be wise to remain appropriately sceptical. There is now a very long history of criminal justice reforms that fail to deliver on the hype that initially surrounds them – the Wrexham super-prison, HMP Berwyn, being only one prominent example. Not only that, but there is a further disconcerting trend in recent data on female imprisonment that calls into question the likelihood of meaningful change in outcomes even if government strategies proceed according to plan.

Post-Corston, much effort has been directed towards trying to end the use of short-term custodial sentences. This has only been partially achieved: since 2013, the overall number of Welsh female prisoners has stabilised rather than declined and, in 2019, 1 in 5 females sentenced to custody were still being sentenced for a period of one month or less. But at the other end of the spectrum, even excluding those serving life sentences, almost a quarter (23 per cent) of all Welsh women in prison are now serving sentences of 4 years or more (Ministry of Justice 2020x).[46] This in part reflects the fact that, in 2019, 4.9 per cent of all women sentenced to immediate custodial sentences in Wales were sentenced to 4 years or more as compared to 2.8 per cent in 2013 (Ministry of Justice 2020a). This increasingly large and troubled group will remain unaffected by the opening of the proposed residential centre, no matter how welcome that development might otherwise be.

## YOUTH JUSTICE

Compared with the areas considered thus far, there can be little doubt that youth justice is the most thoroughly researched, commonly written about and best understood part of the Welsh criminal justice system (see inter alia Deering and Evans 2021; Drakeford 2010; Evans et al. 2020; Field 2015; Haines 2009; Haines and Case 2015; Haines et al. 2013; Thomas 2015a). Not coincidentally, it is also a part of the criminal justice system that features not only extensive devolved responsibility, but also a sustained attempt by the Welsh Government to forge its own distinctive policy approach towards children (under 18s) in conflict with the law. This is an approach best summarised as 'children first and offenders second' (Welsh Government and Youth Justice Board 2004), and has been inspired by both principled and pragmatic considerations.

In terms of the former, the Welsh Government is committed to the view that children are agents-in-themselves with their own rights rather than simply subjects for or cyphers of the views of adults, an outlook consistent with the 1989 United Nations Convention on the Rights of the Child (Case et al. 2005; Haines et al. 2004).[47] In purely pragmatic terms, there is also a recognition that diverting children away from the criminal justice system is better for everyone (including the system itself) over the long run: the aim should be to break the cycle or spiral that leads so many to a lifetime of entanglement with the police, courts, prisons and the probation service.

We will return to what Mark Drakeford (2010: 151) writing in his academic guise once described as the 'Welsh experiment' in youth justice policy, namely the attempt to develop a distinctive and distinctly progressive approach, even within the confines of a single England and Wales jurisdiction (Evans et al. 2021; Thomas 2015a). At this stage, we need only point out, first, that the distinctiveness of the Welsh approach has become less marked as the UK Government's more 'punitive' attitude to youth justice in England (cf. Goldson 2010; Scraton 2005) has been replaced by an approach that has arguably moved closer to that embraced in Wales.[48] Secondly, and relatedly, it is also clear that there are significant local variations within both Wales and England in terms of approaches to youth justice; these differences reflect the nuanced and complex inter-relationships between different layers of government, agencies and, indeed, individual personalities (Evans et al. 2021; Goldson and Briggs 2021; Smith and Gray 2019).

Yet even entering those caveats does nothing to diminish the fact that in the area of youth justice there is, for once, good news to report: the number of Welsh children entering the secure estate has fallen dramatically. In December 2019, there were just twenty-three Welsh children in prison compared to 108 a decade earlier (Youth Custody Service 2020; Youth Justice Board 2011). This decline can be attributed to an 80 per cent reduction in the number of immediate custodial sentences handed to under 18s in Wales and to a 76 per cent decline in the number of child arrests in Wales between 2010 and 2019 (Howard League for Penal Reform 2020).[49]

The Welsh Government's continuing commitment to a children-first and rights-based approach to youth justice is prominent in the Welsh Government and Ministry of Justice's (2019b) joint strategy on youth justice in Wales. Indeed, it may plausibly be argued that the Welsh approach has effectively been mainstreamed as a result of an increasing awareness right across the UK and beyond of the impact of adverse childhood experiences (ACEs) later in life (e.g. Bunting et al. 2019; Hetherington 2020; Lewer et al. 2020; for the impact on youth justice in Wales, see Evans et al. 2020; Skuse and Matthew 2015).[50] Whatever its possible limitations (see Anderson 2019; Jahanshahi et al. 2021; Kelly-Irving and Delpierre 2019), given

**Figure 2.13** Children (under 18s) in custody per 100,000 children in England and Wales (based on region of youth offending team), 2002 to 2020

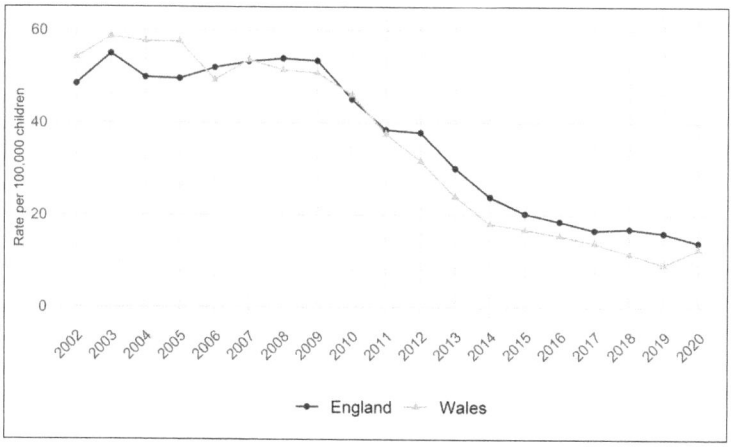

*Source:* Office for National Statistics (2020g, 2020h); Youth Custody Service (2020)

**Figure 2.14** Rate of assaults by children on children at young offender institutions in England and Wales per 100, 2017 to 2019

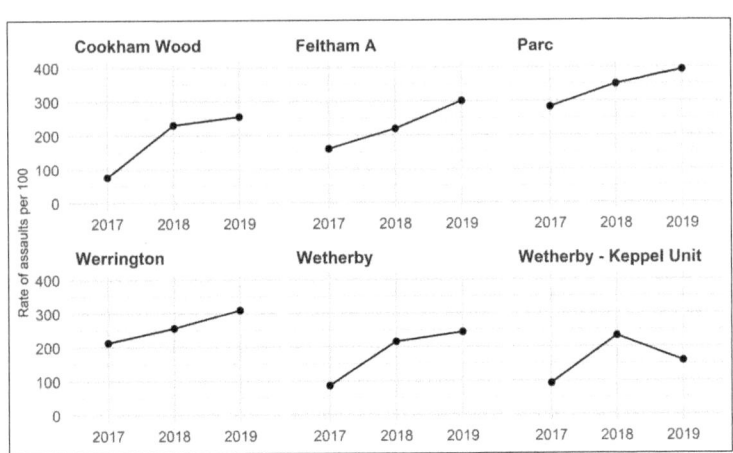

*Source:* Ministry of Justice (2020y)

the obvious potential of the criminal justice system to further amplify the effects of trauma on vulnerable young people, this increasing awareness bolsters the evidential underpinnings of the Welsh Government's approach.

Any doubts about the wisdom of seeking to divert as many children as possible away from the criminal justice system are likely to be tempered by the available evidence on safety within custodial institutions for children in England and Wales (HMI Prisons 2017; Taylor 2016). In Wales, there are currently two such institutions: Hillside Secure Children's Home in Neath and HM Young Offender Institution (YOI) Parc in Bridgend.[51] In November 2019, the then HM Chief Inspector of Prisons, Peter Clarke, described the latter as 'easily the best' young offender institution in England and Wales (HMI Prisons 2020b: 6). Yet even here, disaggregated data (Figure 2.14) show that HMYOI Parc recorded the highest rate of child-on-child assaults of all young offender institutions in England and Wales in each of the three years between 2017 and 2019. In the same inspection report on HMYOI Parc, HM Inspectorate of Prisons (2020b) also raised concerns about the experiences of children from a BAME background: this included reports of discriminatory treatment by staff, as well as being more likely to be subjected to the use of force when compared with other children held at HMYOI Parc.

**Map 2.3**  Youth offending team areas in Wales and the secure estate

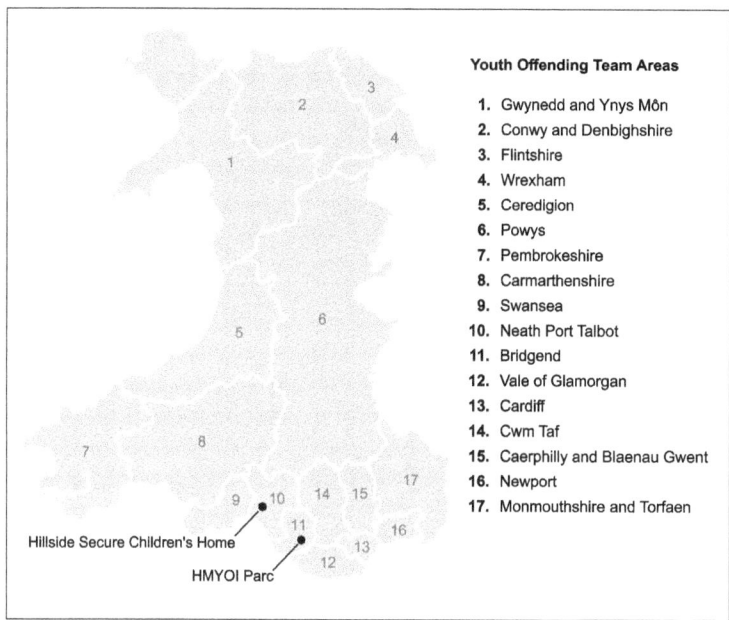

Unsurprisingly, distance and dispersal often exacerbate the 'feelings of isolation, loneliness and vulnerability' that children experience in custody (HMI Prisons 2016a: 19). We glimpse the extent of this problem from a recent inspection at HMYOI Parc: just under a third (30 per cent) of the children being held there at the time were from Wales; a broadly similar proportion (31 per cent) were being held at least 100 miles away from home (HMI Prisons 2020b). During an earlier visit to the same institution, the HM Inspectorate of Prisons' review team were told of one child from England who had received regular visits from their caseworker when held in an English institution, but who had not received a single visit after being transferred to a facility in Wales (HMI Prisons 2016a). Research also confirms that Welsh-speaking children held in custody face additional difficulties, including feeling 'isolated and under threat' when held in an 'unfamiliar linguistic environment' (Hughes and Madoc-Jones 2005: 378). More generally, a study of Welsh girls in custody also showed that 'isolation from their home country' is a major problem for Welsh children held in England (Hughes et al. 2012: 523).

There are two further considerations that serve to qualify the comparatively rosy picture of the development of the youth justice system in Wales presented thus far in this chapter. First, while there is indeed clear evidence of a reduction in the number of children entering the youth secure estate, this decline is unevenly distributed. While the number of White children first entering the criminal justice system fell by 87 per cent between 2010 and 2019, the decline among children from an Asian background across the same period was 69 per cent, and for children from Black backgrounds it was 59 per cent (Ministry of Justice 2020z). This in turn helps explain why, by 2020, 13 per cent of Welsh children in custody were from a BAME background compared with 7 per cent in 2012 (Youth Justice Board 2021b).[52]

Secondly, at 10 years old, the age of criminal responsibility in England and Wales remains one of the lowest in Europe (Brown 2020). This state of affairs has been frequently lamented by the United Nations Convention on the Rights of the Child Monitoring Group, who recommended in 2015 that the Welsh Government should seek to persuade the UK Government to increase the minimum age of responsibility (Croke and Williams 2015: 62). Reporting in 2019, the Thomas Commission (2019: 203) also recommended that the age of criminal responsibility in Wales be increased to 12. Absent the devolution of justice, such a reform requires action by the UK Parliament and Government acting in their England and Wales guise – action that it has refused to take (Brown and Charles 2021). Youth justice may be the area in which devolved involvement in the Welsh criminal justice system is most marked, yet even here there remain hard constitutional limits on the extent of the 'Welsh experiment'.

## CONCLUSION

At the start of this chapter we noted how Wales's incorporation into the English criminal justice system has served to render Wales effectively invisible; a situation that has not changed in any fundamental way since the still relatively recent tendency to append 'and Wales' to various official titles associated with the institutions of that system. The task we set ourselves was therefore to collect, collate and marshal official data in order to ensure that Wales would become visible. Using official statistics we have traced a broad arc through arrests, prosecutions, imprisonment, probation, and on to reoffending. As we have done so we have touched on data relating to the police, courts, prisons and probation. We have also provided separate treatments of women in the criminal justice system and youth justice. Throughout the chapter, we have sought to indicate how the situation in Wales compares with that found in England or across England and Wales as a whole.

At this juncture it is important to restate the limitations of our approach. We claim no more than to have provided a top-line overview. There is no doubt that a great deal of complexity would be uncovered if we were to delve deeper. Our analysis has been constrained not only by considerations of space, but also by the availability of data. To repeat a point that we made in the introduction to this chapter, acquiring even basic information about the operation of the Welsh criminal justice system requires very substantial effort, including extensive utilisation of the rights afforded to putative researchers by Freedom of Information legislation.

Nonetheless, even after entering all the necessary caveats, the picture of Wales that now stands revealed due to this analysis is clearly a deeply troubling one. Lower crime rates than our English neighbour, perhaps, but higher rates of violent offences; disturbing data on race throughout the system; higher conviction rates than in England emanating from a courts system that is increasingly physically inaccessible across much of the country; extraordinarily high rates of incarceration; again, what is surely an extraordinarily high proportion of the population subject to some kind of probation supervision from a service that has been comprehensively mismanaged by the UK Government; disappointing data on reoffending; more deeply troubling data on female imprisonment with all the attendant implications for dependents – the list grinds on. Even in those parts of the system where there are positive trends in evidence, such as youth justice, there remains cause for very significant concern.

Yet, precisely because most of this is largely unnoticed and unknown we have no – or at least very few – explanations as to *why* any of this might be the case. There are few academics who take an interest, and the same is true for those campaigning organisations who do such otherwise excellent work in the field. As will become clearer in subsequent chapters, because of the constitutional underpinnings of the Welsh criminal justice system, neither is there much by way of political or policy interest devoted to understanding the issues at stake. Moreover, even if knowledge and understanding were present and the political will could be summoned up to try to address the problems of the Welsh criminal justice system, the same constitutional structures mean that implementing any transformational change is nigh-on impossible. The Wales revealed here is not only troubled, but – as we shall see – is incapable of attending to its troubles.

# 3
# WHITEHALL AND THE WELSH CRIMINAL JUSTICE SYSTEM
*What power reveals*

THE STARTING POINT for this book is that the Welsh criminal justice system is distinct, even as it remains part of what is ostensibly a single England and Wales criminal justice system. This distinctiveness reflects the ways in which the institutions and practices of any criminal justice system will inevitably interact with the wider realm of social policy and its attendant institutions, which in the Welsh context are usually subject to devolved control. As a result, the Welsh criminal justice system straddles what we have characterised as a jagged edge of devolved and reserved (or non-devolved) powers and responsibilities. The following is the first of two linked chapters examining in more detail both sides of this jagged edge. Here we examine the role played by ministers and their civil servants in Whitehall, as well as England and Wales criminal justice institutions, in the operation of the Welsh criminal justice system.[1] Given that Whitehall remains overwhelmingly the dominant 'partner' in this system, with that dominance underpinned by the Welsh devolution statutes, we aim to be particularly attentive to the ways in which it exercises the power and control that it enjoys.[2] According to arguably the greatest modern political biographer, Robert Caro, 'Power does not always corrupt ... But what power *always* does is reveal' (2019: 206). As will become clear in the following pages, an examination of the ways in which Whitehall exercises its powers in the Welsh criminal justice system reveals a great deal about how Whitehall views Wales.

The chapter consists of two main parts. Initially we engage in what might be termed an institutional mapping exercise, where we provide an overview of the formal roles played by Whitehall departments and their associated agencies in the operation of the Welsh criminal justice system. Two main themes are highlighted in this exploration. The first is the quite extraordinary level of centralisation (in London) that characterises the upper echelons of those criminal justice institutions whose reach extends over England and Wales. The second theme is the (limited) extent to which some of these departments and related agencies have developed Welsh-level administrative arrangements. Where they do exist, these various Welsh-level arrangements tend to act as the interface with the Welsh Government and its associated agencies.

In the second part of the chapter we draw heavily on interview evidence to examine how the 'England and Wales' side of the Welsh criminal justice system operates in practice. Here we identify and explore the impact of three structural factors shaping Whitehall's relationship with the Welsh criminal justice system. The first is already familiar, namely centralisation. A second and related factor is that Wales-specific considerations enjoy only very limited salience among politicians and senior policy makers responsible for England and Wales institutions. This should not come as a surprise. While the Welsh frame adopted in our previous chapter served to raise fundamental questions about how well Wales is served by its criminal justice system, viewed from the perspective of Whitehall it is all – not to put too fine a point on it – small beer. Even if Welsh imprisonment rates are strikingly high on a per capita basis, knife crime in London or the challenges of policing Greater Manchester, for example, loom far larger as social and political priorities. Wales is largely out of sight and out of mind.[3]

The third structural factor we identify is the dizzying pace of change to which the institutions of the England and Wales system have been subjected in recent decades. This final point will be all too wearily familiar to those readers who are already conversant with the recent history of criminal justice policy across England and Wales. Successive UK governments of all political persuasions have been active – indeed, hyperactive – in their role as stewards of the England and Wales criminal justice system (see Allen

2006; Charman and Savage 2007; Goldson 2010; Loader 2006; Ramsbottom 2010; Sasse et al. 2020; Tonry 2004, 2007). New initiative has been piled on new initiative, all weighed down by veritable rafts of new legislation;[4] reorganisation has been followed by restructuring followed by yet more reorganisation. All this has reflected the interaction of various pressures and influences, including the embrace of marketisation and the related nostrums of so-called New Public Management (McLaughlin et al. 2001), as well as the austerity-driven decision to slash spending on justice (Ford 2017; Newman and Dehaghani 2022). But also of central importance has been the desire of successive administrations to be seen to be 'tough on crime'. Criminal justice policy has often been shaped by performative considerations rather than by judicious evaluation of the evidence as to what actually works (see Garland 2001; Simon 2007). As Barry Goldson argues in his account of New Labour's youth justice policy legacy in England: 'the political imperative to appear "tough", exercises greater influence over policy formation than criminological expertise, research-based knowledge and/or practice-based experience' (2010: 171). As such, an important part of the story set out in the latter part of this chapter reflects the challenges faced by those charged with rendering functional the highly anomalous constitutional configuration of the Welsh criminal justice system, in a context characterised by well-nigh constant churn and the pursuit of performative rather than evidence-led policy agendas.

MAPPING 'ENGLAND AND WALES'

The Home Office and the Ministry of Justice are the key departments of state overseeing the institutions that make up the England and Wales criminal justice system. In broad brush terms, the Home Office is responsible for policing, crime and drugs policy, while the Ministry of Justice is responsible for courts, prisons, probation services and youth justice. The Home Secretary has overall ministerial oversight of and responsibility for the former, while the Justice Secretary and Lord Chancellor (a combined role) plays the same roles in the context of the latter.[5] Both departments are surrounded by a dense thicket of non-ministerial departments, executive agencies and various other kinds of public bodies, which together form key nodes of executive power and administrative responsibility across the criminal justice system.

Underlining the extent of this complexity, the Thomas Commission's (2019: 554–5) attempt to map what it terms Wales's 'justice infrastructure' includes no fewer than fifty-three separate agencies and bodies, ranging alphabetically from the Advisory Board on Justices of the Peace to the Youth Justice Board. Meanwhile, working from the list of reserved matters in the Welsh devolution legislation, in our own previous work we have identified no fewer than seventy-four different agencies and public bodies playing different roles in Wales's wider justice system, forty supporting the work of the Home Office and thirty-four supporting the Ministry of Justice (Jones and Wyn Jones 2019: 260–4). These different estimates reflect the fact that we cast our net wider, including the security service (MI5) as well as immigration policy and enforcement-related activities in our accounting. Common ground is that both lists are extensive and cover a very diverse group of organisations, some of which are large in terms of budgets and staff complements (e.g. HMPPS), while others are very small indeed (e.g. Criminal Injuries Compensation Authority).

Focusing here more narrowly on policing and criminal justice, Table 3.1 lists forty-eight different organisations associated with the Home Office and Ministry of Justice, or otherwise performing some criminal justice-related function (for example, we have included the Health and Safety Executive which falls under the ambit of the Department of Work and Pensions).[6] In each case we have noted: (i) which Whitehall department they are accountable to; (ii) their territorial coverage (i.e. which parts of the constituent territories of the UK are covered in their remit); (iii) where they are headquartered; and, (iv) whether or not they have some Welsh-level administrative structure or arrangement in place (i.e. the extent to which there has been any internal administrative devolution in order to allow Wales to be treated as a territorial unit). Continuing a consistent theme throughout this book, constructing this table required multiple requests under the terms of the Freedom of Information Act 2000.

**Table 3.1** Departments, agencies and public bodies (reserved) with responsibility for criminal justice in Wales, 2020

| Organisation | Ministerial department | Territorial coverage | Location of headquarters | Wales as an administrative unit? |
|---|---|---|---|---|
| **Executive agency** | | | | |
| Criminal Injuries Compensation Authority | Ministry of Justice | England, Scotland and Wales | Glasgow | No |
| HM Courts & Tribunals Service | Ministry of Justice | England and Wales | London | HM Courts and Tribunals Service Wales |
| HM Prison and Probation Service | Ministry of Justice | England and Wales | London | HM Prison and Probation Service Wales |
| Legal Aid Agency | Ministry of Justice | England and Wales | London | No |
| **Executive non-departmental public body** | | | | |
| Health and Safety Executive | Department for Work and Pensions | UK | Bootle | Wales & South West (offices in Cardiff, Carmarthen and Wrexham) |
| Disclosure and Barring Service | Home Office | England and Wales | Liverpool (policy department) | No |
| Gangmasters and Labour Abuse Authority | Home Office | England and Wales | London | No |
| Independent Office for Police Conduct | Home Office | England and Wales | Sale | No[7] |
| Security Industry Authority | Home Office | UK | London | No |
| Criminal Cases Review Commission | Ministry of Justice | England, Wales and Northern Ireland | Birmingham | No |
| Judicial Appointments Commission | Ministry of Justice | England and Wales | London | No[8] |

| Organisation | Ministerial department | Territorial coverage | Location of headquarters | Wales as an administrative unit? |
|---|---|---|---|---|
| Legal Services Board | Ministry of Justice | England and Wales | London | No, but features Welsh provisions (e.g. a staff member with responsibility for Welsh language; a member of staff with responsibility for Welsh legal developments) |
| Parole Board | Ministry of Justice | England and Wales | London | No |
| Youth Justice Board for England and Wales | Ministry of Justice | England and Wales | London | Youth Justice Board Cymru (Swansea) |
| Advisory non-departmental public body | | | | |
| Advisory Council on the Misuse of Drugs | Home Office | UK | London | No |
| Police Advisory Board for England and Wales | Home Office | England and Wales | London | No |
| Police Remuneration Review Body | Home Office | England, Wales and Northern Ireland | London | No |
| Advisory Committees on Justices of the Peace | Ministry of Justice | England and Wales | London | Yes |
| Criminal Procedure Rule Committee | Ministry of Justice | England and Wales | London | No |
| Independent Advisory Panel on Deaths in Custody | Ministry of Justice | England and Wales | London | No |
| Law Commission | Ministry of Justice | England and Wales | London | Yes[9] |
| Prison Service Pay Review Body | Ministry of Justice | England and Wales | London | No |

| Organisation | Ministerial department | Territorial coverage | Location of headquarters | Wales as an administrative unit? |
|---|---|---|---|---|
| Sentencing Council for England and Wales | Ministry of Justice | England and Wales | London | No |
| **Tribunal** | | | | |
| Police Discipline Appeals Tribunal | Home Office | England and Wales | London | No |
| **Independent monitoring body** | | | | |
| Independent Anti-slavery Commissioner | Home Office | UK | London | No |
| **Non-ministerial department** | | | | |
| National Crime Agency | | UK | London | No |
| Serious Fraud Office | | England, Wales and Northern Ireland | London | No |
| Crown Prosecution Service | | England and Wales | London | CPS Cymru-Wales (Cardiff, Mold and Swansea) |
| Supreme Court of the United Kingdom | | UK | London | No (although sat in Cardiff in June 2019)[10] |
| **Other** | | | | |
| Biometrics Commissioner (criminal matters) | Home Office | England and Wales | London | No |
| College of Policing | Home Office | England and Wales | | No |
| Commission for Countering Extremism | Home Office | England and Wales | London | No |
| Forensic Science Regulator | Home Office | England and Wales (in collaboration with Scotland and Northern Ireland) | Birmingham | No |

| Organisation | Ministerial department | Territorial coverage | Location of headquarters | Wales as an administrative unit? |
|---|---|---|---|---|
| HM Inspectorate of Constabulary and Fire & Rescue Services | Home Office | England and Wales (police) | London | No |
| Investigatory Powers Commissioner's Office | Home Office | UK | London | No |
| National Counter Terrorism Security Office | Home Office | UK | London | No |
| National Crime Agency Remuneration Review Body | Home Office | UK | London | No |
| Office for Communications and Data Authorisations | Home Office | UK | Manchester | No |
| Surveillance Camera Commissioner | Home Office | England and Wales | London | No |
| HM Inspectorate of Prisons | Ministry of Justice | England and Wales | London | No |
| HM Inspectorate of Probation | Ministry of Justice | England and Wales | Manchester | No |
| Independent Monitoring Boards | Ministry of Justice | England and Wales | London | No |
| Judicial Appointments and Conduct Ombudsman | Ministry of Justice | England and Wales | London | No |
| Judicial Office | Ministry of Justice | England and Wales | London | No |
| The Legal Ombudsman | Ministry of Justice | England and Wales | Wolverhampton | No |
| Official Solicitor and Public Trustee | Ministry of Justice | England and Wales | London | No |
| Prisons and Probation Ombudsman | Ministry of Justice | England and Wales | London | No |
| Victims' Commissioner | Ministry of Justice | England and Wales | London | No |

Given our previous discussion of the territorial constitution of the UK, the information on territorial coverage will come as no surprise. The overwhelming majority (71 per cent) of the organisations listed – fully thirty-four out of forty-eight – are 'England and Wales' in scope, with the Home Office and the Ministry of Justice themselves both largely operating as 'England and Wales' ministries. To further underline this point, it is worth recalling that when calculating the Barnett consequentials that determine changes in the block grant to the devolved territories, the UK Government's own figures suggest that only 8.3 per cent of spending by the Home Office and none at all of the Ministry of Justice's spending relates to Scotland.[11] It is also worth noting that those UK-wide justice-related organisations that do exist operate in ways that recognise the existence of three different legal jurisdictions and (criminal) justice systems within the territory of the state (see, for example, the Independent Anti-slavery Commissioner 2019).

Perhaps unsurprisingly in the context of the historic organisation of the British state, a large majority of these organisations are headquartered in London. Nonetheless, with fully thirty-eight out of forty-eight organisations (79 per cent) headquartered there, the extent to which this is true is particularly striking. And even this does not tell the full story of London dominance, for despite various continuing efforts to move offices and staff away from (in an England and Wales context) the English capital, as noted by the Institute for Government (2019), the civil service's 'efforts at workforce relocation have tended to focus on staff in junior, operational roles'. London remains the nerve centre (Institute for Government 2019). Thus for the UK civil service as a whole, although 20 per cent of staff are based in London, this includes two-thirds (67 per cent) of the most senior (i.e. SCS grade) staff and 45 per cent of those on the next most senior grades (Grades 6 and 7) (Institute for Government 2019).[12] In the case of the Home Office, although 39 per cent of the overall staff complement are based in London, this includes 85 per cent of its SCS staff and 73 per cent of the department's Grade 6 and 7 staff (Home Office 2020h). As for the Ministry of Justice, while 73 per cent of its total staff complement are based in London, this includes 94 per cent of its most senior staff and 82 per cent of those on Grades 6 and 7 (Ministry of Justice 2020zi).[13]

What about the place of Wales in these England and Wales institutions? While the Ministry of Justice established a three-person Justice Devolution Team in 2015 (Ministry of Justice 2020zii), not one of the various institutions that make up the England and Wales criminal justice system is headquartered in Wales. As a result, only 0.6 per cent (twenty-two in total) of the Home Office's SCS level and Grade 6 and 7 staff are based in Wales (Home Office 2020h).[14] The Ministry of Justice, for its part, has zero SCS grade staff based in Wales and only 0.7 per cent (eight in total) of its Grade 6 and 7 staff. Indeed, in August 2019, the total number of Ministry of Justice senior staff (i.e. SCS) based in London (135) was higher than the total number of staff working for the ministry in Wales (116) (Ministry of Justice 2020z). In substance if not in name, this remains an English criminal justice system.

This is not to say, however, that Wales is entirely absent from the institutional scaffolding. Rather, as Table 3.1 also makes clear, some of the institutions concerned recognise Wales as an administrative unit within their overall structures (Pritchard 2016 provided an initial, pathbreaking exploration). Examples include HM Prison and Probation Service (HMPPS) in Wales, Youth Justice Board (YJB) Cymru, a Home Office team in Wales, HM Courts and Tribunals Service (HMCTS) Wales and the Crown Prosecution Service (CPS) Cymru-Wales.

From a Welsh perspective, it is tempting to view the various examples of administrative devolution as a recognition of Wales's 'unique status' and the significance of the changes wrought by the advent of democratic devolution (NOMS Cymru et al. 2006: iii). More often than not, however, Wales appears to have been established as an administrative unit as part of wider processes of institutional regionalisation and reform that had little or nothing to do with Wales itself. Thus, CPS Cymru-Wales was established in April 2011 as one of fourteen regional units across England and Wales (Crown Prosecution Service 2011).[15] Yet while adapting to the reality of Welsh devolution may not have been the main driver for administrative recognition of Wales, on occasion at least, it has played a key role. National Offender Management Service (NOMS) Cymru (now HMPPS in Wales) is a case in point. Originally established in 2004 as part of a wider structure of ten regional directorates across England and Wales (Home Office 2004b), NOMS Cymru was disbanded in 2011 as the attempt to regionalise parts of the Ministry of Justice (of which it formed a part) was abandoned after NOMS was told to reduce the cost of its headquarters' functions by 37 per cent as part of the government's spending review (National Audit Office 2012). Yet only three years later, in 2014, NOMS Wales would be resuscitated (it was the only regional-level organisation to be reintroduced in this way), in explicit recognition of the 'distinct differences arising from devolution' (NOMS 2016: 21).[16]

Herein lies the significance of the admittedly limited and often precarious extent of administrative devolution that characterises some England and Wales criminal justice institutions. The Welsh-level organisational nodes that do exist have tended to become key points of interaction with devolved institutions in Wales on whose cooperation they rely when operating west of the border. Yet the ability of these Welsh-level administrative structures to bear the weight that is being placed on them seems questionable. As we have seen, because there is very little – if any – policy-making influence or capacity in Wales, the units that have resulted from administrative devolution have tended to be operationally focused and relatively junior in the context of a notoriously hierarchical civil service. There remains, therefore, a very strong reliance on London-based policy makers proactively seeking to understand the devolved Welsh context and to act on the basis of that understanding. This would be challenging enough at the best of times, but – as has already been noted – since the early 1990s the criminal justice system has been subjected to a stream of organisational reforms and policy initiatives that has continued more or less unabated until the present day: from Michael Howard to Jack Straw to Chris Grayling and Theresa May to Priti Patel (see Goldson 2010; Garside et al. 2020; Loader 2006; Ramsbottom 2010; Sasse et al. 2020; Tonry 2004). This at a time when Welsh devolution itself has also rotated through four separate constitutional dispensations and endured almost constant iteration and change (see Rawlings 2003; Wyn Jones and Scully 2012).

It is surely wildly optimistic to expect a highly centralised system with almost no senior presence in the country, and one which is being driven by performative rather than evidence-based policy agendas, to take seriously the complex and *sui generis* arrangements that pertain for Wales. Rather, and as we shall observe in the next section, on this side of the jagged edge it has been a case of trying to ameliorate the worst effects of an 'England and Wales' system for which Wales is, at best, an afterthought.

## EXPERIENCING 'ENGLAND AND WALES' IN PRACTICE

Our emphasis so far has been largely organisational, focusing on the structures that make up the England and Wales criminal justice system. Here we draw heavily on interview testimony to explore how these various institutions – with their elements of administrative devolution – operate in Wales in practice. These voices are important. As we have repeatedly noted, criminal justice policy is unavoidably linked to wider social policy, hence the jagged edge between devolved and reserved (non-devolved) policy that characterises and defines the Welsh criminal justice system. Our interviewees (see Appendix) are those tasked on a day-to-day basis with trying to straddle this jagged edge and are therefore uniquely well placed to reveal just how well (or otherwise) the England and Wales structures and adaptations are managing the very significant challenges that they face. Again, our underlying interest is in what power reveals.

\* \* \*

The first point to note is that among some interviewees, at least, there exists a degree of optimism about the ways in which the administrative devolution that has taken place to date allows the criminal justice system to bridge the divide between devolved and non-devolved responsibilities. As well as helping to ensure that Whitehall-based officials have a better understanding of the Welsh context, administrative devolution is credited with improving levels of engagement and understanding among policy makers in Wales and with helping to smooth out any problems that may arise in intergovernmental working.

> **Jonathan:** What's happening now is I think there's a much greater understanding of things that are likely to be different in Wales ... HMPPS senior meetings have got a set template, agenda, purpose ... There is a consideration of 'is there something different we need to do in terms of Wales?'

> **Sam:** It increases the chances that Wales doesn't get randomly missed. HMPPS in Wales have now created forums with Welsh Government, forums with ministers, where they say, 'You know this policy? You know that policy? It's really important that we try and remember offenders in it.'

**Jonathan:** And I think that has helped massively in acting as a bridge between HMPPS in Wales, Welsh Government and the Ministry of Justice . . . The Ministry of Justice sometimes forgets about devolved administration; [but] it happens the other way as well, I think.

**Sian:** Staff can walk into that building [Welsh Government]. They have got a pass. They literally can walk in and go and find who they want to speak to; sit down and explain, 'This isn't about politics. This is the problem. We're going to be accused of this. Can you get four hundred grand out of your minister?' 'Oh, I'll go away and find out' . . . So that sort of thing is where there is real added value of somebody who is on the ground with a very small team . . . who is able to make those relationships and get things done when the politics . . . the devolution stuff, and everything else gets in the way.

It is certainly the case that it is the Welsh administrative arms of England and Wales bodies that tend to be involved in the various fora that have been established to bridge the devolved/reserved divide. These include: the Advisory Panel on Substance Misuse; the All Wales Anti-social Behaviour Co-ordinators Group; the Criminal Justice Board for Wales; the Wales Anti-slavery Leadership Group; Community Justice Cymru; the Integrated Offender Management Cymru Board; the Justice in Wales Strategy Group; the Policing Partnership Board for Wales; the Wales Association of Community Safety Officers; the Wales Extremism and Counter Terrorism Unit; the Wales Home Office Advisory Group; and the Wales Youth Justice Advisory Panel (Jones and Wyn Jones 2019; Thomas Commission 2019; Welsh Government 2017a).

The use of 'Wales', 'All Wales' or 'Cymru' in these various titles may be emblematic of the way that – operationally speaking – certain parts of the England and Wales criminal justice system simply *have* to work differently in Wales. In the field of youth justice, for example, the *All Wales Youth Offending Strategy* was co-produced by the Welsh Government and the Youth Justice Board (2004: 1) in an effort to develop a 'national framework' for preventing youth offending in Wales. A decade later, the Welsh Government and the Youth Justice Board (2014) published *Children and Young People First* in which they restated their joint commitment to reducing the number of children entering the criminal justice system in Wales. In doing so they explicitly recognised that a reduction in re-offending would be 'best achieved' if devolved and non-devolved partners 'work together' (Welsh Government and Youth Justice Board 2014: 4–6).

Other examples of such co-production include the 2006 strategy document *Joining Together in Wales*, which was jointly published by NOMS Cymru, the Youth Justice Board and the Welsh Government (2006: 7–8) and explicitly recognised the 'considerable autonomy' enjoyed by the Welsh Government over policy areas key to reducing reoffending in Wales. More recently, the Welsh Government published a framework designed to help support individuals at risk of offending in Wales. The report was developed in conjunction with HMPPS in Wales, reflecting, it claimed, the 'strong relationships' that exist between them (Welsh Government and HMPPS in Wales 2017: 3). This framework has since been supplemented by the publication of a concordat agreement between the Ministry of Justice and Welsh Government aimed at ensuring 'consultation and co-operation' between them (2018: 1). More recently still, both sides have worked together on blueprints for 'Wales-only' strategies for women and young people (Welsh Government and Ministry of Justice 2019a, 2019b).

For some of our interviewees, these and related developments underline the ways in which the establishment of Welsh-level structures within the England and Wales criminal justice system has improved working relationships between the UK and Welsh governments and helped clarify a complex policy space.

**Kate:** Youth justice is a really good example of where that tension is really clear, but it has been mediated by having YJB Cymru which has been able to put a different slant on youth justice in Wales. [It is] looking to work with the Welsh Government to put something together that supports children in the youth justice system. So, having a joint youth justice strategy is actually an example of where that complexity has been dealt with quite well.

**Jonathan:** In terms of the wider landscape of strategy development, I think there's much more clarity now than there has been. I think that we've got things like the Wales Criminal Justice Board (now Criminal Justice Board for Wales) and IOM [Integrated

Offender Management] Cymru in terms of [a] reference point. I think people understand what those boards are doing and what the contribution is.

These sentiments suggest that the England and Wales criminal justice system is, even if only gradually, successfully adapting to devolution.

In reality, however, the overall tenor of the interviews is far less positive. The sense is rather of relatively small groups of committed individuals desperately seeking to make up for systemic deficiencies and relying on goodwill in order to do so. The following comments are typical.

**Olivia:** At best what we're talking about with the Home Office presence in Wales is three people. And don't get me wrong, I think the three of them are very effective, and they have certainly paved the way with some of that relationship building with Welsh Government. Staff have gone from a position of not even being afforded a desk in Welsh Government and having to sit in the coffee shop across the road to actually being in meetings and being able to engage effectively. But . . . three people can only do so much. And in terms of that knowledge development with Welsh Government . . . and being able to influence? It's going to be limited.

**Sam:** All too often HMPPS in Wales are still acting as a filter on the Whitehall side [checking] whether Wales has been properly thought of, and staff can feel a bit like whack-a-mole in that sense. If they are not quick enough a mole is going to pop up and really HMPPS in Wales will pay the heaviest price, because they tend to damage relations.

**William:** While Welsh Government are working well with them now, and with a set of ministers in the Ministry of Justice that want that to happen, a different set of ministers in Ministry of Justice could want a different thing altogether.

**Olivia:** I think a lot of it on that level comes down to personalities . . . They're sitting round the table because they want to . . . And that it's the right thing to do. But the danger with that is that if you do have an individual who doesn't want to play [along], then it all unravels.

**Kate:** How does that work? It works because individuals make it work, and organisations make it work, but it doesn't work by design.

Officials engaging in bureaucratic 'whack-a-mole', in a system that 'doesn't work by design' but instead depends on the presence of people of goodwill who seek to make the system work *despite* its manifest limitations and failings: this is a damning indictment. This story is not, moreover, one that is confined to those criminal justice professionals working in and for Wales. It is rather one that will be familiar to anyone who has taken an interest in the challenges facing officials and staff working in the England and Wales criminal justice system over the past three decades (Liebling 2010 et al; Souhami 2007; Tidmarsh 2021; Walker et al. 2019). Nonetheless, there is a unique Welsh dimension created by the very structure of a Welsh criminal justice system characterised by a jagged edge between devolved and non-devolved competences and responsibilities.

Interviewee testimony points to a tendency for initiatives to be produced without consideration of the specificities of the Welsh devolved context or the Welsh Government's own pre-existing activities in these areas. These policy initiatives are then launched using timeframes that give officials working in the Welsh administrative arms of the relevant England and Wales bodies almost no notice of their impending arrival, yet nonetheless require them to find ways of bridging the jagged edge to render them operational in Wales. Their testimonies also suggest reasons as to why Welsh devolution appears to present such a challenge to politicians and officials acting as custodians of the England and Wales criminal justice system. They point to weak understanding of the devolved context in Whitehall (a recurrent theme in the literature on devolution, see e.g. Hazell 2015; House of Commons Justice Committee 2009; House of Commons Welsh Affairs Committee 2010a; House of Lords Select Committee on the Constitution 2016; Thomas 2017; Rycroft 2019), a situation that is not helped by the constant churn of Whitehall officials between civil service roles (see e.g. House of Commons Public Administration and Constitutional Affairs Committee 2018: 20; Sasse and Norris 2019: 4–8). Even when devolution-related expertise is built up, it is rapidly lost. In addition, interviewees believe that the problems facing the criminal justice system in Wales are given little weight by policy makers preoccupied with the challenges facing the criminal justice system in large, English metropolitan centres.

The perceptions of our interviewees are supported by evidence from the policy documents themselves. Since 1999 and the advent of democratic devolution, numerous Home Office and Ministry of Justice policies have been published without serious thought being given to the Welsh context or even without reference to Wales at all. At best, a short paragraph or sentence is inserted into a UK Government's strategy to explain that the policy context is different in Wales. For example, during the New Labour government's frenetic period of reform and 'modernisation', the Welsh context was often simply acknowledged in a single sentence (Home Office 2001a, 2001b, 2004a, 2004b, 2006a) or overlooked entirely (Home Office 2003a, 2004c, 2004d, 2004e, 2006b). Twenty years later, government strategies are still failing to engage seriously with the specificities of the Welsh context, despite the development of elements of administrative devolution in the Home Office and Ministry of Justice. Examples include policies focused on prison safety (Ministry of Justice 2016a), serious violence (Home Office 2018a), hate crime (Home Office 2018b), drugs (Home Office, 2021), serious and organised crime (Home Office 2018c), female offending (Ministry of Justice 2018a) and victim services (Ministry of Justice 2018b).

Given this context it is perhaps unsurprising to find our interviewees decrying the UK government's long-standing failure to do more than simply make 'passing reference' to the distinct context that exists in Wales.

> **Emma:** When policy is being developed or officials in Wales get a White Paper or a government response – that level of document, which is giving an indication of the direction of travel – there's always a sentence that says something like, 'and consideration will be given to how this operates in Wales'. And it doesn't matter how far you go back and how many you pick up; you'll pretty much see that. So, policy tends to get set, but the Welsh bit always feels like the 'and Wales' afterwards at the end.
>
> **William:** You had a *Prison [Safety and] Reform* White Paper that made a passing reference to Wales on page thirty-five of the

document but didn't say how they were going to design a different prison system in Wales.

**Jonathan:** [The] Welsh Government interpreted it [the *Prison Safety and Reform* White Paper], and I think with hindsight, rightly, as 'we're just a bit of an add-on, oh, and we'll have to do something about Wales'. And didn't do it. So, I think that is where things have fallen down, perhaps at Ministry of Justice level sometimes rather than HMPPS.

**Jayne:** Or the Welsh Government get a little paragraph on page ninety-two that says, 'Oh and it's different in Wales and we'll work with Welsh Government colleagues to sort it.' That doesn't help at all.

What are ostensibly meant to be England and Wales policies are, in reality, English policies in which Wales features – literally – as an afterthought.

The inevitable consequence of what appears to be a generalised and systematic failure to consider how Wales 'fits' at the policy formulation-stage is that UK government officials based in Wales and Welsh Government staff find themselves engaged in frantic, last minute efforts to ensure that new policies can be rendered workable. Indeed, serving to underline the extent to which 'England and Wales' policy makers ignore the reality of Welsh devolution, in some cases, government strategies are announced or published without any prior notification being given to officials in Wales, rendering the whole process of trying to retrofit Wales into their plans even more fraught. The following provide a sense of the challenges faced by those charged with seeking to make operational in Wales policies that have been designed 'in total isolation' from what is now a very different policy context.

**Jayne:** The *Female Offender Strategy* is one that colleagues from Welsh Government had been asking for over a year to be involved in at the same time, rather than having what we've had in the past [where] lovely strategies have come out from colleagues in London, that have clearly been developed for months and months and months, and officials in Welsh Government get, in some cases, three hours to comment on them before publication.

**Sian:** I'll give you another example. [The] *Serious and Organised Crime* [strategy], which is the one staff have been trying to do for six years . . . Painful, painful, painful. And they've got to a point now where the *Serious Violence Strategy* came out and the Home Office got some serious flack for that from the Welsh Government. 'You didn't engage us! We haven't got a problem with half of this stuff. [But] it doesn't mention the Welsh context in the strategy.' The Home Office did some engagement events. It wasn't the best they had ever done, but I think time was, you know, really racing past. Everyone was very upset about it. It was a big disaster.

**Jayne:** The *Victim Strategy*, for example, that was MoJ Petty France[17] owned, and that was quite a last-minute approach. And the *Female Offender Strategy* – the MoJ one – was definitely done in total isolation until the last minute when the Welsh Government were given an opportunity to comment.

**Craig:** It [the *Serious Violence Strategy*] was just announced and landed. And that, unfortunately, is a trait of central government in London. Things will just get announced, unbeknown to officials in Wales. There's a relatively small window of engagement and opportunity to influence and provide advice and evidence to any changes in policy, strategies or direction of travel. And that again is very frustrating.

**Sian:** And I think the way that the Home Office work is often seen as being very much all behind closed doors. It's all very secret, they don't want to let anybody have any information, and the first that people find out about stuff is when it's actually announced or it's on the television.[18] And I think that's massively frustrating and I can see how that feeds a perception that either the Home Office don't know what they're doing in terms of Wales, or they don't care.

**Jayne:** And sometimes the Welsh Government will have the choice of really trying to retrofit something so it looks like it is truly an England-Wales approach, or they can't do it, in which case they have to publish it as 'England and Wales' and deal with the fallout of colleagues and stakeholders in Wales saying, 'Well, it's an England and Wales report. Where's NHS England in this? Where's the Health and Social Services Act in this? Where's ...?'

Despite the years that have passed since the advent of democratic devolution, ministers and senior officials in Whitehall still struggle to differentiate Wales from England. The result is criminal justice policies that are designed with little or no consideration of the specific legislative and policy context pertaining in Wales. It is not surprising that this apparently endemic failure to 'appreciate' legislative and policy differences between Wales and England when designing 'national' policies is the cause of very obvious frustration among our interviewees.

**William:** They have a responsibility for England *and* Wales for the justice system, but design systems that are only fit for England.

**Jamie:** If they do have a viewpoint on what's going on in Wales, from a service perspective, I think it would be based on what they perceive is just going on in services in England.

**Emma:** I think the other thing that's important is the officials who are advising ministers don't always appreciate that there is a difference. So, for example, staff [in Wales] have recently been reviewing the strategy documents written by colleagues in London, and they are looking at the dragonisation element. 'Well actually you've mentioned Ofsted, Ofsted doesn't cover Wales. We have something else, it's not quite an equivalent. This is what it looks like. So that responsibility won't exist here.' So for officials in Wales, whether in the Youth Justice Board or the Welsh Government, there's a continual job of raising awareness with your colleagues that actually things are different.

**William:** Ministry of Justice will work with Whitehall departments and people like NHS England and Public Health England developing their strategic approach to the management of prisons and offenders. So that immediately doesn't take account of the devolved legal context in Wales or the devolved policy context in Wales. So, you've got a central government department saying, for example, 'We need better mental health support so what we'll create is mental health hubs, support hubs, in London, Birmingham, Manchester, which are acute support hubs.' But then they say, 'Health is devolved to Wales, so you just do your own thing.'

One of the clearest examples of the Ministry of Justice's failure to understand or navigate differences between Wales and England surfaced in 2016 after Charlie Taylor (now HM Chief Inspector of Prisons) published his recommendations for secure schools following a review of the youth justice system in England and Wales (Taylor 2016). While Taylor's recommendations were immediately welcomed by the Ministry of Justice (2016b), which quickly announced its intention to roll out the proposals across England, they were just as quickly rejected by Welsh Government's Cabinet Secretary for Communities and Children who declared the Welsh Government's intention to devise 'Welsh solutions' to the problems facing the youth secure estate in Wales (National Assembly for Wales Debate, 14 December 2016). For a number of our interviewees, this was further evidence of the way in which the Ministry of Justice still tends to view England and Wales as an undifferentiated whole.

> **Emma:** So if we take Secure Schools as an example. Secure is a justice responsibility; school in Wales is a devolved responsibility. 'We'll have secure schools and we will work out how this is going to work in Wales.' So of course, the first thing that happens is an objection from the Welsh Government to a Secure School in Wales: they don't think it's the right model.

> **William:** In terms of legislation, they refer to and use legislation which doesn't exist in Wales. So, to give a practical example, on the youth side, the whole concept of Secure Schools is based on the academies legislation and the Care Act. Well, the Care Act doesn't exist in Wales, it's the Social Services and Wellbeing Act, and we don't have academies and never will because our education system is designed differently.

**Jayne:** This is one of the things that I keep on hearing about all the time from Ministry of Justice, making reference to Secure Schools as their principal [vehicle] for youth justice and ongoing education provision. They don't exist here. Similarly, Secure Training Centres. We don't have those here. And so therefore principles and commitments given to those do not align with the education provision that we have in Wales.

Twenty years and more later, policy makers clearly still find the implications of 'and Wales' remarkably difficult to grasp.

In addition to what we might term the 'England and Wales = England' mindset, another set of practical difficulties arises from the way in which the civil service in Whitehall operates. In particular, the regular 'churn' of officials from one function and, indeed, from one department to another tends to mean that any understanding and expertise on how criminal justice policy operates in a devolved landscape is quickly lost.[19] During an inquiry by the House of Commons Public Administration and Constitutional Affairs Committee (2018: 20) members were told that a 'rapid turnover' of staff means that officials often have less knowledge about policy issues than the ministers they are expected to advise. A report by the Institute for Government also found that high staff turnover can be 'damaging', with the loss of 'knowledge' and 'expertise' potentially undermining the policy-making process as well as the quality of the advice given to ministers (Sasse and Norris 2019: 4–8). What this tends to mean in practice is that officials in Wales are forced to continually remind new staff at the Ministry of Justice and Home Office about how policy works in Wales. Of course, it is not just officials that 'churn'. When Brandon Lewis was appointed justice secretary in September 2022, he was the ninth person to undertake that role since 2010. It is well attested that a change of minister often adds to the difficulties faced by civil servants who are tasked with bringing them up to speed *and* adapting to a new minister's way of working (Freeguard et al. 2018; House of Commons Justice Committee 2019a; Sasse et al. 2020; Thompson 2020).[20] In combination, this churn in both officials and ministers, all in the context of little-understood additional complexities engendered by devolution, militates against the creation of policy that is appropriate for the Welsh context.

It was certainly the source of frustration for our interviewees who discussed the impact of churn (among officials and ministers) on those staff working to bridge the jagged edge.

**Sam:** If you have a change of Secretary of State, or ministers, it takes people a while to understand the complexities that they're dealing with. As you know, that has happened more than is usual over the last couple of years.

**Jayne:** The problem that people find is that there's such a churn with staff, particularly in Whitehall, especially in [the] Ministry of Justice, that you just about get to the point of explaining what is devolved and breaking that down into the four main themes[21] and how that impacts on criminal justice and the services required to achieve good outcomes, and then they move on. And so, you have to start from scratch over and over again.

**Sam:** Liz Truss being [an] example – when she was Secretary of State for Justice – wanted a prisons change. She wanted to deliver that at pace. I really do think they struggled with the Welsh context at that time, because there was this desire to move at pace, there was this desire to have big change. And often in those things – and certainly in that case – the complete understanding of the Welsh context was lost a bit in the desire to move forward very quickly.

A final factor that helps explain Whitehall's continuing failure to take the Welsh context seriously is Wales's relatively small size within the England and Wales jurisdiction. Research on policing, for example, has shown that government policy is often largely directed towards the 'problems' associated with densely populated urban areas (Mawby 2004; Wooff 2015). Other studies have also demonstrated how developments in larger towns and cities can have a considerable influence over the trajectory of national policy (Brewster 2017; Shiner et al. 2013; Shute et al. 2012).

According to our interviewees, Wales's relatively small size means that it is frequently overlooked, with the larger conurbations of England likely to be higher on the agenda amongst officials in Whitehall. The fact that the 'crime problem' in Wales is not as prominent as in other parts of the jurisdiction also contributes to Wales being overlooked (Sian). In the 12 months prior to December 2019, for example, Wales comprised just 5 per cent of all police-recorded crime in England and Wales (Office for National Statistics 2020b).[22] With 263,447 offences recorded by Welsh police forces, Wales had the fewest number of recorded criminal offences in absolute terms of any 'region' in England and Wales.[23] Another interviewee pointed to the Home Office's *Serious Violence Strategy* as an example of the precedence given to larger urban centres in England in criminal justice policy. Although the strategy did reference some of the work being carried out in Welsh communities, the Home Office's (2018a) document was replete with references to developments in London, Liverpool and Manchester, including specific concerns about recorded knife crime, gang activity and the phenomena of county lines in urban areas like Birmingham, London and Liverpool.

**George:** Wales is quite small when it comes to the whole of England and Wales policing. We're four forces out of forty-three. 3.2 million out of a population of England and Wales of some 60 million. So, we are quite small, and therefore perhaps we are not at the forefront of their mind. The bigger conurbations of London, West Midlands, Merseyside, etc., are the ones that they have more focus on, and us and some of the outlying areas are not as high on the agenda. So that does cause us problems.

**Emma:** I don't think there is adequate consideration [of Wales]. If you look at youth justice statistics, Wales represents something like 5 per cent of youth justice activity across England and Wales, so we're a small partner in the whole [system].

**Sian:** The counter to that is: do the Home Office care? Is there a big enough crime problem in Wales for the Home Office to get really upset about this? Is there a big enough immigration problem that the Home Office absolutely have to include Wales in everything that it does? Is there any real terrorist threat ... from Wales, that they would worry about? ... So that has traditionally been, 'We need you to do this, but if you don't do it, is the world going to end? Maybe not.'

**Craig:** But that is a strategy [*Serious Violence Strategy*] that fits England. And it doesn't actually fit the whole of England. It fits the urban areas of England and London in particular, possibly Birmingham, Manchester, and a few other larger cities. So again, that doesn't fit what we would have in Wales. And we would have a completely different serious violent crime strategy in Wales, in my opinion. So, from the outset, none of that was taken into consideration, or very little was taken into consideration.

Indeed, one of the striking elements of our interview testimony is the extent to which those staff who are responsible for trying to bridge the jagged edge between Whitehall and the Welsh Government find themselves having to repeat time and again the basic existential point: Wales exists and things are done differently here.

**Sarah:** Quite often you bring in Wales and it feels like you're having to remind people that Wales exists. I've been in that position and I know my manager has, and I've heard other colleagues say they have.

**Sion:** You often have to put your hands up and say, 'That's not quite how it's going to operate in Wales.' 'Ah, yes, yes, we know that.' So, the tensions are there.

**Ross:** You're always having to remind [people] that Wales exists. But it does exist in a different world to the rest of the English services.

**Emma:** At an official level, there is a continual job of saying, 'That's different. You can't say that's "England and Wales".' And, you know, really having to keep on top of that.

**Sion:** But it does mean that there has to be quite a lot of consultation, discussion, information provided – and particularly, reminding the London end that devolution is here in Wales, and that whilst policing is not devolved all our key partners are devolved, including the other emergency services.

Driven by politicians who have demanded constant, performative criminal justice policies and activity at the expense of evidence-informed approaches (Goldson 2010), whilst also being ideologically committed to marketisation (actual or pseudo) as a route to 'efficiency' and/or reduced spending, officials based overwhelmingly in London have produced a torrent of policy initiatives and rafts of new legislation. In doing so, they have rarely considered how these policies might be translated into the particular operational context of Wales, defined as it is by a jagged edge between devolved and reserved (non-devolved) competences that cut across the wider criminal justice policy space. This because Whitehall is generally bad at engaging with devolution; because the officials concerned are working at such frenetic pace with new ministers and new policy ideas; and because Wales has low salience among officials preoccupied with the challenges of crime in the large urban centres.

The result is that policies and initiatives produced with little or no thought about Wales are then funnelled through to officials based in the Welsh administrative arms of England and Wales criminal justice bodies – very few in number, with even fewer on senior grades – who are required, often with no effective notice, to try to make them 'fit' into a Welsh context. Their attempts to do so are further complicated by the fact that the Welsh Government itself has not been set up in a way that makes enacting its responsibilities in this policy area straightforward (a point we return to in the next chapter); this precisely because criminal justice is a reserved matter. It is a system that might well have been designed to fail.

CONCLUSION: WHAT POWER REVEALS?

Whitehall is the dominant power in the Welsh criminal justice system. Its dominance is underpinned by a Welsh devolution settlement that reserves policing and criminal justice in Wales to the UK level, even when those powers are devolved to Scotland and Northern Ireland. This means that Whitehall's dominant position is exercised via ministries and associated bodies that act primarily on an England and Wales basis. It is these England and Wales institutions and structures that have been the focus of this chapter.

Our first step was to provide an overview of its various constituent parts. While they form a complex institutional web, common ground (literally) between them is that they are largely located in or headquartered in London. Relatedly, London is also – overwhelmingly – home to their policy-making capacity. But in addition, we have also stressed the extent to which this England and Wales system has experienced almost constant upheaval during the period that has coincided with the establishment and development of democratic devolution. This because of successive 'reforms' animated by a desire to get tough, or to be seen to get tough on crime, and an apparently unshakeable belief in the positive impact on public services of marketisation, 'transforming' agendas and the related nostrums of New Public Management.

We have explored how these England and Wales institutions have risen to the very substantial, if still largely unrecognised, challenge of seeking to make work the highly anomalous constitutional design that is embodied by Welsh devolution. Specifically, we have examined the role of the Welsh administrative arms of some of the main England and Wales criminal justice institutions in seeking to bridge the jagged edge between devolved and non-devolved competences. This is an organisational structure whose emergence has coincided with democratic devolution, even if not necessarily inspired by it, and has become the means by which the England and Wales criminal justice system tends to interact with devolved government and its associated institutions and agencies.

Drawing mainly on interview evidence, we examined how well this interaction works in practice. Our conclusions are sobering, if perhaps unsurprising. No matter how dedicated the professionals involved, they find themselves engaged in an extended game of 'whack-a-mole'. That is, they are continually forced to react to an apparently endless torrent of reforms and new initiatives designed by Whitehall policy makers who have little knowledge of, let alone interest in, the distinctive policy context created by Welsh devolution. Given the serious criminal justice-related challenges facing Wales highlighted in Chapter 2, this can hardly be said to be a system that is set up to take Wales seriously.

In the introduction to this chapter we recalled political biographer Robert Caro's dictum that 'what power always does is reveal'. Having reviewed the way that those responsible for the England and Wales criminal justice system use their dominant position within the Welsh criminal justice system, we are forced to confront an unpalatable truth: Wales counts for very little in and for the institutions of the England and Wales criminal justice system. Despite the 'and Wales' addendum, it remains in essence an English system in which Wales is all too often an afterthought. Given the way that its basic design flouts constitutional first principles, making the post-devolution Welsh criminal justice system work was always going to present a major challenge. What is truly damning, however, is that most of those at senior levels in the England and Wales institutions have failed even to try.

# 4
# THE WELSH GOVERNMENT AND CRIMINAL JUSTICE
*Responsibility without power*

IN THE PREVIOUS chapter we focused on one side of the jagged edge of competences and powers that run through and define the Welsh criminal justice system, namely on those England and Wales institutions that are a part of – or ultimately accountable to – the UK-level of government. These are, of course, the dominant players in the system, with that dominance underwritten by the devolution settlement itself. In this chapter we focus on the other side of the jagged edge; that is, the role of devolved government and its associated institutional web, including Welsh local government.

Even though devolved government plays a subordinate role in the Welsh criminal justice system, it is not an insignificant one. Far from it: the system is in fact heavily reliant on the devolved level. Nor is the devolved level without its own agency in the system. Rather, in seeking to carry out its various responsibilities (which we detail below), devolved government has sought to develop policies designed to ameliorate some of the problems that characterise the Welsh criminal justice system. In doing so, it has – in fairness – tended to act with a seriousness of purpose. Some of the resulting policies have even been heralded as examples of best practice. Yet the results have been disappointing, often failing to meet initial expectations; not only because criminal justice tends to have more than its share of intractable or even so-called 'wicked' problems (Edwards 2002: 152). As will become clear in the course of this chapter, these disappointed hopes and expectations also reflect the fact that the agency of devolved government is so constrained: its efforts are hamstrung by the very structure of the Welsh criminal justice system.

We shall proceed in three substantive steps. First, we attempt to map the activities of devolved government in the criminal justice space. Given what we have already said about the ways in which criminal justice functions are umbilically linked to wider social policy, it should come as no surprise that the list of relevant bodies, policy initiatives, partnerships (and so on) is extensive. As part of this mapping exercise we also seek to identify where these various activities 'sit' within Welsh Government. Unsurprisingly, perhaps, given that policing and criminal justice are formally reserved, we find that the Welsh Government's criminal justice responsibilities lack a locus and are instead widely dispersed across its various directorates, with implications to which we return in Chapter 6, in particular.

Following from this, our second substantive section explores, in broad-brush terms, how the Welsh Government has sought to make use of its policy competences in the area of criminal justice. We argue that it is difficult to generalise. There are significant differences between policy areas, reflecting not only the specific extent of devolved policy competence but also their political salience. In the case of policing, for example, the extent of devolved involvement and influence is far greater than might be expected when viewed purely through the lens of formal constitutional powers. Nonetheless, when the Welsh Government has engaged seriously in a given area, it is clear that it has sought to develop policies that are both evidence-based and avowedly progressive in intent. While we should not overstate the degree of progressiveness achieved compared to some international comparators (Jones et al. 2019), nonetheless the contrast with the performative toughness discussed in the last chapter could hardly be more marked.

The third and final section of the chapter draws heavily on interview testimony in order to examine how the devolved government's approach has worked in practice. We reveal a story of good intentions and potentially good policies being frustrated or otherwise undermined. This because of the ways in which the very constitutional underpinnings of the Welsh criminal justice system serve to ensure that Welsh Government, despite its best efforts, is inevitably a *policy taker* in the area of criminal justice. It simply does not control enough of the policy levers to make good on its avowedly progressive intentions.[1] In the same way that Robert Caro's injunction that 'power reveals' helped guide our analysis in the previous chapter, here we draw our inspiration from closer to home. Aneurin Bevan remains not only the quintessential Welsh Labour hero; he was also one of the most effective wielders of executive power on the progressive left in the history of the state. As such, we may assume that he spoke with authority when he claimed that 'Responsibility without power is the most dangerous of all situations for a political party with progressive pretensions' (Bevan 1952: 26). To examine the role of devolved government in the Welsh criminal justice system is to be struck forcibly by the limitations – for progressive actors, in particular – of responsibility without power.

## WHAT'S DEVOLVED IN CRIMINAL JUSTICE?

Given that policing and criminal justice are formally reserved, the obvious starting point for this discussion is what – precisely – does the devolved level do in the policy area?[2] The answer, in simple terms, is that it has responsibility for crime prevention and community safety arising from its responsibilities for functions like local government, children's services, tackling substance misuse and education; it provides important services within Welsh prisons, including health and education; it helps provide 'Through the Gate' services designed to transition prisoners back into the community; and it provides a number of important services (though not all) for offenders in the community that – ideally – assist them in reintegrating successfully (Jones and Wyn Jones 2019).

There are three points to note here. First, these responsibilities are wide-ranging, extending right across the criminal justice system. Secondly – and this might perhaps be regarded as obvious, but nonetheless needs to be clearly stated – these responsibilities are important. Put simply, crime prevention matters and, indeed, as we shall see in Chapter 5, approximately two-thirds of all funding for Wales's ostensibly non-devolved police services derive from devolved sources. Health and education services in prisons matter, with the importance of the former having been recently underlined by the experience of the COVID-19 pandemic (Coker 2020; Neil 2020). The 'reform and rehabilitation of offenders', to cite the words of the 2003 Criminal Justice Act, is one of the fundamental aims of the criminal justice system. In other words, the role of Welsh Government in the Welsh criminal justice system is not some bolt-on, 'nice to have' addition to its 'real' business; it is rather an integral part of it. Thirdly, without exception, as the deliberately conditional language of the previous paragraph serves to emphasise, the devolved level operates alongside the various institutions that make up the England and Wales criminal justice system. Thus, whilst the Welsh Government plays a series of important roles in the Welsh criminal justice system, it cannot undertake any of them independently of, and without being subject to, the actions of England and Wales institutions. We return to the implications of the latter point later in the chapter, but for the moment we will focus on providing a more detailed map of devolved activity in and around criminal justice.

Given its extent, providing a concise, readable summary of all devolved activity in the area of criminal justice is a nigh-on impossible task (for overviews, see Pritchard 2016; Jones and Wyn Jones 2019). But while eschewing any claim to comprehensiveness, we can gain at least a flavour of these activities and their constitutional basis in the current devolution arrangements. In order to do so, we shall again sketch an arc from policing and crime prevention, via the courts and prisons to 'Through the Gate' services intended to both support and supervise people who have offended with the aim of reintegrating them successfully into broader society.

### The prevention, detection and investigation of crime

As the explanatory notes of the Wales Act 2017 point out, 'the prevention, detection and investigation of crime and policing are reserved – such that the Assembly [sic] cannot confer, impose, modify or remove functions on/of the police' (Wales Act 2017 c.4).[3] Yet it is clearly also the case that multiple areas of devolved competence – from education to taxation – ensure that Wales's devolved government and legislature have significant influence on all of these reserved activities, including over Wales's four police services.

Finance is fundamental. The Welsh Government provides a component of the Police Settlement via the (devolved) Revenue Support Grant and (devolved) National Non-Domestic Rates (NDR or 'Business Rates'). In 2019–20 the Welsh Government component of the 2019–20 Police Settlement was worth £143.4m (StatsWales 2020b). In addition, police and crime commissioners raise money through the council tax precept, again a fully devolved tax. In 2019–20 this amounted to an additional £318.8m

(Welsh Government 2019b). As previously noted in Chapter 2, since 2011 the Welsh Government has also provided direct financial support for an additional 500 police community support officers (PCSOs), intended to play 'a pivotal role not only in making our communities safer, but in making them feel safer' (Welsh Government 2011: 25). In 2019–20 the cost to the Welsh Government of these PCSOs amounted to £16.7m (Welsh Government 2019c). Given that the total revenue expenditure for policing in Wales in 2019–20 was £753.5m (StatsWales 2020c), the proportion that derives from devolved sources is very substantial indeed.

The everyday activities of Wales's police services – the only one of the emergency services that is non-devolved – are also shaped by close cooperation with the Welsh Government or those institutions and agencies that fall under its auspices. Cooperation is coordinated by a police liaison unit set up as early as 1999 and facilitated through a web of agreements and concordats – both national and locally focused – through which the Welsh Government seeks to facilitate various policy aims (Jones et al. 2022). The *Mental Health Crisis Care Concordat*, for example, is an agreement that brings together Welsh Government, the police, the (Welsh) NHS, the Welsh Ambulance Services, local authorities and various third-sector organisations in Wales to improve responses to people in crisis because of a mental health condition. One of the Welsh Government's commitments is to work with the police to reduce the number of people being detained under powers within sections 135 and 136 of the Mental Health Act 1983 (Welsh Government 2016b). At a more local level, community safety partnerships bring together police and devolved actors as part of the Welsh Safer Communities programme (Welsh Government, 2017a).

Community safety partnerships are the product of the Crime and Disorder Act 1998, which enshrined the concept of statutory partnership working between local authorities, police forces, health, fire and probation services in order to prevent and reduce 'crime and disorder' in particular communities. The establishment of democratic devolution only a year later meant that most of the relevant partners would inevitably be devolved. But Welsh Government has not been content to simply inherit obligations in this area. Over time it has actively sought to develop its own initiatives. Public service boards (PSBs), for example, were formed as a consequence of the (devolved) Well-being of Future Generations (Wales) Act 2015 and offer another mechanism for partnership working between devolved and non-devolved agencies. Although the police forces are not formal members of these boards (recall that the devolved level has no formal responsibility for policing), both they and the non-devolved probation services are invited to attend their meetings and participate in their activities.

In November 2018, the Welsh Government established a Policing Partnership Board (initially Policing Board) for Wales 'to discuss policing issues across the devolved and non-devolved aspects of the service' (Davies 2018a). The board's membership includes Welsh chief constables and police and crime commissioners as well as Welsh Government ministers and officials (Davies 2018a). The Welsh Government's initial invitations also extended to the Secretary of State for Wales, the Home Office and Ministry of Justice, as well as NHS Wales and the Welsh Local Government Association. While the Welsh Government views the board as facilitating its involvement in this area and a sign of its commitment to cooperating with non-devolved actors, this interpretation was initially rejected by some at the England and Wales level. Neither HMPPS nor the Home Office's representatives in Wales attended the initial meeting, and while details are not publicly available, a number of those involved in the process have made it clear that this was at the instance of another non-attender, namely the then Secretary of State for Wales, Alun Cairns. While this stand appears to have been intended as a signal that the Welsh Government should stay away from territory that remains the rightful preserve of Whitehall, the board has since enjoyed greater success after attempts were made to appease Whitehall concerns about the board's intended role. This included adding the word 'partnership' to the board's title (Davies 2018a; Policing Partnership Board for Wales 2018).

All of which may be interpreted as confirming that, whatever those who would dogmatically assert Westminster's constitutional prerogatives might wish for, the Welsh Government is inevitably involved in the Welsh criminal justice system. In addition to policing, there are multiple other examples of Welsh Government activity in the area of crime prevention and community safety that might also be pointed to. They include, inter alia:

- 'The Wales Police Schools Programme' (previously the All-Wales Schools Liaison Programme), which claims to provide 'vital support' to schools educating children on substance misuse and per-

- sonal safety issues (Welsh Government 2018b: 14). In its draft 2019–20 draft budget the Welsh Government allocated £1.98m to the programme, which also receives match funding from all four police forces in Wales.
- The Welsh Government has taken a proactive approach to tackling violence against women, which has included the publication of strategies in 2005, 2010 and 2022 as well as the passage of the 2015 Violence against Women, Domestic Abuse and Sexual Violence (Wales) Act (Welsh Government 2005a, 2010, 2022b). This legislation was accompanied by the launch of a *National Training Framework* designed to try to affect a fundamental shift in attitudes towards offending behaviour while, unsurprisingly, identifying the criminal justice system as playing a central role in tackling violence against women (Welsh Government 2016c). The Welsh Government's final budget for 2019–20 allocated £5m to support its activities in this area.
- Modern slavery is another area that has seen the Welsh Government take the initiative even while the legislative context is formed by Westminster legislation, in this case the Modern Slavery Act 2015. The Wales Anti-Slavery Leadership Group provides strategic leadership for tackling slavery in Wales facilitating collaboration between devolved and non-devolved partners and the third sector. It is chaired by the Welsh Government's head of community safety with other members including policing officials, police and crime commissioners, Home Office, Crown Prosecution Service Wales, National Police Chiefs' Council,[4] National Crime Agency, National Probation Service Wales and a range of third-sector groups and organisations (see Welsh Government 2022c).
- While the misuse of and dealing in drugs (as well as their classification) is reserved to the UK Government, responsibility for addressing the effects of substance misuse falls on the devolved level (including the health service and local government). Again, this is an area in which the Welsh Government has – of necessity – been active. Part of this activity is specifically focused on offenders, to which we return. But it also has an active prevention agenda. The sum total allocated to the Welsh Government's Substance Misuse Action Plan in the 2019–20 budget was £26.3m.

Substance misuse is a good example of a policy area in which, over time, the devolved government has developed its own distinctive policy stance after initially inheriting or adopting an approach developed in Whitehall. Thus, its initial strategy *Tackling Substance Misuse in Wales*, published in 2000, whilst not being identical to the UK Government's *Tackling drugs to build a better Britain strategy* (Home Office 1998; Welsh Government 2000b), clearly drew heavily upon it (Brewster and Jones 2019). Since 2008, however, the Welsh Government's (2008b, 2019d) approach has placed greater emphasis on public health and harm reduction. It is an approach that, at least in the view of Welsh Government, has been 'widely applauded' for covering both drug and alcohol misuse as well as focusing upon all stages of the 'harm reduction journey' (Welsh Government 2019d: 1–5). It is certainly an approach that contrasts sharply with that of the Home Office, which emphasises 'robust enforcement' and focuses on steps to tackle supply and related crime (Brewster and Jones 2019). The Welsh Government's most recent strategy continues its emphasis on tackling the harms associated with substance misuse by improving prevention, treatment and recovery services across Wales (Welsh Government 2019d).

### The courts

Given that the courts stand at both the legal decision-making and symbolic heart of the England and Wales justice system and jurisdiction, it is perhaps not a surprise that this is where devolved influence is most muted. While the Welsh Government and Senedd can and do opine on matters related to the role of courts, they cannot determine nor apparently successfully influence key elements of the service, such as sentencing guidelines, court closures or cuts in criminal legal aid; even where, as in the latter case, they have a disproportionately negative impact in Wales (Thomas Commission 2019: 124–31). This is not to suggest, of course, that there are no links between the Welsh legislature and executive and the England and Wales judiciary. In fact, on either side of this particular jagged edge, there have been proactive attempts to build bridges in ways that demand more detailed analysis and explanation than is possible here. But neither can we escape the fact that these relationships are a courtesy rather than a constitutional requirement.

Despite the limits to joint working, services that fall under the purview of the Welsh Government play a key role in ensuring the functioning of the courts. This includes the role played by local health boards and mental healthcare teams to provide support to court custody staff in Wales (HMI Prisons 2016b).[5] The Welsh Government has also provided funding to Victim Support Cymru, the body which gives vital assistance and support to victims of crime appearing in courts across Wales (James 2019a). Finally, the Welsh Language Commissioner has worked alongside HM Courts and Tribunals Service (HMCTS) to help promote the rights of people to use Welsh in court settings in Wales, and to ensure that the Welsh language is included as part of its digitising agenda (HMCTS 2019).

Prisons

Responsibility for healthcare within public sector prisons (*sic*) was transferred from the Home Office to the Welsh Government in 2003 and represents devolved government's most significant set of (direct) responsibilities for prisoners in Wales. Devolution was accompanied by a funding transfer from the UK Government to the Welsh Government based on historic patterns of spending on prisoner healthcare. This figure has not been updated since 2004/5 and does not take account of inflation or population changes (Senedd Health, Social Care and Sport Committee 2021).[6]

In practical terms this has meant that, since April 2006, Wales's local health boards have been responsible for healthcare at public sector prisons in Wales. Primary healthcare at HMP Parc in Bridgend is provided by the prison's private operator G4S Care and Justice Ltd (G4S), with secondary healthcare services delivered by the local health board. The Welsh NHS is also responsible for promoting best practice throughout public sector prisons in Wales.

Public Health Wales established the Wales Custodial Public Health Advisory Board (WCPHAB) in 2012 to provide advice to the partnership boards responsible for prisoner healthcare, and to the Welsh Government on policy development and the maintenance of prison healthcare standards in Wales (Jones 2017). In September 2019, the Welsh Government, Public Health Wales, the Welsh local health boards and HM Prison and Probation Service (HMPPS) published a partnership agreement outlining the shared priorities for prison healthcare in Wales (Welsh Government et al.

2019). Subsequently, the Welsh Government and HMPPS in Wales established the Prison Health and Social Care Oversight Group to help deliver on its shared priorities for prison healthcare in Wales (Senedd Health, Social Care and Sport Committee 2021).

Mental health is one of the most challenging issues facing the Welsh criminal justice system. In recent years, police forces across Wales have seen a rapid increase in the number of incidents involving mental health issues. The scale is enormous: South Wales Police, for example, receive a report relating to a mental health concern every 13 minutes (Jukes 2018). In response, all four Welsh forces have introduced mental health triage protocols which see psychiatric nurses placed in police control rooms to help improve responses for people in mental health crisis. Except for South Wales Police, the local health boards provide funding support for these schemes (Broome and Davies 2020: 10–11; Thomas Commission 2019: 179).

All too often, prison has become the 'default setting' for dealing with those experiencing mental health problems (HMI Prisons 2007: 7). According to the findings of a recent study in England, fully two-thirds (67 per cent) of prisoners screened positive for clinical symptoms of at least one form of mental disorder and over half reported that they had been in contact with mental health services either in prison or in the community (Tyler et al. 2019).[7] In Wales, the Welsh Government plays a key role in trying to address the mental health crisis in the country's prisons. The Welsh Government's *Raising the Standard* strategy, published in 2005, pledged to improve 'in-reach' mental health services into prisons across Wales (Welsh Government 2005b). After introducing its new mental healthcare strategy in 2012 to incorporate the requirements of the Mental Health (Wales) Measure 2010 (Welsh Government 2012b),[8] the Welsh Government published guidance in May 2014 aimed at providing support to those involved in the provision of primary and secondary mental health services in prisons (Griffiths 2014). The Welsh Government's 2015 suicide and self-harm prevention strategy identified prisoners as a 'high-risk' group and recognised prisons as 'priority places' for suicide prevention services (Welsh Government 2015a: 19–23).

Formal responsibility for prison education was transferred to Welsh ministers in 2009. Operating under the terms of section 47 of the Prisons Act 1952, ostensibly at least, the Welsh Government has a key role to play in the strategic planning and management of delivering prisoner education in Wales (Hanson 2019: 5). This transfer of responsibilities was accompanied by a concomitant transfer of funding, which amounted to £6.9m per annum, according to the most recently available figures (Hanson 2019: 5). Operationally, however, this represents a particularly convoluted example of the type of complexity that characterises the interaction between the England and Wales and Welsh systems of government in the area of criminal justice. While executive responsibility for prisoner education has been transferred to Welsh ministers, practically speaking it is the Welsh administrative arm of an England and Wales body, HMPPS in Wales, that carries out this work on the Welsh Government's behalf. HMPPS in Wales is not only the main education provider in three of Wales's prisons (Cardiff, Swansea, Usk & Prescoed) but, according to a report produced by former Labour MP, David Hanson, it has 'a stronger role [than the Welsh Government] in formulating and delivering [education] policy in Welsh prisons' (Hanson 2019: 9). Education in HMP Parc is supervised by HMPPS in Wales but provided by the private operator of the prison, G4S, while HMPPS in Wales has contracted out education provision at HMP Berwyn to an external provider (Novus Cambria). In other words, while executive responsibility for prison education has been formally devolved, the leading role in formulating policy and delivering services is actually undertaken by a non-devolved England and Wales body, in some cases abetted by outsourced providers. Little wonder perhaps that Hanson, despite being broadly supportive of this arrangement, notes that 'in discussions with senior representatives of both the Welsh Government and HMPPS, it became clear that both formulation of policy and scrutiny of proposals submitted could be improved' (Hanson 2019: 9).

### 'Through the Gate' services, rehabilitation and reintegration

Health and education provision within prisons impact on the ability of prisoners to reintegrate successfully into the community post-release. But there are, in addition, specific services designed to aid rehabilitation and reintegration, and ultimately – it is hoped – reduce levels of reoffending. These so-called 'Through the Gate' services extend from prison back into wider society itself and include social care, housing support, support in tackling substance misuse, and mental health services. In all of these, the

Welsh Government plays a key role. Indeed, the Ministry of Justice itself is clear that 'much of the work' being done to support Welsh prisoners upon release is carried out by the Welsh Government (Ministry of Justice 2014b: 8). Yet despite its extensive responsibilities, this continues to be an area in which devolved government remains – as previously noted – very dependent on, and indeed subject to the whims of, the England and Wales level.

Most obviously, over the past few years, rehabilitation and reintegration work in Wales has been negatively impacted by the chaos that ensued from the UK Government's attempts to privatise much of the England and Wales probation service under the guise of *Transforming Rehabilitation*. The paradox of the Welsh Government's position – responsibility without power – is highlighted (unintentionally, no doubt) in the consultation document published by the Ministry of Justice in July 2018 as it sought to exit from the disastrous attempt to privatise large parts of the service. It acknowledged not only the 'distinct needs of Wales', but also the 'fundamentally different delivery landscape' created by devolution (Ministry of Justice 2018c: 36). Yet while it is to be earnestly hoped that National Probation Service Wales, which in early December 2019 assumed responsibility for the management of all low-, medium- and high-risk offenders in Wales, proves more efficient and successful than its immediate predecessor, devolved influence on the shape of these new arrangements has been negligible. It remains to be seen how relationships are managed more informally. Given the impact of the pandemic it is premature to offer any assessment at this point.

Reviewing the first two decades of devolution, housing is one of the areas in which the Welsh Government has been most heavily engaged in terms of seeking to support rehabilitation and reintegration. As this is the focus of an extended case-study discussion in the next chapter, we shall not elaborate here beyond pointing out that, in the early years of devolution, the Welsh Government sought to take a very different approach to that of the UK Government (acting in its English capacity) in seeking to provide housing support to offenders. The policy it adopted was a quintessential evidence-based policy and was lauded as such by external observers (HMI Prisons 2010, 2014). Yet, for reasons that we will explore in detail, it was a policy that the Welsh Government abandoned with the passage of the Housing (Wales) Act 2014. Understanding why this occurred tells us a great deal about the relationship between the apparently abstract question of the constitutional underpinnings of the Welsh criminal justice system and the all-too visible impact of the failure of efforts to provide adequate housing support for prison leavers.

## Women and criminal justice

While many of the areas we have discussed so far relate to services for both men and women, the 'distinct set of issues' facing women in contact with the criminal justice system has led to the establishment of distinct Welsh government policies and legislation (House of Commons Welsh Affairs Committee 2007: 19). In 2005 and 2010, for example, the Welsh Government (2005a; 2010) introduced national strategies to tackle domestic abuse in Wales. This was followed in 2022 by a renewed commitment to try to 'change attitudes' towards violence against women in Wales (Welsh Government 2022b). In 2015, the Violence against Women, Domestic Abuse and Sexual Violence (Wales) Act was introduced to try to ensure consistency in service provision across Wales. In the wake of its passage, the Welsh Government (2016c) launched a *National Training Framework* to help deliver the goals of the legislation across Wales.

The scope of the Welsh Government's activity in this area also extends to distributing funding to third-sector organisations to provide support to sex workers and victims of abuse (Welsh Government 2017b). It has also funded research into the relationship between sex work and substance misuse in Wales to help generate an evidence-base upon which to develop future policy around sex work and drug and alcohol misuse (Sagar et al. 2015). The Welsh Government's *National Strategy on Violence against Women, Domestic Abuse and Sexual Violence* (2016d) underlined its commitment to protecting women and improving access to support for those involved in sex work in Wales. But while the cost of assisting individuals is devolved, legislating and regulating sex work is reserved to the UK Government.

The Welsh Government has also been active in attempting to address the problems facing women already in contact with the criminal justice system. Through its *Substance Misuse Delivery Plan*, for example, the Welsh Government pledged to ensure that HMP Eastwood Park would be included as part of its plans to deliver a 'coordinated, transparent and consistent service for those with substance misuse problems in prison, based on best practice' (2019d: 13). Later that same year, the Welsh Government and Ministry of Justice published its joint blueprint strategy to improve services for female offenders in Wales (2019a: 1). The strategy includes a commitment to ensuring that fewer women are victims of crime, and to developing a public health approach in Wales consistent with the Well-being of Future Generations (Wales) Act 2015. That said, the UK Government's decision (in May 2020) to site a women's residential centre in Wales (albeit supported by the Welsh Government) serves as yet another reminder that it is the UK/England and Wales level that continues to control the overall shape and trajectory of criminal justice services in Wales.

Youth justice

A final area in which devolved responsibilities necessitate – and indeed obligate – substantial Welsh Government involvement in the criminal justice system is the area of youth justice (Drakeford 2010; Haines and Case 2015). Here again, devolved involvement spans a number of specific responsibilities, including education, training, health and local government. It should also be recalled that, from very early on in the era of democratic devolution, the Welsh Government set out its commitment to ensuring that 'the needs of children and young people' are provided for (Welsh Government 2000a: 3), a commitment that has remained something of a touchstone ever since. It extends to the needs of those children and young people who come into contact with the criminal justice system. A key focus has been on prevention via the *All Wales Youth Offending Strategy*, with Welsh Government funding being directed via the Safer Communities Fund (Cardiff University et al. 2009). Cooperation between England and Wales institutions and the devolved level is maintained through bodies such as the Wales Youth Justice Advisory Panel, which was established in January 2017 to facilitate dialogue and cooperation between the Welsh Government and the Youth Justice Board (Youth Justice Board 2019a). In 2019, the Welsh Government and the Ministry of Justice (2019b) published a joint blueprint strategy to outline its shared commitment to diverting children away from custody and improving youth justice services in Wales. Despite this partnership, there have been some notable disagreements between UK and Welsh levels, reflecting their fundamentally different approaches to criminal justice issues to which we shall return shortly.

\* \* \*

At this juncture it is worth reiterating that this survey makes no claims to being comprehensive. It has nonetheless served to demonstrate that the Welsh Government is, overall, an important and indeed essential actor in the Welsh criminal justice system. This reflects both the sheer extent of devolved competences and, relatedly, the unavoidable and, indeed, equally essential links between criminal justice and multiple other areas of social policy. The Welsh Government's extensive activity in and around the Welsh criminal justice system is matched in turn by extensive financial commitments in a policy area that is formally reserved to the UK level. These two apparently contradictory points – namely that criminal justice is reserved yet requires action and engagement right across devolved government – has one significant structural implication that is important to tease out before we conclude this part of the discussion.

Table 4.1 identifies the location of various criminal justice-related activities across Welsh Government, which in 2021 was divided into four directorates (the Office of the First Minister group, the Health and Social Services group, the Economy, Skills and Natural Resources group, and the Education and Public Services group) as well as the Permanent Secretary's group. The results serve to underline just how widely they are dispersed: all five of these elements feature in this table. The other side of the coin, however, is that there is no real locus for criminal justice policy within Welsh Government. Notwithstanding the recent establishment of a Justice Policy Division (in 2021), the construction of Welsh devolution as a two-legged stool means that Welsh Government lacks one of the standard institutional accoutrements of democratic governments all over the world, namely a justice ministry or ministries.[9] In its report, the Thomas Commission lamented the lack of a 'clearer focus on justice in the Welsh Government' and recommended '[B]ringing together the current justice functions held by the Welsh Government within a single portfolio' (2019: 13, 474).

In reality, however, the absence of a central coordinating locus for criminal justice in the executive would seem to be the inevitable consequence of the flouting of normal Westminster family constitutional practice in the construction of Welsh devolution. Moreover, even if the Welsh Government were so minded and sought to establish such a locus within the confines of the current dispensation, the suspicion and initial reluctance to engage with the Policing Partnership Board reminds us that the UK Government response would likely be one of deep unease; the governmental equivalent of the apocryphal farmer's cry of 'get off my land'. Yet, the absence of a central locus within the Welsh Government that might coordinate its criminal justice-related activities not only has implications for the ways in which those various responsibilities are discharged. It also has significant implications for the ability of the Senedd to hold policy makers to account (as elaborated upon in Chapter 6, below).

Table 4.1 The location of criminal justice functions in the Welsh Government, 2021

| Teams or units | Minister | Responsibilities |
|---|---|---|
| **Office of the First Minister group** | | |
| **European Transition, Constitution and Justice** | Counsel General and Minister for the Constitution | Justice Policy Division<br>• Development of Welsh Government policies on matters relating to the operation of justice in Wales<br>• Engagement with justice agencies<br>• Oversight of the implementation of the Thomas Commission recommendations<br>• Advice on justice impact assessment<br><br>Constitutional Affairs and Tribunals Division<br>• Management of the Welsh Tribunals Unit to support the administration of the devolved tribunals in Wales<br>• Monitoring constitutional developments and how they impact Wales<br>• Advising on matters relating to UK Parliamentary Bills and UK secondary legislation relating to devolved competence |
| **Office of the Legislative Counsel** | Counsel General and Minister for the Constitution | Drafting and amending Senedd Bills<br><br>Delivering the government's legislative programme and improving the accessibility of Welsh law |
| **Welsh European Funding Office** | | Implementing the European Structural Fund programme in Wales, the European Social Fund, and the European Regional Development Fund. Includes £3.9m investment in Legal Innovation Lab Wales at Swansea law school from 2019 to 2022 |

| Teams or units | Minister | Responsibilities |
|---|---|---|
| Legal services | Counsel General and Minister for the Constitution | Providing legal advice to ministers and officials across the Welsh Government |
| | | Drafting secondary legislation |
| | | Instructing legislative counsel in relation to Senedd Bills |
| | | Procurement of legal services through the NPS Solicitors Services Framework (with ESNR commercial procurement) and the Welsh Government panel of counsel |
| **Health and Social Services group** | | |
| Mental health, vulnerable groups and NHS governance | Minister for Health and Social Services/ Deputy Minister for Social Services/Deputy Minister for Mental Health and Wellbeing | Coordination of policy, funding and delivery of health services for vulnerable groups, including prisoners |
| | | Offender health and the Partnership Agreement for Prison Health |
| | | Substance misuse policy |
| Cafcass Cymru | Minister for Health and Social Services/ Deputy Minister for Social Services/Deputy Minister for Mental Health and Wellbeing | Providing child-focused advice and support, safeguarding children, and ensuring the voices of children are heard in family courts across Wales |
| Social services and integration | Minister for Health and Social Services | Delivery of the Improving Outcomes for Looked After Children work programme |
| | | Working with the Ministry of Justice to implement family justice policy |
| | | Supporting the performance of local authorities and family courts in Wales |
| | | Safeguarding and advocacy |
| **Education and Public Services group** | | |
| Housing and regeneration | Minister for Climate Change/ Deputy Minister for Climate Change | Homelessness prevention and housing resettlement |
| | | Improving housing outcomes for offenders |
| | | Youth homelessness |

| Teams or units | Minister | Responsibilities |
| --- | --- | --- |
| Communities and tackling poverty | Deputy Minister for Social Partnership/ Deputy Minister for Mental Health and Wellbeing | Children and families<br>• Tackling adverse childhood experiences<br>• Implementation of the Children (Abolition of Defence of Reasonable Chastisement) (Wales) Act 2020<br>Communities Division<br>• Equality and human rights<br>• Violence against women, domestic abuse and sexual violence<br>• Hate crime<br>Prosperous Futures Division<br>• Advice services, including implementation of the Information and Advice Action Plan |
| Care Inspectorate Wales | Minister for Health and Social Services/Deputy Minister for Social Services/ Deputy Minister for Mental Health and Social Services | Domiciliary care at HMP Usk & Prescoed<br>Contribute to HMI Prisons and HMI Probation inspections (including thematic review of social care in prisons in England and Wales in 2018) |
| Health Inspectorate Wales | Minister for Health and Social Services/ Deputy Minister for Mental Health and Wellbeing/Deputy Minister for Social Services | Contribute to HMI Prisons and HMI Probation inspections<br>Contribute to investigations by the Prisons and Probation Ombudsman into deaths in prison custody by undertaking a clinical review for all deaths within a Welsh prison or approved premises |
| Local government | Minister for Social Justice | Community safety<br>• Prisons and probation<br>• *Female Offending Blueprint*<br>• Youth justice<br>• *Youth Justice Blueprint*<br>• Policing, relations with police and crime commissioners, police, and other criminal justice agencies<br>• Community safety partnerships<br>• Police liaison unit – provide advice on policy affecting operational policing |

# THE WELSH GOVERNMENT AND CRIMINAL JUSTICE

| Teams or units | Minister | Responsibilities |
|---|---|---|
| | | Civil contingencies and national security |
| | | • Cyber resilience and cyber security |
| | | • Coordination of the Welsh Government's involvement in the development and delivery of the UK Government's Counter Terrorism, Serious and Organised Crime and Modern Slavery strategy |
| | | • Representation on the CONTEST and Extremism Board Wales |
| **Economy, Skills and Natural Resources** | | |
| Business and regions | Minister for Economy | Increase growth of a strong and sustainable economy, including support for the legal profession through Business Wales and digital economy work streams |
| Skills, Education and Lifelong Learning | Minister for Economy/ Minister for Education and Welsh Language | Employability and skills |
| | | • Response to the David Hanson review on offender learning |
| | | • Offender Learning and Employability Stakeholder group |
| | | • Youth employment policy |
| | | Further education and apprenticeships |
| | | • Apprenticeship policy and programmes, including legal and policing apprenticeships and roles in the criminal justice system |
| **Permanent Secretary's group** | | |
| Knowledge and analytical services | All ministers | Providing information and analytical services to ministers and officials |
| | | Statistical Services Division include a social justice statistics team, supporting with criminal justice data in Wales |

## ON 'PROGRESSIVE PRETENSIONS'

The discussion in this chapter thus far has focused on mapping the extent of the Welsh Government's involvement in the country's criminal justice system. What devolved government has done with those various powers and responsibilities is the focus of this second substantive section. Our fundamental argument is that, where the Welsh Government has taken a sustained interest, its approach to policy-making has tended to be evidence-led, holistic and progressive in intent. But as our caveating implies, a devolved role in a given part of the Welsh criminal justice system does not necessarily translate into sustained interest, let alone policy success. As a result, not all of the actions of the Welsh Government in the Welsh criminal justice system can be characterised as evidence-led or progressive. Given that the limited academic literature dealing with the role of devolved government in the criminal justice system tends to focus on precisely those areas in which it is most active, it is important that we do not lose sight of the fact that this is not the whole story.

The Welsh Government's responsibilities for health and education in some Welsh prisons are good examples of where devolved responsibilities have not translated into meaningful policy engagement. In this case, the executive powers of Welsh ministers are divorced from any legislative powers residing in the Senedd. Indeed, for practical purposes these ministers are agents of the UK level. Moreover, prison education is, notoriously, a 'Cinderella service', with the proliferation of short-term sentences and the regular movement of prisoners from one over-crowded prison to another rendering meaningful education programmes very difficult to deliver (Criminal Justice Alliance 2012; UK Department for Education and Skills and Department for Work and Pensions 2005: 28). Healthcare provision for prisoners has also tended to be a low political priority – a situation left largely unaffected even by the COVID-19 pandemic (Jones 2020a). This combination of tightly constrained formal influence and a lack of political engagement has had the effect of ensuring that devolved activity has been very limited in scope. Indeed, in the area of prison education, the Welsh Government's well-known and much advertised hostility to outsourcing/contracting out has apparently been insufficient to counteract the 'marketisation' predilections of the institutions of England and Wales criminal justice that are responsible for delivering this service at HMP Berwyn on behalf of Welsh ministers.[10] The result is that prison education is one of the few parts of the education system in Wales in which private or outsourced providers play a leading role. Well over a decade since a 'Welsh-specific policy for prisoner education in Wales' was promised, policy remains functionally identical to that found in England (Explanatory Memorandum to the Welsh Ministers (Transfer of Functions) Order 2009, No. 703: 4).[11]

There are a number of potential explanations as to why certain areas of policy have elicited so little apparent policy interest at the devolved level.

The kinds of very complex governance arrangements in place for prison education and health are likely to act as a major deterrent. Budgetary pressures and civil service capacity may also act as limiting factors (Evans et al. 2021; Jones and Wyn Jones 2019), especially in a context in which there is no overarching locus for criminal justice in the government. In the case of certain parts of the criminal justice system, the absence of any real external interest (including among academics) may also reduce the pressure on policy makers to engage. Lack of powers is, of course, another factor (Brewster and Jones 2019). But as already noted, we should resist the temptation of suggesting too simple a correlation between formal devolved powers and devolved engagement. Policing has already been identified as a prime example of an area where the Welsh Government's formal powers are limited, yet in which political imperatives have led to significant devolved investment (especially in resource terms).[12]

That being said, while it is important to enter the appropriate caveats, there are also multiple examples of the Welsh Government using its powers, responsibilities and influence in the Welsh criminal system in ways that demonstrate a fundamentally different approach to the one that has been adopted by successive UK governments since the early 1990s. As discussed in the previous chapter, performative (though not only performative) punitiveness has dominated at the England and Wales level (Goldson 2010; Tonry 2007). In this context, generating positive headlines and/or embarrassing political rivals have been considered more important metrics for measuring policy success than reducing crime or its associated harms. Evidence as to what might help secure the latter outcomes – especially 'expert' evidence that contradicts the punitive agenda – has been dismissed or overlooked (Garland 2001; Goldson 2010). By contrast, there appears to be consensus among those scholars who have studied those parts of the Welsh criminal justice system in which the Welsh Government has been active that the latter has attempted to develop evidence-based policy that is self-consciously progressive in terms of its approach. This reflects its wider approach to social policy in general (on which see Chaney and Drakeford 2004; Drakeford 2007; Scott and Mooney 2009). In other words, and to return to our Bevan quote, this is an actor with 'progressive pretensions'.

There are multiple examples to which we might point to buttress this claim. In those areas in which it does not have direct responsibility, it opposed the (ultimately failed) privatisation of part of the probation service (Wales Online 2013), the programme of court closures (Welsh Government 2015b) and (eventually) an attempt to site a new prison in Port Talbot (Davies 2018b).[13] It has sought to mitigate the impact of cuts on police budgets (such as its investment in PCSOs) (Lowe et al. 2015). Where it has direct responsibility it has, for example, attempted to develop a harm reduction approach to substance misuse (Bennett and Holloway 2011; Brewster and Jones 2019); secured legislation to remove the defence of reasonable chastisement in Wales (cf. 'the smacking ban') (Welsh Government 2021), abolished imprisonment as a sanction for non-payment of council tax (Drakeford 2018), and has unveiled legislative plans for what will be, if enacted, the most progressive prisoner voting policy in the UK (Welsh Government 2020). Its attempts to ensure that those departing prison were not left homeless through a policy that was widely lauded as being evidence-based and notably progressive will be discussed in more detail in the next chapter.

But perhaps the best known – and certainly the most studied – example of devolved engagement in the Welsh criminal justice system relates to youth justice. Reflecting a rights-based 'children first, offender second' philosophy, the Welsh Government has used its relatively extensive powers in this area to emphasise 'maximum diversion' and, where possible, avoiding the criminalisation of children (Drakeford 2009: 8; Welsh Government and Youth Justice Board 2014). While there is clear evidence to show that progressive practices exist across different parts of England (Thomas 2015a; Smith and Gray 2019), the Welsh Government's approach has been characterised as 'superior' to England's because of its focus on supported rehabilitation and firm commitment to non-custodial alternatives (Morgan 2009: 20). The difference in approach between the England and Wales and Welsh levels was nicely illustrated when, in 2016, amid growing concern about the state of custodial institutions for children, the chair of the Youth Justice Board called for the development of 'secure schools' to replace young offender institutions and secure training centres across England and Wales. This proposal was rejected by the then Welsh Cabinet Secretary for Communities and Children, Carl Sargeant, who declared that the Welsh Government would instead seek to find 'Welsh solutions' to the problems facing young people in the secure estate in Wales (National Assembly for Wales Debate, 14 December

2016). More recently, the Welsh Government and Ministry of Justice's (2019b) joint *Youth Justice Blueprint for Wales* included a commitment to promoting rehabilitation and to reducing the number of Welsh children in custody. This strategy once again underlines the Welsh Government's commitment to a 'children first' approach and to the relevant articles of the United Nations Convention on the Rights of the Child.

In the academic literature, the development of a distinctive approach in Wales towards youth justice that is progressive in intent has been dubbed 'dragonisation' (see Field 2015; Haines 2009). The term is a deliberate echo of 'tartanisation', as used in the criminological literature on Scotland (see, for example, McAra 2006; McAra and Mcvie 2015; Mooney et al. 2015). It should be noted, however, that more recent scholarship has questioned the extent to which 'dragonisation' has been more aspirational than actual. Could it be that the intention to do things differently in Wales has not always been delivered upon, or at least has been delivered upon to different degrees in different parts of the country (see Evans et al. 2021; Thomas 2015a)? We explore the difference between aspiration and actuality in the third and final part of this discussion, where we draw on interview evidence to explore how the Welsh Government's 'progressive pretensions' fare in the context of a criminal justice system in which the dominant actor is committed to a fundamentally different approach.

## DEVOLVED RESPONSIBILITY IN PRACTICE

Thus far in this chapter we have demonstrated that even while the Welsh Government is very clearly the subordinate partner in the Welsh criminal justice system, its responsibilities within that system are nonetheless extensive. We have also pointed to the ways in which, in shouldering many (though, as we have seen, not all) of these responsibilities, the Welsh Government has sought to adopt a progressive approach that is almost diametrically opposed to that which has dominated at the England and Wales level for the past three decades. It will be immediately obvious, however, that even if the Welsh Government's progressive pretensions require no apology – they are, after all, buttressed by a democratic mandate from the people of Wales – this combination of policy ambition and constitutional subordination is fraught with the possibility of dysfunction, to say nothing of deep frustration.

In this final section, we draw on interviews with policy professionals active in the Welsh criminal justice system to explore devolved responsibility in practice. What this testimony suggests is that, from youth justice to tackling substance misuse, whenever the Welsh Government tries to shoulder its responsibilities in the Welsh criminal justice system, it is quickly confronted by the constitutional limitations of its role. Indeed, it is striking how frequently interviewees refer – unbidden – to the constitutional underpinnings of criminal justice policy in Wales when discussing the challenges of and barriers to practical policy implementation.[14] The jagged edge of divided responsibilities and competences not only defines the Welsh criminal justice system in an academic sense; it circumscribes the daily lives of those working within it. This all the more so because when the Welsh Government attempts to act in ways that are unapologetically progressive, it is going against the grain of an England and Wales criminal justice system whose guiding force – the UK Government – has, since the mid-1990s, tended to scorn evidence-based policy, viewing performative 'toughness' not only as an end in itself but arguably the most important aim of criminal justice policy (Garland 2001; Goldson 2010; Simon 2007).

Youth justice cuts across many of the Welsh Government's wider responsibilities and it has long been actively engaged in seeking to prevent youth offending via the *All Wales Youth Offending Strategy* and other related strategies (Welsh Government and Youth Justice Board 2004, 2014). More recently, the Welsh Government's commitment to tackling adverse childhood experiences (ACEs) has seen it focus on the relationship between childhood trauma and future offending – as is obvious in the *Youth Justice Blueprint for Wales* co-produced by the Welsh Government and Ministry of Justice (2019b; Welsh Government 2017c). But as Mark Drakeford – writing in his then academic capacity – observed, while most of the 'core services' drawn together in youth offending teams are devolved, some of the most important areas affecting children in contact with the youth justice system are reserved to the UK level (Drakeford 2010: 139). This includes control over the youth secure estate, the age of criminal responsibility and guidelines on sentences that are handed down to children. Interviewees are clear about the limitations placed on the Welsh Government's ability to develop an alternative approach to youth justice.

**Anthony:** I think the fundamental issue about the constitution is that if you want to take a different approach to England – a less punitive, more socially responsible approach, and do things like start tackling adverse child experience and all of those issues – but you don't have the levers to be able to fully control that, then it makes it quite difficult.

**Emma:** You're probably designing something that you have no control over or have limited control over. It's the kind of statutory justice elements, if you like, within the operation of the system. What age do you [want] criminal responsibility? What type of court orders? It's the whole custodial responsibility. It's the bricks and mortar. The capital and the revenue costs.

The limitations imposed by a lack of access to or control over key policy levers is a recurring theme.

In fulfilment of its responsibilities for community safety, health and local government, the Welsh Government has launched a number of initiatives aimed at combating domestic abuse. As previously noted, national strategies to combat domestic abuse were published in 2005 and 2010, followed more recently by a strategy designed to challenge public attitudes towards violence against women in Wales (Welsh Government 2005a, 2010, 2022b). In 2015, the Violence against Women, Domestic Abuse and Sexual Violence (Wales) Act was passed. This legislation seeks to improve consistency in service provision across Wales and enhance the quality of 'needs-based' approaches to tackling domestic abuse and sexual violence. The Welsh Government's *National Training Framework* further underlines its commitment to tackling violence against women (2016c).

Once again, however, the Welsh Government and its officials face hard constitutional constraints when seeking to develop their own approach to the problem. Lacking control over criminal law and sentencing, they are unable to introduce alternative sanctions, provisions or protections that might correspond more closely with Welsh Government's own policy and legislation in this area.

**Anthony:** We've had a recent Act passed from a Welsh Government perspective [The Violence against Women, Domestic

Abuse and Sexual Violence (Wales) Act 2015]. The one thing it couldn't do was specify different sanctions for offenders or different protections for victims beyond what was already in existence for England and Wales. But, obviously ... the aspiration from Welsh Government's point of view is why don't we do something different? Why don't we take more restorative approaches? Why don't we invest more in perpetrator programmes? Those sorts of things. Because, as we know, what happens with perpetrators, particularly of domestic violence, is that they just do it time and time again. They go through, they get sentenced, they serve the sentence, they come out, and lo and behold you've got another victim.

In other words, a 'whole system approach' to policy-making in which all the elements align in the pursuit of a unified vision or goal is debarred because of the structure of the Welsh criminal justice system.

Resettlement and rehabilitation of former prisoners is also part and parcel of devolved government's wider responsibilities for social policy. As acknowledged in a joint strategy published by NOMS Cymru, Youth Justice Board Cymru and the Welsh Government in 2006, 'many of the mechanisms' for reducing reoffending in Wales fall under the purview of the latter (NOMS Cymru et al. 2006: 7). Here again, however, we find the efforts of the Welsh Government being stymied by its inability to align some of the most important policy levers in order to forge a coherent overall approach.

One hugely significant barrier to successful resettlement of prisoners is the widespread dispersal of Welsh prisoners across the England and Wales prison estate. The resulting, often very significant, distances between prisoners and family members make maintaining family connections very difficult. As will be discussed in more detail in the next chapter, it also makes providing meaningful 'Through the Gate' support challenging, if not, at times, impossible. All this in a context in which the research is clear that maintaining family links and securing accommodation on release are key factors in avoiding reoffending on, or soon after, release (e.g. Maguire et al. 2010; Niven and Stewart 2005; Quilgars et al. 2012; more generally on the challenges of distance in the context of Welsh prisoners, see Jones 2017). While the Welsh Government has no power to determine where Welsh prisoners are being held, the issues created by distance have a huge bearing on its ability to carry out its own responsibilities in an area that, as we saw in Chapter 2, Wales has particularly severe problems (see also Madoc-Jones et al. 2018a: 81 on housing). One interviewee summarises the situation in the following terms:

> **Michael:** I would imagine that there is an issue in that you're looking at the best ways to support and rehabilitate someone but then you've got no control over, say, sentencing guidelines, or the locations of prisoners. And you also have no control over the laws under which they're incarcerated. I suppose if you identify that a certain behaviour results from certain circumstances, you might view it differently as a criminal offence. You might recognise, 'this pattern of behaviour indicates substance misuse or it indicates mental ill health. We don't wish to treat it so harshly as a criminal offence.' But you can't change that. So, you're dealing with people who are incarcerated under laws you haven't made, according to sentences and sentencing guidelines you haven't written, and then you've got to help them out.

As this account makes clear, distance is only one, albeit fundamental, issue undermining Welsh Government efforts.

The issue of substance misuse raises other, equally fundamental questions. As noted earlier in this chapter, while the misuse of and dealing in drugs (as well as their classification) is reserved to the UK Government, responsibility for addressing the effects of substance misuse falls on the devolved layer of government. This is also an area in which, over time, the Welsh Government has developed a distinctive perspective and approach focusing on harm reduction. The Welsh Government's latest *Substance Misuse Delivery Plan 2019–2022*, published in October 2019, commits to ensuring that all prisons in Wales have a 'coordinated' substance misuse service based on existing evidence of 'best practice' (2019d: 13).[15] However, with the key legislative levers for the regulation of drugs and alcohol – as well as sentencing, held by the UK Government – there are hard constitutional constraints on the ability of the Welsh Government to pursue such an approach in a systematic fashion (Brewster and Jones 2019). In recent years, these have prevented the introduction of safe-site injecting rooms in Wales despite growing evidence that they can help reduce drug-related deaths (e.g. Kaleidoscope 2017; Marshall et al. 2011; Milloy and Wood 2009; Otter 2017).[16] Welsh policy makers have also been prevented from legalising the medical use of marijuana, despite Members of the Senedd having voted to support such a change in January 2018 (BBC News 2018).

> **Jamie:** In terms of where policies need to change, when you're looking at more generalised harm, you're looking at imprisonment in relation to drug-related crimes. You're looking at drug-related deaths. Legislation needs to change around that, and obviously that isn't devolved. That's dictated by Westminster. So, I think that's where the challenge comes.
>
> **Sarah:** I think of safe injecting sites... That's a perfect example of a limitation. If Welsh Government did want to pursue that, they would probably struggle because of legislation.
>
> **Ross:** Injection rooms are an example of what they [Welsh Government] can't do. They can't change the system where we're putting people in prison unnecessarily because of their drug use. Yes, they can work with police and crime commissioners to look at where we caution people and where we don't caution people. But again, that would be the responsibility of the police and crime commissioner and not Welsh Government, even though the Welsh Government can influence. So, I think those bits of work are more difficult.

While the Welsh Government – supported by the Senedd – may wish to focus on harm reduction, including the 'more generalised' harms generated by criminalisation and the problems associated with becoming entangled in the criminal justice system (on which, see Padfield and Maruna 2006; Scraton 2007), its ability to do so effectively is severely constrained.

One possible response, of course, is to lobby for changes at the UK level. Our interviewees were, however, uniformly sceptical about how much influence the Welsh Government, the 'minor partner' in the Welsh criminal justice system, could realistically hope to have.

> **Emma:** They [Welsh Government] will always want to express a view, and be taken seriously when they express that view. But then their ability to influence perhaps is a bit more questionable, because inevitably the policy is for England and Wales, and Wales is the smaller – you know – the minor partner.

> **Michael:** I suppose there are probably certain aspects of policy in Wales that we would just think, 'Oh well that's Department for Culture, Media and Sport, or that's Home Office. We're not shifting them.' My colleagues in London have tried to go and see them. They can't shift them. So, we just let it go. We work with what we've got.

David Brewster and Robert Jones (2019: 11) also find that Welsh officials tend to give up trying to 'advance more liberal or progressive' approaches in dealing with their UK level counterparts. Hard constitutional reality and the dictates of *realpolitik* mean that either ambitions have to be scaled back; more promised than can reasonably hope to be delivered; and/or policies that appear to be well founded dropped altogether. The following interviewee testimony makes the point across a range of different issue areas.

> **Michael:** I guess we just drop certain topics. We don't expect to see movement from the UK Government, so we work on the topics which are obviously devolved, because there's a chance for movement there.

> **Sarah:** If I think of some of the work with women exploited through prostitution. Say you wanted to go, 'Do you know what? We need to create a policy where those women are protected ...' Say they wanted to do a zoning of it. Because that crosses devolved and non-devolved areas, it suddenly may minimise or change the vision ... It's an example where you may have a willingness from one statutory body wanting to do something ... but then you have the police saying, 'We can't because ...' And they use the instructions and the guidance and the policies that are coming out of ACPO [now renamed the National Police Chiefs' Council], etc. So that means that Wales wouldn't be able to achieve its vision.

**Jamie:** When talking about [the] development of services, bringing it back to the likes of drug consumption rooms, that isn't something that the Welsh Government, from a legal perspective, can give that go-ahead for. They can't change the law around that, which makes it incredibly frustrating, because you've got evidence-based interventions ... They have got a huge amount of evidence behind them to suggest that they do work, in relation to their aim and objectives.

**Michael:** Certainly, it came up in the original substance misuse strategy, in that there was a lot of talk about – well, there was a whole section on alcohol in the community, availability of alcohol in the community. And there's a certain amount you could do simply by working with people. But pretty much all of the legislative levers were not devolved. So, you couldn't reform the Licensing Act in any kind of creative fashion. You couldn't manage the price of alcohol. You couldn't manage opening hours. You couldn't manage advertising practice. So that whole section of the substance misuse strategy was a bit more hopeful than it was determined.[17]

'[A] bit more hopeful than it was determined' may well be euphemistic, but the meaning is clear enough and – sadly – might well serve as an epitaph for the Welsh Government's progressive pretensions in this policy field. Time and again, Welsh Government attempts to shoulder its various criminal justice-related responsibilities in ways that are not only consistent with the values that it seeks to embody, but are also evidence-based, have been frustrated. Frustrated, above all, by the very nature of the constitutional structure that underpins the Welsh criminal justice system.

## CONCLUSION

In the introduction to this chapter we cited Aneurin Bevan's dictum that 'Responsibility without power is the most dangerous of all situations for a political party with progressive pretensions.' As we conclude we return to consider what light it sheds on the role of devolved government in the Welsh criminal justice system. In doing so, the first point to make is that, even if its role clearly varies between policy areas both in terms of formal responsibilities and the extent of its influence, taken as a whole the Welsh Government's role is extensive. Even if it had no interest in doing so – and given the statistics revealed in Chapter 2 one might hope that indifference would itself be unthinkable – the nature of Wales's devolution settlement means that devolved government *inevitably* has a vital role to play in the functioning of the Welsh criminal justice system. Equally clearly, however, by reserving the single England and Wales criminal justice system and legal jurisdiction to the UK level, that same settlement serves to ensure that in carrying out those responsibilities, the Welsh Government is, also inevitably, always the subordinate or 'minor partner'. In other words, while its formal responsibilities are extensive, its power is closely constrained by the fact that so many of the basic policy levers are beyond its control or influence.

A second point to make is that, given that devolved government has no choice but to get involved in criminal justice – as might indeed be expected given that it is a democratically elected government accountable to a parliament and, ultimately, the wider Welsh electorate – it has sought to develop its own approach to the exercise of its responsibilities. Equally unsurprisingly, that approach has been consistent with the values espoused by a Welsh Labour Party that has been self-consciously progressive – recall the 'clear red water' between Welsh and New Labour – as well as committed to evidence-based policy-making (Drakeford 2007; Davies and Williams 2009). In the specific context of criminal justice, it has sought to focus on prevention and harm reduction rather than criminalisation and punishment – in other words, its approach has, in the main, been the antithesis of the dominant approach in the England and Wales criminal justice system as a whole since the advent of democratic devolution.[18] But as we have seen, the result in practice has been frustration. Indeed, based on the analysis in both this and the preceding chapter, we cannot avoid the conclusion that such frustration is the inevitable outcome of the constitutional underpinnings of the Welsh criminal system and devolved government's place within it: frustration is structurally overdetermined.

All of which serves to bring into sharp, even pitiless, relief the perpetual dilemma facing the Welsh Government when seeking to enact its responsibilities towards the Welsh criminal justice system. It is a dilemma that is as much ethical as it is practical. The Welsh Government may choose to ignore its own values and separate electoral mandate by simply echoing in Wales those England and Wales policies that the UK Government is enacting in England: an approach that, in terms that Bevan would doubtless recognise, risks its soul. Alternatively, the Welsh Government can continue to try to use its tightly constrained powers to endeavour to do things differently in Wales, doing so in full knowledge of the fact that the very structure of the system militates against any realistic chance of success. An approach that must surely, over the longer term at least, risk its credibility. Such is the fate of a progressive government charged with significant responsibility but endowed with only very limited power.

# 5
# ON POLICY-MAKING AND POLICY TAKING
## *Two case studies*

GIVEN THAT an important aim of this book is to provide for the first time an overview of the operation of the Welsh criminal justice system – a system whose very existence as a constitutionally distinctive arrangement of powers and responsibilities remains widely overlooked – the previous chapters have necessarily ranged widely. But there is a resulting danger that the breadth of coverage has served to eclipse depth. In this chapter, therefore, we focus our attentions on two specific case studies, namely housing provision for former prisoners and the funding arrangements for Wales's police forces. Doing so allows us to explore in much greater detail the ways in which these distinctive arrangements impact on the operation of the criminal justice system.

These two cases are, deliberately, very different from each other. The first is high profile and highly emotive. The second is more technical and even (we must reluctantly admit) rather dry, even if still operationally vital. In addition, while housing provision straddles both criminal justice and other areas of public policy, police funding relates to the arrangements for part of the Welsh criminal justice system that is (ostensibly) completely non-devolved. But in addition – and even more importantly for present purposes – housing provision for prison leavers is an area in which, from the early years of democratic devolution, devolved government has actively sought to develop its own distinctive and, yes, evidence-based and progressive approach. Police funding, by contrast, is an area in which devolved involvement is an inevitable consequence of the entanglement of the reserved and devolved in a constitutional context in which normal, Westminster-family rules do not apply.

Superficially at least, the stories that emerge from both case studies are quite different. In the case of housing provision, it is a case of a high-minded and evidentially well-founded policy floundering on the rocks of the structural inability of the Welsh Government to enact the kind of 'whole system approach' that public policy experts regard as the *sine qua non* of transformational change. The end result, to be blunt, has been an abject policy failure with baleful human consequences that are all too visible on the streets of towns and cities right across Wales. Police funding, by contrast, is a story of constant negotiation in which decisions made by the UK Government that make perfect sense in the context of its English responsibilities, once transposed into the devolved context, end up having major implications for police services in Wales as well as the Welsh Government. On the one hand, therefore, a deliberate attempt at policy differentiation instigated from Wales; on the other hand, policy differentiation that is an unintended but nonetheless unavoidable consequence of the operation of a criminal justice system that remains (formally) a wholly owned subsidiary of the UK Government but which – post-devolution – now operates in a very different context in Wales.

Yet both case studies ultimately serve to underline the same basic if, for many, discomforting truth about the dysfunctional nature of the Welsh criminal justice system. The retention of so many of the key policy levers in London means that the Welsh Government is ultimately a policy taker rather than a policy maker; even in those areas of criminal justice policy (like housing for prison leavers) where it has a clear locus. Also, no matter how jealously it guards its constitutional prerogatives, the UK Government's writ over the Welsh criminal justice system, and therefore its powers as a policy maker within that system, are also constrained by the reality of devolution. Indeed, when the limitations of its own power and influence are reached, it finds itself reliant on the understanding and goodwill of the Welsh Government. The decision to break from the traditional Westminster-model alignment of governmental and justice institutions thus leaves the Welsh criminal justice system stranded in limbo – or purgatory – with the possibility of effective policy-making being one of the prime casualties.

## CASE STUDY ONE: HOUSING AND THE DEMISE OF A FLAGSHIP POLICY

The introduction of the Homeless Persons (Priority Need) (Wales) Order 2001 was one of the first major Welsh Government initiatives relating to the criminal justice system. Its provisions ensured that 'unintentionally homeless' prison leavers were included within the categories of people for whom local authorities 'must provide housing support' (for an overview, see NOMS Cymru et al. 2006: 12). This included offering support to prisoners with a 'local connection' to Wales without the 'additional burden' of having to prove their 'vulnerability' (Shelter Cymru 2004: 3).

This policy reflected a growing body of international research evidence that had underlined the critical importance of securing accommodation for prisoners upon release. In 1996, a Joseph Rowntree Foundation report concluded that prisoners were more likely to reoffend if they did not have suitable accommodation to which to return (Joseph Rowntree Foundation 1996). The UK Government's Social Exclusion Unit's report on *Reducing Re-offending by Ex-prisoners* found that stable accommodation helped reduce the risk of re-offending by some 20 per cent (2002). Indeed, given the subsequent fate of the policy, it is notable that the evidence base underpinning the Welsh Government's 2001 policy has continued to strengthen (e.g. Maguire and Nolan 2007; O'Leary 2013). A survey carried out by the Ministry of Justice in 2012, for example, reported that three out of five (60 per cent) prisoners felt that having a place to live was key to preventing them from offending in future (Williams et al. 2012b; see also Roman and Travis 2006; Prison Reform Trust and Women in Prison 2018). Further confirming the link between homelessness and reoffending, more than three-quarters of prisoners (79 per cent) who reported being homeless prior to entering custody were reconvicted within the first 12 months after release, as compared to less than a half (47 per cent) of prisoners with some form of accommodation prior to entering custody (Williams et al. 2012b). A report published by HMI Probation found that prisoners who are released as homeless are 'significantly more likely' to reoffend and return to prison. Inspectors found that the number of service users recalled or resentenced to custody within 12 months of release was almost double for those without any settled accommodation to return to (HMI Probation 2020: 4).[1]

Practitioners were certainly conscious of the evidence base underpinning the 2001 policy and its significance:

**Holly:** The Welsh Government were very aware of the international evidence around reoffending and the importance of a home ... If you haven't got a home, your chances of getting back on your feet are so incredibly slim that we felt, in Wales, that we could do something positive by creating an automatic priority need for people coming out of prison.

**Holly:** We felt that it was progressive because we knew there were a lot of people coming out of prison into homelessness, and into street homelessness. And as we saw it the first twenty-four to forty-eight hours post-release are so important for getting someone established. And if you don't get that right, if people don't have a roof over their head in that critical time, then it can be a trigger that ends up with people going straight back in. Because they end up falling off the wagon. It's a really critical time to get right.

An evidence-based, self-consciously progressive policy: priority need was indeed 'dragonisation' writ large.

As a result of the 2001 order, housing provision for Welsh prisoners became markedly different from that available to prisoners from England. Whereas unintentionally homeless prison leavers from England had to prove that their period of incarceration had left them particularly vulnerable before they could be allocated priority need status, prison leavers with a local connection to Wales were not required do so.[2] Instead, they would be automatically allotted priority need status if they were about to become unintentionally homeless.

The Welsh approach was widely lauded. In 2010, following an inspection of HMP Altcourse in Liverpool,[3] HM Inspectorate of Prisons described Welsh services as 'an example to the English authorities' of the kinds of support structures needed to help resettle English prisoners upon release (HMI Prisons 2010: 5). Following a repeat visit to HMP Altcourse in 2014, the inspectorate referred to the policy as something that 'sets Wales apart from England' (HMI Prisons 2014: 6). Indeed, research at the same prison revealed that prison staff had been made aware of threats of possible violence against Welsh prisoners resulting from resentment at the additional support being made available to them by 'in-reach' Welsh housing services (Jones 2017).

Despite all this, in 2013 the Welsh Government announced plans to remove prisoners from the list of those given automatic priority need status. From this point, as had already been the case for English prisoners, being unintentionally homeless would not be enough: they would also have to prove their 'vulnerability'.[4] The Welsh Government's volte-face was fuelled by criticism of the cost of maintaining priority need for unintentionally homeless prisoners; in particular from Welsh local government. Research published by the Welsh Local Government Association (WLGA) in 2008 had already warned about the future sustainability of the policy (Humphreys and Stirling 2008). The WLGA's evidence to the Welsh Government's consultation on its plans to remove prison leavers from the priority need category estimated that during 2012/13 the average cost of accommodating a former prisoner was over £2,100, with a total of just under £2m spent to accommodate former prisoners in Wales in the same financial year (Welsh Government 2013: 5).

The financial burden on local authorities in Wales arising from the 2001 policy had grown as demand for housing services from Welsh prison leavers increased. Between 2001 and 2012, the number of households across Wales where a member was vulnerable due to being released from custody without accommodation to which to return had grown by 142 per cent (StatsWales 2015). In the period between 2008/9 and its peak in 2011/12, this meant a real-terms increase from 640 to 955 households in 2011/12 (StatsWales 2015). As well as the direct financial costs involved, local authorities were concerned that other vulnerable groups were being overlooked because of the need to cater for prison leavers (Mackie and Hoffman 2011; Mackie et al. 2012). Operationally, the 2001 duty also generated what were undoubtedly serious challenges for local authority staff who were required to provide immediate support for homeless prison leavers arriving at their offices with little or even no notice. Of the eighteen local authorities that responded to the Welsh Government's consultation on what was to become the Housing Act (Wales) 2014, all were either partly or wholly in favour of removing automatic priority need status from prison leavers (Welsh Government 2013).

Responding to the same consultation, third-sector organisations also raised a number of wider concerns, including the problems created for service providers by insufficient housing stock, a lack of data surrounding the success of priority need for prison leavers, and the difficulties of accessing housing benefit. In addition, however, they raised serious questions about the role of some local authority staff in the implementation of the policy. Indeed, Shelter Cymru made clear that some Welsh local authority staff were actively subverting the policy, with staff telling prison leavers that they would be found to have become intentionally homeless or that they would not be considered a priority (Shelter Cymru; see also Jones et al. 2021).

Notwithstanding their various concerns and reservations, third-sector organisations were largely opposed to the Welsh Government's proposals amid fears that 'many vulnerable former prisoners' would be denied access to accommodation if the 2001 approach to priority need were abandoned (e.g. Gofal 2014: 8; also Cymorth Cymru 2013; Shelter Cymru 2013).

One of our interviewees draws out the ways in which the 2001 policy tended to polarise opinion between the criminal justice sector and local authorities.

> **Joshua:** I think criminal justice will say, 'Yes this has been brilliant, brilliant for us, we can focus on other things.' The local authorities would say, 'We've been spending maybe a quarter of our budget in terms of actual cash and in terms of staff time trying to resolve this fairly small cohort of people. This is actually undermining our intention to try to prevent homelessness across this much wider spectrum.'

> **Joshua:** Prisoners started arriving generally on a Friday, sometimes late in the afternoon and sometimes after they've had a visit to the pub as well. So, local authorities were unable to plan in terms of what support they could provide. And with them being priority need it meant there was a definitive duty to provide something. Which often meant, at that late notice, probably unsuitable bed and breakfast accommodation, probably with other prison leavers who presented at roughly the same time. On a Friday afternoon, again.

The objections of the local authorities prevailed. The Housing Act (Wales) 2014 established a regime that ensured that those prison leavers with a local connection to Wales and who were set to become unintentionally homeless on release from prison would only be granted priority need status if they could also prove that they were 'vulnerable' as a direct result of their time in custody (Shelter Cymru 2021). Rather than England emulating Wales, as suggested by the prisons' inspectorate, as far as priority need entitlement for homeless prison leavers was concerned, it would instead be a case of 'for Wales, see England'. The requirement that Welsh local authorities 'help to prevent' homelessness by providing assistance in securing accommodation for prison leavers at risk of homelessness (a policy to whose subsequent fate we shall return) was no substitute for the duty that had been in place since 2001.

The result was predictable and indeed predicted:

**Holly:** We took what we thought was a real step backwards by removing that [2001 duty] and creating this new tiny little category [of priority need] that hardly anyone is fitting into. And we did predict that it would lead to an increase in rough sleeping. And funnily enough, we've had a great increase in rough sleeping. Not just because of that – there's been a lot of factors in that – but we've just been doing this study where we've gone out round Wales, we've spoken to a hundred currently street homeless people, and a lot of them are prison leavers.

The statistics on homelessness among prison leavers – to which we will return – bear out the impressions of this practitioner. All of which begs the obvious question, why did the Welsh Government make the decision to scuttle its own flagship policy? Is it simply a case of the lobbying power of local authorities trumping other considerations?

It is worth returning here to the 2008 WLGA research report discussed earlier. It cites a number of criticisms aimed at the 2001 policy, some of which appear to be less than compelling in retrospect. It is clear, for example, that some local authority staff were resentful at having to engage in tasks for which they were not trained or not accustomed, and which they regarded as rightfully falling under the purview of those working in the criminal justice system (Humphreys and Stirling 2008). Viewed from the perspective of this writing, the substantial additional workload burden on local authority staff generated by the subsequent rise of rough sleeping (which includes, of course, a related emotional toll) puts a different gloss on these complaints.

More substantively, however, the authors, Caroline Humphreys and Tamsin Stirling, warned that the 'complex' intersection between UK criminal justice policy and the Welsh Government's housing responsibilities might eventually undermine the 2001 policy (2008: 46). Here critics were on stronger ground. There is indeed no doubt that the organisation of the England and Wales prison system did cause significant and, indeed, intractable operational difficulties for those charged with implementing the 2001 duty.

The England and Wales prison system operates as a single system, with prisoners from Wales dispersed across it very widely, including (during the operation of the priority need policy, in particular) on release (Jones 2017).[5] This made it nigh-on impossible to predict who was about to turn up in Welsh local authority offices looking for support in order to avoid becoming homeless. Relatedly, research from one of the current authors confirms that distance from place of release to place of residence plays a significant role in determining the willingness and ability of prison leavers to access support (Jones 2017). Stories of prisoners from south Wales being released from prisons in south-west England and ending up engaging in substance misuse in transit through Bristol, before seeking potential support networks closer to home, are not merely apocryphal (Jones 2017: 175–8). Moreover, the belief that prison leavers tended to present on a Friday was also statistically well founded (Selous 2015).[6]

Another development that was to render the 2001 duty ever more challenging was the ever-rising prison population and the resulting increase in the number of prison leavers. Between 2001 and 2013, that is between the introduction of the duty and the Welsh Government's announcement of its demise, the prison population in England and Wales increased by a quarter (26 per cent).[7] Even without the other problems that helped undermine the policy, this alone was bound to make delivering on the 2001 policy more difficult, especially in a context in which the social housing stock was under severe pressure (e.g. Essex et al. 2008).

While the negative and ultimately short-sighted attitudes of (some) local authority staff may have accelerated the end of the duty, the real issues were more deeply seated. The reality was (and remains) that the Welsh Government had no means of controlling or even influencing the upstream factors that would impact the rate or timing of demand for housing support for prison leavers. As such, the absolute duty imposed in 2001 was almost certainly destined to become regarded as too burdensome, especially when the UK Government that *did* control those upstream factors was pursuing priorities that were not only very different but inimical to the ones prioritised by the Welsh Government. Indeed, one can to some extent sympathise with local authority staff who were, in effect, being expected to make good on the contradictions at the heart of the Welsh criminal justice system – a nigh-on impossible task. Were the Welsh criminal justice system structured differently, a determined, whole-system approach incorporating all the relevant agencies may well have been able to secure different results. Instead – as we have seen – this is simply not possible given the jagged edge of divided responsibilities and competences that currently characterises this policy space in Wales. Lest there be any doubt about the matter, the fate of the Welsh Government's much less ambitious replacement for the 2001 duty stands as further testimony to just how limited its *effective* policy competences in this field really are.

The distinctive Welsh policy on automatic priority need was replaced by a 'preventative duty', intended to help ensure that the prison leavers did not find themselves unintentionally homeless (responding, of course, to the now further strengthened evidence base clearly demonstrating the link between homelessness and reoffending). It relied heavily on 'Through the Gate' services to assist the transition from prison back into the wider community. It is important to recall here that the decision to drop the 2001 rules on priority need status for prison leavers coincided with partial privatisation of the England and Wales probation service. Twenty-one community rehabilitation companies (CRCs) were given responsibility for managing low- and medium-risk offenders, alongside a National Probation Service (NPS) tasked with supervising high-risk offenders. In Wales, this meant that the Wales CRC – the contract for which was awarded to Working Links – would have primary responsibility for delivering on the 'preventative duty', as set out in the Welsh Government strategy document on housing provision for prison leavers (Welsh Government 2015c); especially in the light of the (in itself, welcome) UK Government decision to extend supervision to prison leavers who had been sentenced to less than 12 months.

The complete debacle that was the attempt to partially privatise probation has been well documented elsewhere and there is little point in rehearsing the litany of disastrous mis-steps here (for early indications of impending failure, see HMI Probation 2016a, 2016b; for subsequent confirmation, see House of Commons Public Accounts Committee 2019; National Audit Office 2019; for academic accounts, see Deering and Feilzer 2015; Robinson et al. 2016; Walker et al. 2019). The failures of the Wales CRC in relation to housing serve as a microcosm of these wider problems. An inspection in February 2019 by HMI Probation (2019b: 32) found that its 'Through the Gate' services were 'inadequate'. Indeed, resettlement planning focused on individual needs and circumstances, which was meant to be at the heart of the new system, had taken place in under half (just 45 per cent) of cases examined by the inspectors. Part of the problem with *Transforming Rehabilitation* was that it had been drastically 'underfunded' because of the UK Government's unrealistic expectations about likely demand (House of Commons Public Accounts Committee 2019: 5). Indeed, having faced 'financial pressures' from the outset of the contract, Working Links went into administration in February 2019 (HMI Probation 2019b: 13).

Housing services were one of the things that suffered in all of this. An evaluation led by Iolo Madoc-Jones found that the Wales CRC was failing to properly complete housing applications and assessments, with problems identified at prison reception and 'poor' services being delivered at the pre-release stage (Madoc-Jones et al. 2018a: 2). Consequently, despite the change in the priority need rule, housing service providers in Wales once again found themselves facing heavy workloads with insufficient time to address the accommodation needs of those preparing to leave prison and return to the community (for interviewee testimony on the operation of the Wales CRC, see Jones and Wyn Jones 2019: 114–21).

It would appear that some of the pressure was generated by the fact that, in tendering for the Wales CRC contract, Working Links had failed to appreciate the additional work that would be required to respond to the Welsh Government's prevention agenda (Madoc-Jones et al. 2018a, 2018b). This suggests, bluntly, an absence of even the most basic constitutional literacy among contractor and contracting authority alike. The result was that the Welsh Government was left to use its own funds to try to alleviate some of the pressures (Jones and Wyn Jones 2019: 120–1; see also Clinks 2018 for an analysis of the role being played by the voluntary sector); this included making additional funding available to Prison Link Cymru to ensure that resettlement services were being properly delivered at HMP Altcourse in Liverpool – a designated resettlement prison for Wales since 2013 (Ministry of Justice 2014c; Madoc-Jones et al. 2018a).[8] But although the Welsh Government may have viewed itself as having no choice but to try to prop up the failing service, even when it recognised that 'the levers for effective implementation' of its own housing policy for prison leavers 'primarily rest with the UK Government' and the CRCs (James 2019b), there was a price to pay that was not only financial. In addition to the opportunity costs arising from the diversion of the Welsh Government's scarce resources, it is also worth considering the moral hazard involved. It seems highly likely that the use of Welsh Government resources to try to maintain the service in Wales may well have had the inadvertent effect of helping at least one CRC meet its performance targets (Madoc-Jones et al. 2018b). Given the way that privatisation was structured, this in turn would have helped that particular CRC to maximise revenue.

Crucially, it is not only the failings of *Transforming Rehabilitation* that have served to undermine even the much more limited ambitions of the 'preventative duty'. The broader operation of the England and Wales criminal justice system continues to act as a major obstacle to attempts to ensure that prison leavers do not end up homeless. The use of short-term sentences (often for relatively minor offences) means that existing tenancies are regularly lost only for prisoners to be released – homeless – shortly afterwards.[9] Despite an indication in early 2019 that the Ministry of Justice was seeking to review the use of short-term sentences (Gauke 2019), no consequential changes have yet been introduced. Similarly, the dispersal of Welsh prisoners across the England and Wales prison estate also militates against the Welsh Government's ability to successfully deliver on its housing policy. Even though the UK Government has introduced designated resettlement prisons to help move prisoners closer to home a minimum of three months prior to their release (Ministry of Justice 2013b), in 2019, 3,857 prisoners across England and Wales were released from establishments not designated as resettlement prisons, the equivalent of fourteen prison releases a day (Ministry of Justice 2020ziii). Figures on the whereabouts of Welsh prisoners at the time of release are not publicly available – itself an indicator of the continuing absence of basic information – but we do know that at the end of 2019 Welsh prisoners were being held in 105 prisons across England (Jones 2020b). Despite the fact that there are now more prison places in Wales than there are Welsh prisoners.[10] An inevitable consequence of this situation is that Welsh housing service providers are still forced to deal with Welsh prisoners dotted around England's (extensive) prison estate. All of which militates against the effectiveness of attempts to deliver 'Through the Gate' support to ensure that prison leavers do not find themselves homeless upon release (Jones 2017; Quilgars et al. 2012).

It is clear that the termination of the 2001 approach to priority need has seen a very significant reduction in the level of support being provided for Welsh prison leavers who find themselves homeless. In 2014/15 (i.e. in the final year of operation of the 2001 duty) it was calculated that 860 'households' were awarded priority need status because they contained a prison leaver; by the 2018/19 that number had fallen to only fifty-one (StatsWales 2019). We have already seen evidence that the delivery of the subsequent 'preventative duty' fell woefully short as a replacement. Estimating the human costs of these various policy failures is difficult, but after analysing the Welsh Government's *National Rough Sleeper Count Survey* in 2017, Shelter Cymru calculated that 13 per cent of rough sleepers in Wales first became homeless after being released from prison with no accommodation to return to (Jackson 2018b). The same research also found that people were often recalled to prison because they had no fixed address – an utterly Kafkaesque situation. Unsurprisingly, the report's author argues that the evidence 'strongly suggests' that the removal of automatic priority need for prison leavers had been a 'contributing factor' to the growth of street homelessness (Jackson 2018b: 29). More recent Welsh Government estimates suggest that a total of 405 people were rough sleeping in Wales in 2019/20 (StatsWales 2020d), while during that same period Ministry of Justice data show that 148 people managed by Welsh probation services were rough sleeping following release from prison (2020zv). Moreover, as we know, rough sleeping is only one manifestation of homelessness. For an indication of the scale of the wider problem as it relates to prison leavers, we simply note that – again in 2019/20 – fewer than half (45 per cent) of those released from prison custody who were managed by probation services in Wales went into settled accommodation (Ministry of Justice 2020zv). Rough sleeping is the tip of the iceberg.

Given the surge in rough sleeping that became such a visible feature of every city and town across Wales prior to the Coronavirus pandemic (Jackson 2018b), and the widespread view that the demise of automatic priority need for prison leavers contributed to this development (e.g.

Mackie 2017; Shelter Cymru 2017), it is perhaps not surprising that there have been calls to reinstate the previous policy (National Assembly for Wales Equality, Local Government and Communities Committee 2018). However, given that even the less ambitious 'preventative duty' has been so thoroughly undermined by many of the same factors that, ultimately, capsized the preceding flagship policy, advocates of such a move should perhaps give pause. In seeking to ensure that Welsh prison leavers do not become homeless, the Welsh Government finds itself to a very significant extent responding to decisions made by the UK Government in its role as custodian of the institutions of the England and Wales criminal justice system. Constitutional realities mean that it is the UK Government that is overwhelmingly the dominant partner in criminal justice policy, with the Welsh Government camped out on the other, subordinate side of the jagged edge: ultimately, a policy taker rather than a policy maker. As a consequence, successfully delivering even minor departures from 'English policy' is extremely difficult, no matter how well intentioned and well founded the approach is adopted (see also Brewster and Jones 2019).

## CASE STUDY TWO: POLICE FUNDING

In the previous chapter we briefly discussed the role of devolved government in supporting Wales's four police forces. It will be recalled that even though this part of the criminal justice system is reserved to Westminster, the devolved level nonetheless makes a significant contribution to the funding of policing in Wales. Partly because of this, but also because of the intimate ties between policing and other (devolved) public services, we posited that Wales's devolved institutions enjoy more influence on policing in Wales than the formal constitutional position might imply. This is not to suggest, however, that this relationship is necessarily a straightforward, let alone a harmonious, one. Rather, as an unavoidable consequence of the jagged edge of divided powers and responsibilities that defines the Welsh criminal justice system, the police, devolved government and UK Government find themselves caught in an often rather fraught three-way relationship that requires constant negotiation. This in a context in which the formal machinery for managing these relationships has been notable largely by its absence; in part, it would seem, because the establishment of such machinery would involve a tacit admission that the UK level's dominance over this part of the criminal justice is not – indeed, cannot be – as total as the provisions of the devolution legislation might suggest.

In this second case study we will unpack the funding arrangements for policing in Wales before we consider what has become a running sore in the relationship between the two governments in Cardiff and London and the Welsh police forces, namely the Apprenticeship Levy. By doing so we can draw two key issues into focus. The first is the considerable additional complexity that the constitutional order underpinning the Welsh criminal justice system imposes on professionals tasked with operating that system. The caveating is important here, and needs to be spelled out explicitly. We do not mean to imply that there exists somewhere a land where all is ease and crystalline simplicity in dealing with these matters: the public policy equivalent of *Tir na nÓg*. Public policy is inherently complex, especially so in multi-level systems (on the latter point, the literature includes, inter alia, Bache and Flinders 2004; Conteh 2013; Hooghe and Marks 2003; Howlett and Newman 2010; Obinger et al. 2005; Scharpf 1988). Our claim is rather that the Welsh criminal justice system is particularly complex because of the way it straddles two different executives and legislatures and a jagged edge of divided responsibilities and powers.

The second point we bring into focus is the extent to which the UK Government is reliant on the goodwill and cooperation of Welsh Government to ensure the smooth running even of its ostensibly 'wholly owned' elements of the criminal justice system. Here we have the opposite side of the coin to the one examined in the previous case study. There we saw how the ability of devolved government to act as an effective policy maker was constrained and, ultimately, undermined by the fact that the UK Government controls most of the key policy leavers and is intent on pursuing other, incompatible policy priorities. Ultimately, even in the case of those criminal justice-related matters that clearly lie within its field of competence, devolved government is more policy taker than policy maker. But in the case of police funding, it is the UK Government that requires the Welsh Government's cooperation to ensure that its reserved policing responsibilities are carried out effectively. When, for whatever reason, that cooperation is not forthcoming (and there may well be good reasons why it is not), problems will ensue.

It is important to make clear that we are not implying that this is an equal relationship: co-dependency is not synonymous with equality. As we have stressed time and again in the preceding pages, Whitehall and Westminster acting in their England and Wales guise are without doubt the dominant force in the Welsh criminal justice system. Our point is rather that the highly unorthodox constitutional order that characterises this policy space in Wales also imposes real limitations on the potential effectiveness of the UK level as a policy maker.

Let us start by considering a basic question. How are Wales's police forces funded? The simplest answer is that in 2019/20, they received around £751m of total funding derived from three principal sources: £319m from the police precept that accompanies council tax bills; £214m from the Home Office police grant; and another £143m from Welsh Government through a revenue support grant and redistributed non-domestic tax rates (Ifan 2019c; cf. Johnston and Politowski 2016; Allen 2019). In addition, they received £74m in specific grant funding from both the UK and Welsh governments. These sources sit on different sides of the devolved/reserved divide.

The Home Office police grant is allocated by and paid from the budget of one of Whitehall's largest departments. In other words, this is UK-level funding – although it is worth recalling that the Home Office's policing activities are overwhelmingly focused on England and Wales rather than the state as a whole. The level of the grants is determined by the Police Allocation Formula which considers such factors as local population size and crime indicators (Johnston and Politowski 2016). The other two principal sources of funding are closely aligned to and/or dependent on the funding arrangements for local government, which are a devolved responsibility, or on funds that are otherwise controlled by the Welsh Government.[11]

Although police and crime commissioners set the rate of the police precept, it is within a legislative and policy framework controlled at the devolved level, with the Welsh Government able to place caps on any increases. Indeed, the Welsh Government could decide to completely replace the precept with an alternative funding arrangement – a not unthinkable prospect in a context in which various possibilities for replacing council tax are regularly canvassed. The final element of police funding is also controlled at the devolved level in that the revenue support grant is allocated from the devolved budget, and non-domestic tax rates are fully devolved. The Welsh Government notes that its 'approach to setting and distributing the Welsh Government component of police funding provision [*sic*] is based on a principle of ensuring consistency and fairness across England and Wales' (James 2020). In practice this means that the Welsh Government simply adopts the Police Allocation Formula 'decided by the Home Secretary as part of a common formula covering Wales and England' (Holzinger 2018). But this is a choice on its part: in statutory terms it has the power to adopt a different approach should it so wish (see Annex 3 of James 2020).

Even if policing in Wales is ultimately controlled at the England and Wales level, approximately two-thirds of their funding derives from the devolved level. Which is, we might agree, a rather extraordinary state of affairs that underlines one of our central points about the reliance of the UK level on cooperation from the devolved level to carry out reserved functions. This is not in itself, however, a necessary cause of actual (as opposed to potential) complexity for Wales's police services themselves, particularly given that the Welsh Government has followed the lead of the Home Secretary in determining the Police Allocation Formula. To grasp the additional complexity produced by the constitutional underpinnings of the Welsh criminal justice system, we need to view police funding arrangements through a different lens. For however convoluted our initial model of police funding may appear, the reality is even more labyrinthine.

Another way of understanding police funding is to differentiate between those parts of police-force budgets that can be considered core and those that are more discretionary in nature. Focusing on the former, these funds are derived from different sources at both the UK and devolved levels and are also allocated via different mechanisms, be that the Police Allocation Formula or the police precept. It is also important not to gloss over the real difficulties caused by the swingeing cuts to the Home Office budget brought about by the UK Government's commitment to austerity; cuts that have had far-reaching consequences for police budgets in England and Wales. Nonetheless, from the perspective of Wales's police force managers and financial officers, core funding is – relatively speaking – the least complex element of the overall budgetary picture.

The real difficulties arise in the context of discretionary funds; that is funds allocated for particular purposes or to support specific schemes or initiatives. In the case of Welsh police forces, three different nodes of political and fiscal authority are relevant: the UK Government, the Welsh Government and Wales's four police and crime commissioners. Much has been made of the fact that the decision to introduce police and crime commissioners in Wales was made against the direct wishes of Welsh Government and Parliament (BBC News 2011; Welsh Government 2012c). More pertinent to the present discussion is that the UK Government pressed ahead with this development despite the fact that there was already an additional actor engaged in this space in Wales as the result of devolution. It cannot even be claimed that creating police and crime commissioners in Wales was a way of ensuring uniformity of treatment across England and Wales's police services. For even if that position had any intrinsic merit, in the cases of both London and Greater Manchester the UK Government has decided that powers invested in police and crime commissioners elsewhere should be invested in directly elected mayors; presumably because in those cases the creation of such commissioners as additional roles would over-complicate matters.[12] In Wales, however, this proved to be no barrier; this even though the powers of Welsh Government and Parliament far exceed those of the metropolitan mayors.

All three of these actors use finance as a tool with which to promote their various policy priorities. As a result, the police are constantly engaging with a plethora of different schemes to which funding is attached; all with different aims and adopting different metrics for success (on the latter see Thomas Commission 2019: 182; Wales Audit Office 2016). As our primary interest in this discussion is the respective roles of the UK and Welsh governments, we do not propose to discuss that of the police and crime commissioners in any detail, although throughout what follows it is important to recall that their role is significant and includes, inter alia, liaising with the two governments, holding the chief constable to account, setting the police and crime objectives for their force area, as well as establishing the force budget and determining the precept.

We have already encountered some examples of discretionary spending by Welsh Government on policing in the previous chapter. Perhaps the best known is Welsh Government funding for 500 additional police community support offices (PCSOs), a budgetary commitment of £16.7m in 2019–20 (Welsh Government 2019c). The context for this is set by the austerity-driven cuts to the Home Office's budget – down by a quarter from its 2010–11 level (Ifan 2019c) – and the resulting cuts in police numbers across England and Wales of 14,624 (10 per cent) (Home Office 2020b).[13] Even if PCSOs are not as well trained as police officers and, by comparison, enjoy only 'limited powers' (Loveday and Smith 2015: 75; O'Neil 2014), they clearly represent a net gain for Welsh police services and have been welcomed as such (Jukes 2018; see also Cosgrove and Ramshaw 2015; Lowe et al. 2015: 71–2; Merritt 2010; O'Neil 2014; Thomas Commission 2019: 175). Meanwhile, the fact that local authorities in England provide funding for PCSOs in their own areas provides plenty of constitutional cover for Welsh Government spending money in this way. Unsurprisingly, our interviewees were positive in their assessment.

>**Sion:** The Welsh Government very generously, voluntarily, provides support for policing and community support officers: five hundred across Wales. So, they are prepared to put their hands in their pockets even though they don't have to.

>**Jayne:** Welsh Government provide significant funding for things that fall under the heading of justice that I don't think is to be sniffed at. They provide the funding for the additional five hundred PCSOs. Welsh Government don't in theory have to do it.

But while the role of Welsh Government in funding PSCOs may gain positive reviews, views of its overall role are much more mixed.

The key issue – and the nub of the additional complications associated with police funding in Wales – is the multiple ways in which policing is umbilically linked to other public services. Much of the discretionary funding available for police services is tied to schemes that seek to improve these links. The potential benefits of these schemes for all parties are obvious. Returning to mental health, given that the police are often the first responders to those suffering mental health crises, ensuring smooth cooperation between police and mental health services is clearly eminently sensible (HMICFRS 2018a; Vitale 2017). It is an example that can be multiplied many times over across different policy spaces, including education, housing, and support and treatment for substance misusers. Indeed, so valued are such links that they are regularly funded, at least in part, from the budgets of those other relevant departments or agencies rather than from the budgets of the police services themselves or even the Home Office.[14] But of course, as should be immediately obvious by this point in our discussion, even though they are part of a single England and Wales police service, Wales's four police forces find themselves lodged in a very different public service environment than that surrounding their English counterparts. Most public services in Wales, including the other emergency services, are devolved. Which means in turn that Wales's police forces also find themselves in a very different context as far as discretionary funding opportunities are concerned.

Sometimes, the same arrangements apply in both England and Wales – although establishing whether or not this is the case is often not straightforward not least because, even two decades and more after the establishment of democratic devolution, many Whitehall departments remain notoriously unclear about the geographical extent of their various announcements and initiatives (Rycroft 2019). Often, however, they do not. The question then arises for Wales's police forces is whether there is an equivalent devolved scheme – and associated pot of funding – to any given English scheme? In addition, there are schemes supported by some part or other of the Welsh Government that seek to support other types of linkage between policing and public services through the use of discretionary spending. The complexities are all too readily apparent. As is the potential for conflict and blame-shifting.

It is important to underline that we are not seeking to suggest that all is straightforward for English police forces. There would in fact appear to be widespread consensus at the UK level that the police funding system for England and Wales is overdue for reform (for recent developments, see Allen 2019). Which is to say that while the following interviewee comments all emanate from and focus on Wales, we would expect to hear similar comments being made in England and, indeed, in Scotland and Northern Ireland.

> **William:** I think that the criminal justice system is a significant drain on Welsh devolved public services, when you look at all the ACEs [adverse childhood experiences] agenda, and the preventative agenda.

> **John:** Currently all four forces are using their own budget – police money – to fund community psychiatric nurses to sit in police control rooms to help us better manage the demand of mental health.

**Harry:** The [Welsh] health minister took a decision to take half a million pounds out of [Operation] TARIAN. That money was going from the health budget because of TARIAN's part in tackling drugs, which of course is a problem that's a drain on the health service. But it's 'No, that's policing, so I'm taking the money out.' We've got the threat that next April they'll take out the money for police officers in schools [now renamed the Wales Police Schools Programme].[15]

**Craig:** And the police have actually got to a position where there's even been a little bit of pushing and pulling of funding purely because Welsh Government have pulled funding from certain activities and, as a result of that, police have made a decision to pull funding from other aspects. So that relationship is a difficult one purely from a funding point of view.

Disagreements over who benefits most from cooperative relationships, and who therefore should be paying for what, are a constant in all democratic political systems, especially during periods of spending constraint. There is no reason to be surprised or unduly alarmed by the existence of such 'pushing and pulling': it would be far more surprising if it did not feature.

Potentially more serious is the perception among some involved in policing in Wales that, despite the allocation of additional resources (such as the funding for 500 PSCO) and the fact that the Welsh Government has allowed police and crime commissioners in Wales to raise the police precept at higher rates than has been allowed in England, the net impact of the complex funding environment which they inhabit has been to leave Welsh police forces worse off than their English equivalents.

**John:** Because of our devolved nature, there are inevitably pots of money that are made available to English forces, via the Department of Health, Department of Education, Department of Communities and Local Government in Westminster, that are closed to Welsh forces. Now, you could say, 'but there's pockets of money available through Welsh Government that's not available to English forces'. That would be a correct statement. But the scale of that means that police forces in Wales probably, on balance, lose out compared to English forces.

We shall not seek to provide authoritative adjudication on this claim. With so many assumptions to question and counterfactuals to ponder, such an exercise is likely to prove less than illuminating.

More germane to the current discussion are our interviewees' neat summary of the different funding environment faced by police forces on either side of the Welsh-English border. This reflects the reality faced by all England and Wales criminal justice institutions with an active, on-the-ground presence in Wales, and not just those working in Wales's police services. To illustrate the point here are reflections on the areas of youth justice and mental health respectively:

> **Richard:** You've got the Youth Justice Service. It's the only children and young people's service that's not devolved to Wales. I don't know how many youth justice partnerships you've got [in Wales]. You've got four in north Wales and they're all funded differently. So, you get a pot of money from the Ministry of Justice, you get one from the Welsh Government, your local authorities will do something, North Wales police and the police and crime commissioner will do something . . . But it's inconsistent. You look at Gwynedd and Ynys Môn Youth Justice [services], and you look at Flintshire Youth Services . . . They'll have different pots of money from different organisations.

> **Rhys:** In England you have Department of Health and Ministry of Justice [who] work very closely together. Ministry of Justice decides that there's a health need; Department of Health agrees; Department of Health funds Ministry of Justice to do a health programme . . . That gets announced. Welsh Government ask the question, 'So when is that happening in Wales?' The message tends to be, 'Health is a devolved matter. It's for the Welsh Government to find the money if they wish to carry out those measures.'

This senior official is clearly aware of the difficulty:

> **William:** I think the issue with funding is the myriad of different funding streams that operate in this area, coming from Welsh Government, coming from Ministry of Justice, coming from Home Office, sometimes even [UK Department of] Housing, Communities and Local Government.
>
> **William:** The Welsh Government create new programmes. They create additional initiatives, because politicians like those things, but that creates yet more complexity. For example, they have a Positive Engagement for Young People Fund which funds all of the preventative activity. You've got youth service funding going in. You've then got the Home Office saying to police and crime commissioners, 'Do you want to bid for money on a Youth Intervention Fund on serious violence?' And then you've got [the] Ministry of Justice coming in with different funding around young people.

The ensuing complexity is clearly labyrinthine. But it is equally obviously a manifestation of the structure of the system rather than the 'fault' of any particular actor within it. The UK Government has, constitutionally speaking, a perfectly legitimate right to launch policy and associated funding initiatives in its areas of responsibility: indeed, it has a responsibility to do so. But so too does the Welsh Government as, indeed, do Wales's police and crime commissioners. While we may wish to quibble with this or that policy or this or that initiative, the fact of the matter is that no one is behaving unreasonably let alone irresponsibly in trying to get things done or by utilising financial levers to achieve their policy aims. Yet the net effect is an overall funding regime for those working in the Welsh criminal justice system that is extraordinarily convoluted and dysfunctional.

To further illustrate this, our fundamental point, let us briefly consider the controversy that has arisen around the funding of apprenticeships in Wales's police forces. The context is straightforward. Since April 2017, the UK Government has imposed an apprenticeship levy on all employers, both private and public, with a wage bill of over £3m per annum. In England, these employers are in turn given an apprenticeship allowance to be used to pay for training their workforces. The intention is to encourage employers to offer more training opportunities and thus, ultimately, to ensure a more skilled and more productive workforce. In the rest of the UK, the situation is complicated by the fact that the levy, which was apparently introduced without consultation with devolved governments (National Assembly for Wales Economy, Infrastructure and Skills Committee 2017: 9), cuts across devolved responsibility for education and training. In the devolved territories, therefore, the UK Government transfers the funds generated by the levy to the devolved government for onwards distribution. They, in turn, utilise the resulting funds to support their own approaches to training and skills development, which in the Welsh case involves channelling resources into specific sectors reflecting the government's economic development and other policy goals, as opposed to providing all employers with an allowance.

While finding the additional funds with which to pay the levy has been a challenge for cash-strapped Welsh public services, there is at least some evidence that the Welsh Government's approach to the use of the resulting funds has been more effective than the UK Government's in terms of ensuring take-up of apprenticeships (see National Assembly for Wales Economy, Infrastructure and Skills Committee 2018). Without seeking to be complacent, it is plausible to argue that in the main this system has worked reasonably well. Except, that is, for Wales's police forces who have found themselves caught trapped between the Scylla of UK control over policing and the Charybdis of Welsh control over training and education.

The Home Office has taken the position that, in a context in which training is a devolved responsibility and that the Welsh Government has anyway been in receipt of central government funds, it is Cardiff's responsibility to pay the apprenticeship allowance to Wales's police forces. The latter's counter position is that, given that policing is reserved to the UK level, it is obviously the UK Government's responsibility to pay for the training of future police officers. Moreover, it is not for London to dictate or direct how the devolved level should be carrying out its own responsibilities in relation to training (which is effectively what the Home Office is demanding). The result has been an impasse. While Wales's police forces pay the apprenticeship levy to the tune of some £2m pounds per annum, who pays them the equivalent of the allowances received by English forces in order to fund training – which if set at the equivalent level to England's police services would be worth an estimated £2.8m per annum – remains hotly disputed (National Assembly for Wales Economy, Infrastructure and Skills Committee 2018: 30–1). While a one-off funding package for 2018–19 was agreed between the Home Office and the Welsh Government and has been replicated in subsequent years, the sum falls well short of the amount that Welsh forces would be receiving for training if they were being funded on the same basis as England's. It is unsurprising, therefore, that the situation remains a source of deep concern and frustration for those responsible for policing in Wales. As is made crystal clear by our interviewees:

> **Sion:** There have been difficulties at both ends to get the two respective governments to agree where the money is and how it's to be resolved. I think we are now making progress. We've had some money given from the Home Office that enables us to make progress. But it's been a tortuous process.

> **John:** The four Welsh police forces, until very recently, have been stranded without the funding that's given to the remaining thirty-nine forces in England to fund police training. That money wasn't available to the four Welsh forces because education is devolved in Wales, and the routing of the apprenticeship levies [is different]. Welsh forces pay into the levy, but they weren't able to access it because of this anomaly. Nobody thought about it when the legislation was passed. So, they were stuck, 'til the absolute eleventh hour, not being able to access funding to train and recruit officers. They've just got an interim fix, but it's still one that's outstanding.

> **Sion:** Clearly this is a very important matter for policing in Wales because if it isn't finally resolved – and it's only partially resolved at this point – then you could end up with different professional standards this side of the border compared with the other side, which would be no use whatsoever ... Until that matter is finally put to rest – and we don't know exactly how much money Welsh forces are going to have and how we can draw it down, regardless of where it comes from – only then will we be able to relax properly and to get on with the professional training of future police officers.

Not only is the dispute time consuming, but – *in extremis* – it risks a situation where police in Wales are not as well trained as police personnel in England. At the time of writing, this dispute has yet to be resolved but rather remains the subject of high-level negotiation between ministers and officials in Cardiff and London.

Yet even when the problems surrounding the operation of the apprenticeship levy in the context of policing in Wales are finally put to rest, the problems that have been highlighted will remain. They are in fact inherent to the very structure of the Welsh criminal justice system as it is currently organised. The implications are, we suggest, profound for the potential effectiveness of that system. As noted by one observer:

> **Kate:** I think criminal justice in Wales is really hampered by the different sources of money and this constant fight about who is in control, who is setting priorities for the criminal justice system.

It will be clear from the preceding discussion that we concur with this assessment, though it is also important to re-emphasise that this state of affairs is structural in origin rather than the product of deliberate malice or machination. Indeed, while there are plenty of examples of poor communication and disregard for partners, especially on the part of the UK Government, we find little evidence that any of the actors are spoiling for a 'fight'. The difficulty is rather that the very organisation of the Welsh criminal justice system means that conflict and, of course, enormous complexity are inherent. This situation is further exacerbated by the fact that mechanisms for inter-governmental relations (IGR) in this area are particularly poorly developed, even in an overall context in which there is widespread consensus that the UK's mechanisms for IGR in general leave much to be desired (see Kenny et al. 2021; McEwen et al. 2020).

## CONCLUSION

This chapter has focused on two very different case studies serving to lay bare some uncomfortable truths about the impact of the constitutionally unorthodox way that the Welsh criminal justice system is organised. On the one hand we have seen that, whatever its pretensions, even in those areas of criminal justice policy such as housing for prison leavers where it has a clear locus, the Welsh Government is ultimately a policy taker rather than a policy maker. Whitehall and Westminster remain in charge of too many of the key policy levers to allow for anything else. On the other hand, even while it aggressively asserts its dominant constitutional position within the Welsh criminal justice system, the reality of devolution means that the UK Government's powers are far more constrained than its rhetoric might suggest. It is in fact heavily reliant on the goodwill and cooperation of the Welsh Government. And as a direct result of all of this, those working within the Welsh criminal justice system are forced to shoulder very substantial additional burdens, costs and complexities.

As noted in the chapter's introduction, by breaking from a Westminster model of institutional organisation that aligns governmental and justice institutions, the Welsh criminal justice system has been stranded in a kind of limbo or no-man's-land: neither quite Westminster's nor Cardiff Bay's, this is a policy area in which the writs of both levels of government are constrained not only by problems inherent to criminal justice, but as a direct consequence of a unique set of constitutional arrangements. Were all well in the Welsh criminal justice system then perhaps this could be dismissed as a minor quirk or inconvenience. But as we have seen so clearly in Chapter 2, this is not the case. Moreover, the difficulties of effective policy-making that have been explored here have as their corollary, real and perhaps intractable issues around ensuring proper accountability. It is to this that we now turn our attention.

# 6
# SCRUTINY AND ACCOUNTABILITY ACROSS THE JAGGED EDGE

B Y DISPENSING WITH the orthodox alignment of legislature, executive and justice system, Wales has been left with a powerful devolved legislature and executive lodged within an England and Wales legal jurisdiction and criminal justice system that is the jealously guarded preserve of the United Kingdom parliament and government. But because criminal justice is umbilically linked to a wider set of social policies and public institutions, most of which *are* devolved, the Welsh criminal justice system is inevitably different from England's. It is characterised by the division of powers and responsibilities between the England and Wales and Welsh levels which were mapped and analysed in chapters 3 and 4. The implications of this for policy-making were explored in more detail in the previous chapter, Chapter 5, where we found that even in those areas in which it has a clear constitutional locus, the Welsh Government is effectively a policy taker rather than a policy maker because most of the relevant policy levers are controlled in Whitehall. By the same token, it is clear that the jagged edge also limits Whitehall's ability to act as an effective policy maker in its areas of responsibility because of its reliance on the devolved level.

In this chapter we consider the implications of the constitutional underpinnings of the Welsh criminal justice system for the accountability of that system. That these implications are likely to be far-reaching should be obvious simply on the basis of first principles. The basic Westminster model of parliamentary democracy is premised on the alignment of legislature and executive. Acting on behalf of the electorate, the democratically elected legislature is tasked with scrutinising and holding to account an executive formed from the members of that legislature. The judiciary stands at one remove from this relationship. Charged as it is with interpreting the laws created by the legislature while also ensuring that the executive does not over-reach the powers that have been conferred upon it, its 'independence' from both is (or at least, should be) highly valued. This is not true, however, of the wider justice system. Rather, the various institutions that form that system – that is, the police, prisons, probation and youth justice services – are part of the executive, and as such are scrutinised and held accountable by the legislature.

If institutional alignment of the kind just sketched is precisely what is absent from the design of Welsh devolution, this in turn raises profound questions about how and by whom is the Welsh criminal justice system scrutinised and held to account?[1] On the one hand, the country's devolved institutions have been constructed as a two- rather than three-legged stool, with England and Wales criminal justice institutions answerable to a London level that remains dominant in this particular field. This surely makes it constitutionally as well as politically problematic for Wales's devolved executive and legislature to seek to hold those institutions accountable for their actions in Wales. On the other hand, and as has been discussed at length, actors and institutions accountable to the devolved level are – not only legitimately but inevitably – implicated in the functioning of the criminal justice system in Wales; to the extent that the system cannot function without them. But, again, it would seem constitutionally as well as politically incongruous for the accountability mechanisms that exist at the England and Wales level to extend their reach to cover their roles. The obvious danger in all of this is that, in the absence of alignment, no one is properly holding to account or accountable for the Welsh criminal justice system.

But even if first principles suggest that ensuring accountability in the unusual, even unique, constitutional circumstances of the Welsh criminal justice system is likely to prove difficult, this does not preclude the possibility that effective ad hoc solutions have been found. In this chapter we will therefore investigate how the various mechanisms that might ensure scrutiny and the accountability of that system operate in practice. Our discussion is divided into two main parts. First, we focus on the role of those institutions that scrutinise and render accountable the England and Wales criminal justice system as a whole. We then turn our attention to the devolved level and, in particular, the efforts of the Senedd to scrutinise and hold the Welsh criminal justice system to account. The chapter will conclude by considering the extent to which the inherent barriers to effective accountability arising from the constitutional order have been overcome. As will become clear, our conclusion on this score is negative. In the same way that it serves to undermine the possibility of effective policy-making, the jagged edge of divided powers and responsibilities that characterises the Welsh criminal justice system also serves to undermine the possibility of holding it properly accountable.

## SCRUTINY AND ACCOUNTABILITY AT THE ENGLAND AND WALES LEVEL

In modern societies, criminal justice systems express and embody the state's power over individuals and communities in its starkest form. Various mechanisms have evolved that seek to act as a check on the use, and potential abuse, of this power. In the England and Wales context these include a relatively extensive inspection regime that operates on behalf of the executive, but which also serves to provide vital evidence for the UK parliament's (largely) committee-based oversight activities. But in addition, other actors sitting outside governmental structures also play a vital role in ensuring accountability. The latter include civil society organisations such as charities and pressure groups (e.g. Howard League for Penal Reform), trade unions (e.g. National Association of Probation Officers) as well as the media and, indeed, academia. Clearly, to attempt to provide a comprehensive account of all of these activities as they do or do not relate to the Welsh criminal justice system risks making the present discussion hopelessly unwieldy. To delimit the discussion, therefore, we will concentrate our attentions on what are arguably the main formal conduits for ensuring the accountability of the England and Wales criminal justice system, namely the inspection regime to which we have already alluded, as well as the role of select committees of the House of Commons.

England and Wales's police, probation, youth justice and prison services are routinely monitored by Her Majesty's (HM) Inspectorates.[2] While UK ministers are responsible for appointing chief inspectors, the inspectorates regard themselves (with considerable justification) as providing independent scrutiny without fear or favour. HM Chief Inspector of Prisons was formally established through the Criminal Justice Act 1982 and is responsible for inspecting the conditions in prisons and young offender institutions, police and court custody suites, secure training centres and immigration removal centres across England and Wales (HMI Prisons 2021; Stockdale 1983). Probation and youth offender services across England and Wales are scrutinised by HM Chief Inspector of Probation. Having previously operated as a Home Office function, the inspectorate was given a statutory footing through the Criminal Justice Act 1991. HMI Probation provides 'a source of well-evidenced fair comment' for ministers and the public on the effectiveness of existing provisions (Bridges 2010: 1).

HM Inspectorate of Constabulary and Fire & Rescue Services (HMICFRS) was established in 2017 as a replacement for HM Inspectorate of Constabulary (HMIC). It subjects Wales's police services to regular inspections but, unlike in England, its remit in Wales does not extend to the country's devolved fire and rescue services. Rather the latter are inspected by the Auditor General for Wales and the Chief Fire and Rescue Adviser and Inspector for Wales. Finally, joint inspections are carried out by Criminal Justice Joint Inspection to address issues and areas that reach across more than one criminal justice agency. Having been formally established by the Police and Justice Act 2006, the Criminal Justice Joint Inspection brings together the criminal justice inspectorates of constabulary, the Crown Prosecution Service, prisons and probation (Criminal Justice Joint Inspection 2021b).[3]

Although they report to UK Government ministers, given that they operate on an England and Wales basis, it is clearly incumbent on HM Inspectorates to make a serious effort to understand the particularities of the Welsh legislative and policy framework, not least to ensure that inspectors grasp the context in which criminal justice professionals and/or institutions based in Wales actually work. There are, indeed, multiple examples of the inspectorates doing precisely this. This includes England and Wales-level inspectorates concluding formal agreements with devolved-level inspectorate bodies, including Health Inspectorate Wales and Estyn, in order to facilitate prison and probation inspections carried out in Wales (Health Inspectorate Wales and HMI Prisons 2014).[4] In 2019, HMICFRS carried out its first pilot inspection in Wales involving no fewer than five different inspectorates, two of them England and Wales bodies (namely HMICFRS itself and HMI Prisons) and three devolved (Health Inspectorate Wales, Estyn and Care Inspectorate Wales), in order to review child-protection arrangements in Newport (Care Inspectorate Wales et al. 2020).

However, despite these efforts, many involved in the Welsh criminal justice system are doubtful that HM Inspectorates fully understand the Welsh context. We find significant evidence to support this view by perusing the various reports that they publish. Take, for example, some of the recent work of HMICFRS. Its 2018 report on policing and mental health failed to acknowledge the different legislative and policy context in Wales. The report recommends that the (in effect, English) Department of Health and Social Care work alongside the Home Office to 'review the overall state response' to people suffering from mental ill-health (HMICFRS 2018: 25). No reference is made to the Welsh Government. A recent joint report by HMICFRS, the College of Policing and the Independent Office for Police Conduct around violence against women and girls focuses exclusively on the English context (HMICFRS et al. 2021), failing to take into account the Welsh Government's (2016b; 2016c) framework for tackling domestic violence and abuse in Wales.

Given this, it perhaps comes as no surprise that our interviewees describe Welsh police forces having to work hard to ensure that HMICFRS inspectors understand the context in which they are working. Yet despite these efforts, Welsh forces run the risk of being marked down because police in Wales do not always operate in the same way as their English counterparts.

> **George:** There's a lot of scrutiny around policing. More so probably than any other organisation in the country. We've mentioned that sometimes it's not a like-for-like, because police in Wales have the devolved nature of their work. And with HMIC[FRS] the inspectors are not from your own force, and generally won't be from Wales. So therefore you've got English inspectors coming across to Wales who don't have a full understanding.

> **John:** It's often said that police act locally, i.e. within the devolved space from Welsh Government, but they're measured nationally, vis-à-vis Home Office and HMICRFS. And that's a challenge, particularly around inspection. Again, it's incumbent on the four forces

in Wales to engage HMI regularly so that they understand the context in which Welsh forces are operating. In the past they haven't always done that, and Welsh forces [have] been viewed exactly the same as an English force, and there's been a naiveté. They haven't recognised that police in Wales operate in that different space.

**George:** We could be marked down because we are not doing things similar to what the English forces are doing.

Although this is ostensibly an England and Wales system, England provides the norm against which Welsh forces are measured.

A similar set of concerns arise in the context of the inspection regime for probation services. In 2016, for example, a thematic review by HMI Probation into services for female offenders failed to consider whether the standard of provisions in Wales and England were different. This was despite the inclusion of case studies from Rhyl and Wrexham and the explicit recognition by the inspectorate that mental health, substance misuse and housing/accommodation are all important services for women on probation (HMI Probation 2016c: 26–7). A subsequent report by HMI Probation (2018) into domestic abuse and the work being carried out by CRCs in England and Wales acknowledged the existence of distinct legislation in Wales, but failed to go on to assess how this was impacting on the delivery of CRC services.[5] It is telling that, twenty years after the National Assembly for Wales met for the first time, HMI Probation's annual report for 2019 failed to include a single reference to 'devolution', 'devolved', 'Welsh' or the 'Welsh Government', despite the fact that distinct plans for the future of the probation service in Wales were then being drawn up by HMPPS (HMI Probation 2019a).

Again, our interviewees portray inspectors as struggling to understand the devolved context in which probation services operate in Wales.

**Kate:** I don't think they [HMI Probation] pay much heed to devolved contexts. They will see there are certain complications, possibly, in what probation can deliver. That point about local connection, local services, what's available, you know, how much communication is there between housing policy and criminal justice policy?

**Marc:** But I think on a practical level for staff, up to a certain point, it's very difficult for them to keep two systems in their heads. A classic example of that would be, if you come and do an inspection, one week you've been doing prison inspection in Birmingham and speaking to the Transforming Rehabilitation staff there about housing, and the next week you could be at Parc. Individual staff would have to be very, very studious to keep up to date with all the policy changes in Wales that differ from England. I wouldn't expect to find any of the inspectorate staff know, for instance, that there's a prevention agenda regarding housing in Wales, as opposed to England.

**Kate:** They will probably look at that and go, 'There's a problem here. Whether that's due to devolution or not, we don't really care, it's just something that we notice.' In that sense they are probably not set up to take account of that, and point to where the problems lie. The structural problems. They just see the practical problems on the ground and might make reference to some of the structural [problems]. But to be honest, I'm not sure I've ever read anything that referred to the Welsh Government context in particular, unless it was a reference saying that that policy undermines something else.

**Marc:** On a practical level, there's an awareness that Wales is different, and that there's a gap in knowledge about that, and an attempt to do something about it. Funnily enough, in the Ministry of Justice and in England, when they think Wales, they think north Wales . . . They think of difference primarily in terms of language, and occasionally policy.

This is another example of an England and Wales inspection regime that treats England as the norm and, even after two decades of democratic devolution, struggles to understand the various ways in which Wales is now different. Indeed, in a recent report on accommodation support for adult offenders in the community produced during the COVID-19 pandemic, HMI Probation (2020: 16) made it explicitly clear that they had not considered Wales as part of their investigation as the policy context was different and there had been no opportunity to conduct an investigation there. Which at least has the virtue of clarity and honesty. Yet it also serves to further cement the impression that Wales in merely an add-on to the real focus of the inspectorate's attention: England.

In a sense, however, the inspectorates are 'damned if they do' and 'damned if they don't'. This becomes apparent when we consider the work of HM Inspectorate of Prisons. HM Inspectorate of Prisons has arguably set the standard in seeking to take account of the differences that exist between Wales and England. This has included efforts to critically evaluate the Welsh Government's drug detoxification policy (HMI Prisons 2015b) as well as inspection reports – cited in the previous chapter – that have acknowledged the different housing entitlements for Welsh prisoners (HMI Prisons 2008, 2010, 2014).[6] The difficulty arises when it (not unreasonably) seeks to recommend future improvements. In its most recent inspection of HMP Cardiff, carried out in August 2019, HM Chief Inspector of Prisons took the 'unusual step' of making a recommendation to the Welsh Government (HMI Prisons 2019b: 6). This concerned the need to find a solution to the high levels of homelessness found amongst former prisoners: an area, of course, for which the devolved level has direct responsibility. Yet, as we have also seen in the previous chapter, the Welsh Government's efforts to tackle homelessness among prison leavers have been undermined in large part because it does not control enough of the policy levers to act as an effective policy maker. As such, this may be regarded as an example of one of HM's inspectorates seeking to scrutinise and hold the Welsh Government to account for a matter over which its real powers are actually very limited. One of our interviewees contrasted the respective positions of the UK and Welsh governments in the following terms.

> **William:** The people who run prisons are accountable to HMPPS, who are accountable to the Justice Secretary. Yet you can have a HMI Prisons report that's hugely critical of Welsh Government, and puts recommendations on Welsh Government. But they [the Welsh Government] have no ability to say to the Executive Director of HMPPS, or Governor of Swansea, for example: 'As a government, we are expecting improvements, and we will scrutinise you on it.' Because the Welsh Government have got no ability to do it.

**William:** Whereas David Gauke [then Secretary of State for Justice] can sit in Whitehall and say, to the Executive Director of HMPPS in Wales, 'I want to see improvements in Swansea prison by next year or you will be sat here in front of me explaining and you may potentially lose your job as a result of it.' Or he/she could say to the governor, 'I want an improvement plan from you and I'm holding you accountable for it.'

Thus, while HM Inspectorate of Prisons clearly feels entitled to intervene in this way, doing so only serves to raise fundamental questions about the way in which the Welsh criminal justice system is organised and the extent to which its unique constitutional design is fit for purpose.[7]

Turning from the inspectorates to the oversight role of the legislature, it is natural here to focus on the role of the select committees of the House of Commons. Following their introduction in 1979, these committees have been credited with transforming parliamentary scrutiny of the executive, with both their role and status substantially enhanced by the so-called Wright reforms introduced in 2010. Select committees are now the 'principal vehicle' through which Westminster scrutinises government policy (Bates et al. 2017: 782; see also Benton and Russell 2013; Dunleavy and Muir 2013; Geddes 2018; Kelso 2009; May 2015).[8] As far as the operation of the England and Wales criminal justice system as a whole is concerned, the two key committees are the home affairs and the justice committees, the former focusing on the work of the Home Office and the latter on the work of the Ministry of Justice. While the effectiveness and reputation of the various select committees tends to vary over time – reflecting changing memberships, changing political agendas (Geddes 2018) and, indeed, the size of government majorities (White 2015) – there can be no doubt that these particular committees are among the most high profile and most respected.

Yet while their remits cover England and Wales, neither committee has ever conducted a specific inquiry into the operation of the police and criminal justice system in the distinctive context of post-devolution Wales. Not only this, but their 'normal' reports also regularly fail to take into account the distinctive policy context that exists in Wales. In July 2020, for example, the House of Commons Justice Committee (2020c: 34) called for the UK Government to update them on 'the progress of the action plan for social care in prisons in England and Wales', despite the fact that social care in prisons is a devolved responsibility. The committee's (2020b) review into the impact of COVID-19 on the prison estate also failed to include a single reference to Public Health Wales or to the Welsh Government: fully seventeen years after responsibility for prison healthcare was transferred to the Welsh Government and in the context of a pandemic in which the role of devolved government was a particularly high-profile one.

The Home Affairs Committee similarly tends to overlook Wales and the Welsh dimension to policy and legislation. Its report on domestic abuse (2018a) failed to include a single reference to the work being done by the Welsh Government in this area, including the provisions introduced by the Violence against Women, Domestic Abuse and Sexual Violence (Wales) Act 2015. Its 2018 report, *Policing for the future*, also failed to include a single reference to the role being played by the Welsh Government, despite covering issues for which that government is directly responsible, such as mental health and child protection services (House of Commons Home Affairs Committee 2018b). While purporting to conduct inquiries into the policing and justice arrangements across England and Wales, both committees' reports tend to focus more or less exclusively on the legislative and policy arrangements for England.

Close observers certainly struggle to recall any serious engagement with the Welsh context from those select committees primarily responsible for scrutiny of the England and Wales criminal justice system.

> **Sian:** I can't remember a time when the Home Affairs Select Committee have done it. Not to that extent. There was [an example] when the Police and Crime Commissioner in Gwent sacked the Chief Constable.[9] That's probably the only time that Wales has made it into the headlines. But that was not about Wales, it was about how that interaction happened and the actions that he [the PCC] took. I think somebody said in the proceedings, 'What does the Welsh Government think about this?' but that's probably as far as it has gone.

> **Sam:** Officials go and get scrutinised by the committees in Whitehall [Westminster], and that is very system-wide. Apart from maybe some questions about Welsh language ... the questions could be asked of justice officials in any other part of the jurisdiction.

Given, as we have seen, that devolution inevitably means that the England and Wales 'system' operates differently in Wales, this hardly seems like serious engagement from committees whose responsibilities are England *and* Wales wide. Yet when viewed from the perspective of the majority of committee members, the problems of Wales doubtless seem minor and relatively parochial compared to the multiple, high-stakes crises convulsing the wider system. Not only does Wales enjoy only limited salience among policy makers (as we saw in Chapter 3), the same is also true for most parliamentarians.[10]

Most, that is, but not all. There are three select committees whose remits extend beyond the work of particular government departments and are territorial in scope. The Welsh Affairs, Scottish Affairs and Northern Ireland Affairs select committees scrutinise the work of the UK Government in the three respective territories (Torrance and Evans 2019). For the members of the Welsh Affairs Committee, justice and home affairs are among the most genuinely significant of the remaining reserved areas, and it is thus this committee that has taken most interest in the operation of the criminal justice system in Wales.[11] Since 2005, it has undertaken four inquiries into the subject of imprisonment in Wales as well as four inquiries into policing (House of Commons Welsh Affairs Committee 2005, 2006a, 2006b, 2007, 2010b, 2014, 2015, 2019).

This arrangement contains within it several limitations. First, in contrast to Justice and Home Affairs committees, the Welsh Affairs Committee is one of the Commons' least prestigious select committees. Reflecting this, few MPs from the two main parties appear to be eager to serve on it. Indeed, during the 2017–19 parliament, not only did it struggle to attract the full eleven members, but at times its membership fell as low as six (Cornock 2017).[12] Neither do these members tend to be true subject specialists in the way that many members of the Justice and Home Affairs committees are or eventually become. While their superior 'local knowledge' may provide partial compensation – although not all members of the committee necessarily represent Welsh constituencies – it is highly unlikely that the members of the Welsh Affairs Committee can provide the same level of scrutiny and oversight as that provided by the departmental committees proper.[13]

Moreover, in seeking to scrutinise the Welsh criminal justice system, committee members are stymied by a general reluctance to look over the jagged edge, so to speak, and examine the work of Welsh Government. Doing so would be to usurp the scrutiny function that is rightfully the role of the Senedd – and almost certainly spark an unseemly turf war. A final element that only adds to the incongruity of this whole arrangement, is that it is the territorial department – the Office of the Secretary of State for Wales (formerly the Welsh and more latterly the Wales Office) – that remains the select committee's formal interlocutor at UK Government level. This even though, in practice, officials and ministers from those departments actually driving particular policies are invited to give evidence before it.

Despite the best efforts of committee members and staff, it is certainly hard to gainsay the conclusion reached by one our interviewees when summarising the committees' attempts in this area: 'It's kind of surface level. It doesn't get into any of the real stuff.'[14] Little wonder, either, that the Thomas Commission (2019: 476) described this arrangement as 'unsatisfactory'. But the point can be broadened: our review of the main mechanisms for ensuring accountability at the England and Wales level – HM inspectorates and the select committees – suggest that neither can be regarded as operating satisfactorily. For reasons that are perfectly understandable in their own terms, the main focus of both is overwhelmingly the operation of the criminal justice system in England. The specific arrangements that pertain in post-devolution Wales and the particular problems that arise because of them are largely overlooked. In other words, there is ample evidence to suggest that 'in principle' concerns set out at the start of this chapter around accountability appear to be born out in practice. To again quote the words of our aforementioned interviewee, at the England and Wales level at least, 'nobody really gets under the skin of what's happening in Wales'. The question remains, however, to what extent is the devolved level more successful?

## SCRUTINY AND ACCOUNTABILITY AT THE DEVOLVED LEVEL

As noted in the introduction to this book, one way of understanding the story of Welsh devolution so far is a journey in the direction of Westminster-style constitutional orthodoxy. While the book has gone on to focus on an aspect of that journey that has not yet, and indeed may never be completed, substantial distance has been traversed in other areas. None more so than with regard to the role of Senedd committees. Having started out in the very early days of devolution trying to combine both policy-making and scrutiny responsibilities – and with 'cabinet ministers' full members of the very committees that were seeking to hold them to account – Senedd committees now operate in ways that will surprise no one familiar with Westminster or other Westminster-derived legislatures (Rawlings 2003; Stirbu and McAllister 2018; also Mitchell 2010). Their role is to conduct detailed scrutiny of specific pieces of legislation as well as scrutinise the workings of government. But while in the Commons these tasks are undertaken by different types of committees – ad-hoc public bill and delegated legislation committees in the case of the former and select committees in the case of the latter – the relatively small size of the Welsh legislature has seen these functions combined in a series of specialist committees that undertake detailed scrutiny of relevant legislation as well as a more general oversight of government activity in a given subject area. These subject areas mirror in general terms the portfolios of members of the Welsh Government (Expert Panel on Assembly Electoral Reform 2017: 60–89).[15]

We note this because of the far-reaching implications for the way in which the devolved legislature scrutinises the Welsh criminal justice system. Given that justice is formally reserved, there is no Welsh equivalent of the 'England and Wales' Home and Justice secretaries, the Scottish Cabinet Secretary for Justice or the Northern Ireland Justice Minister. Rather, as noted in Chapter 4, responsibility for those devolved roles that form part of the Welsh criminal justice system is divided right across Welsh Government (see Table 4.1). True, since 2003, justice has been identified as a specific ministerial responsibility. But this is by no means a major portfolio; certainly not in terms of the internal organisation of the government.[16] All of which means that, until very recently, the oversight role for Welsh Government's criminal justice-related activities has also tended to be parcelled out across different committees. To illustrate the point, we can simply note the identities of the different committees that have in the more recent parliamentary term (2016–21) published reports with significant criminal justice-related content (see Table 6.1).

**Table 6.1** Senedd committee reports on inquiries with criminal justice-relevant focus (fifth Senedd only)

| Report title | Committee | Date | Issues covered |
| --- | --- | --- | --- |
| UK Government's Wales Bill | Constitutional and Legislative Affairs | October 2016 | The scope of the devolution dispensation including the reservation of policing and criminal justice powers |
| The Emotional and Mental Health of Children and Young People | Children, Young People and Education | April 2018 | Mental health services for those held in youth secure estate |
| Life on the streets: preventing and tackling rough sleeping in Wales | Equality, Local Government and Communities | April 2018 | Prisoner homelessness upon release |
| Voting Rights for Prisoners | Equality, Local Government and Communities | June 2018 | Prisoner voting rights |
| Suicide prevention | Health, Social Care and Sport | December 2018 | Suicide prevention in the prison estate |
| Mental Health in Policing and Police Custody | Health, Social Care and Sport | October 2019 | Police responses to those experiencing mental health crisis |
| Provision of health and social care in the adult prison estate | Health, Social Care and Sport | March 2021 | The state of prison healthcare services in Wales |
| Making Justice Work in Wales | Legislation, Justice and Constitution | March 2021 | The recommendations of the Commission on Justice in Wales |

There is still no justice committee per se, but – apparently in response to the strictures of the Thomas Commission (see also the discussion in the next chapter) – the renaming of the Constitutional and Legislative Affairs Committee as the Legislation, Justice and Constitution Committee in January 2020 means that there is now a committee with specific responsibility for this policy area. It is of course too soon to say what difference this will make; but even if handing the committee this responsibility serves to provide more focus to the work of the legislature in this area, given that responsibility for different criminal justice-related functions will remain scattered across the Welsh Government's different directorates, it is hard to envisage any fundamental change.[17] It is also noteworthy that this remains another ad hoc solution to the problem of parliamentary scrutiny and accountability (if, this time, on the foreshore of Cardiff Bay rather than the banks of the Thames) in a context in which the Welsh criminal justice system simply does not fit into any of the standard structures.

This is not the only way in which the nature of the devolution dispensation shapes the Senedd's engagement with the Welsh criminal justice system. Far from it. Rather, the dispensation structures and, crucially in the context of the current discussion, limits all its activities and interactions in this area. While this should come as no surprise in as much as delimiting the powers and responsibilities of different institutions is one of the core functions of *any* constitutional order, it is nonetheless worth illustrating the ways in which the constitutional underpinnings of the Welsh criminal justice system constrain the ability of the Senedd to conduct meaningful scrutiny of its operation. We will focus on four, in particular.

### Lack of data

We have already had cause to rue the difficulties of accessing even basic data on the operation of the criminal justice system in Wales. It is not only the small group of interested academics who face this difficulty. In 2019 the Thomas Commission argued that more data on the operation of the justice system should be made available 'without delay' to improve justice outcomes in Wales (Thomas Commission 2019: 14). This two years after the Ministry of Justice's own *Justice in Wales Working Group* (2017) acknowledged that data disaggregated on a Welsh basis should be made more easily available. Unfortunately, little seems to have changed in the interim, meaning that – like academics – Senedd members or researchers working on their behalf are still required to make extensive use of Freedom of Information requests to collect data.[18] Our interviewees make the point in the following terms.

> **Claire:** I'd say one of the main challenges, particularly on an Assembly Member inquiry – so the proactive stuff – is getting any data out of the Ministry of Justice. Assembly staff quite often get asked for information, and they will only be able to access that information – because there's obviously hardly anything publicly available for Wales – by putting in a Freedom of Information request to the Ministry of Justice.
>
> **Claire:** They won't accept [Senedd] officials approaching them in any other way, and usually it can take about six months [to access]. It's constant chasing. A colleague did an inquiry for an Assembly Member last year, and I think it took them nine months to get the data, and that data now is two years' old. People constantly get, 'Oh we don't collect that data in that way.' It's quite hard work.

Indicative, perhaps, of a more general cultural suspicion of transparency, there are examples of researchers being required to use Freedom of Information requests even to access data that is readily available within the system; presumably in order to create an 'audit trail'.

> **Claire:** I think within committee inquiries it's slightly different. But with Assembly Members' constituency-type enquiries, the police will make Assembly officials go through FOI as well, just because they like to have that audit trail. It can be quite complicated to get hold of any kind of data, particularly statistical data that they think somebody is going to use. If you're looking for more policy-type data it's a bit easier. But if you're looking for statistics it's very difficult.

As can be seen, the entirely predictable outcome of this state of affairs is delay: delay in accessing data that may be out of date by the time it is made available. Unlike Westminster MPs, Members of the Senedd can do almost nothing (even notionally) to affect the situation. Constitutionally speaking, they are left as supplicants with no ability to demand changes. Meanwhile, the lack of data – or, certainly, readily accessible data – makes meaningful scrutiny and accountability very much more difficult.

## Access

The Senedd has the power to compel Welsh Government ministers and officials to appear before it. But the same devolution legislation and, specifically, Section 37(3) of the Government of Wales Act 2006 also makes clear that it cannot 'impose' a similar duty on UK Government ministers or officials working for UK Government departments. In the context of the Welsh criminal justice system in which England and Wales institutions play the dominant role, that means that the Senedd's access to many of the most important actors that it might wish to consult and scrutinise is reliant, fundamentally, on goodwill and agreement. Our interviewees make clear that such agreement is not always forthcoming, and even when it is eventually given it is often as the result of many months of painstaking negotiation. Unsurprisingly and, indeed, not unreasonably given the constitutional situation, many Whitehall officials seem reluctant to engage on the basis that they view themselves as answerable to the House of Commons and not the Senedd. Yet the result is an equally reasonable sense of frustration (palpable in the following testimony) on the part of those who would try to scrutinise the operation of the Welsh criminal justice system.

> **Sian:** UK bodies can get out of them [i.e. Assembly committee inquiries]. They can't get out of UK ones where the UK parliament scrutinise their own departments. So, Home Affairs Select Committee and the Welsh Affairs Committee and all of that. It is procedural and [they] absolutely couldn't get out of that. But when the Welsh Government or National Assembly ask, it's [an] invitation. They can't force them to come.

> **Anna:** And it's sometimes basic stuff; they [UK officials] won't even respond to phone calls or e-mails or even letters from chairs.

> **Ffion:** Once they [UK officials] twigged what the Assembly committee were looking at and why and how, and we had long conversations about it, they [UK officials] were more amenable. But it took a long time, and it took a few suggestions that the committee could push more publicly for some of this stuff if the more informal approaches were not working.

**Anna:** It's about using those informal routes as well as the official to official routes. But it becomes an incredibly frustrating experience from the Senedd's perspective – as officials but you also see that Members get frustrated as well.

**Claire:** It was one of those areas where the policy position of Wales and their approach to children was very different from England. They called in the UK Government minister on the basis of the fact that, at that time, they were looking at devolving youth justice budgets to local authorities. But obviously they [the committee] wanted the UK Government to come in and talk about the fact that there was a very different policy approach and what that meant for young people who were ending up having to be placed in custody. In the first instance they refused to come and give evidence, and then after quite a lot of negotiating, at the last minute they turned around and said, 'Yes we will come.'

**Anna:** There is a confidence that they [UK officials] can be that dismissive with Assembly committees; that there'll be no pushback ... It's not just data. It's actually getting UK Government representation in [that] can be difficult.

**Ffion:** On the inquiries – the NPS[19] in particular – it took them quite a long time to get Home Office engagement. In the end they did come to give evidence, and actually submitted a very useful paper. But it didn't come easily because the Assembly were the devolved institution, and I think Whitehall – I mean we can't speak for all Whitehall departments – but there was an impression that Whitehall departments answer to [Westminster] select committees.

Again, delays are typical and success (in accessing officials) far from certain. One alternative solution is for Whitehall ministers or officials to provide written evidence to Senedd committee hearings (HMPPS in Wales 2018; South Wales Police 2018; Wales CRC 2018; Youth Justice Board 2019b). If this is the only available alternative, then it may well be better than nothing; yet it also means that the opportunity to ask oral, follow-up questions

– sometimes the more illuminating element of committee proceedings – is lost (cf. Thompson 2014: 397).

It is important to reiterate that the real issue here is structural rather than personal. True, the occasional Whitehall minister or official may be patronising or dismissive. But the fact of the matter is that Whitehall departments answer to select committees of the House of Commons: that is the way that the Westminster system of scrutiny and accountability has been constructed. It may well be the case that those committees do a poor job in the context of the Welsh criminal justice system, in part because the same jagged edge of divided powers and responsibilities that cuts across it also serves as a major disincentive to the specialist committees even trying to engage. Yet to expect the committees of a different legislature to do the job in their place – committees of a legislature that is not only elected on the basis of a different democratic franchise, but whose inferior position within the criminal justice system is literally written into the relevant constitutional legislation – is clearly for the birds.

### Absence of engagement from external civil society actors

Another factor militating against serious engagement by the Senedd in the Welsh criminal justice system is the relative absence of interest from and pressure by civil society organisations. In developed democratic societies, civil society organisations – encompassing the media, academia, as well as all kinds of voluntary organisations including charities and religious denominations – play a key role in wider societal processes of scrutiny and accountability (see, inter alia, Cohen and Arato 1992; Wyn Jones 2008). This not least because of their vital role in buttressing and supplementing the role of the formal processes that focus on the legislature. In the case of Wales, however, such civil society interest that can be identified almost invariably remains focused on the England and Wales unit.

We will not seek to provide a full accounting of the (relative) lack of interest in the operation of the Welsh criminal justice system across Welsh civil society. We have already said enough to indicate that most academic lawyers and criminologists in Wales remain almost entirely focused on the England and Wales unit, with very few engaging with the specificities of the Welsh criminal justice system. With some honourable exceptions,[20] most of the UK media reporting of criminal justice issues also focuses on England

and Wales.[21] But it is worthwhile to note that the absence of serious and sustained pressure group engagement with Welsh criminal justice issues was specifically cited by a number of interviewees as a factor that reduces the amount of attention being devoted to them in the Senedd.

> **Anna:** The other element is that you don't have the same sort of interest groups talking about these issues because it's not seen as devolved. If I was working for the Prison Reform Trust, would I be speaking to Assembly Members about it? I don't know. No, I'd most probably be focusing my attention at a Westminster level, even though it obviously has all these impacts on devolved services. I think that has an impact as well in terms of how prominent it is.

> **Huw:** It might be the case that there's not that many third-sector organisations taking on those issues. Again, and that might be reflective of the grey areas, jagged edges, of the devolution settlement ... We're talking about Members not wanting to take it on because of the lack of impact. It might be that the same is true of third-sector organisations as well.

> **Claire:** Lobbying Assembly Members, sending briefings out to Assembly Members like we see lots of the other [organisations do]. In health there are lots of charities who are all meeting with the chair of the committee constantly to get their subject on the agenda. I just don't think with the Prison Reform Trust and the Howard League of Penal Reform, they don't have a Wales office, so they are not going to be doing that.

It is certainly the case that in other parts of the UK, pressure groups can and do play a key role in highlighting issues in the criminal justice system and encouraging political attention, by publishing data, commissioning research and providing briefings and updates to politicians and officials. Howard League Scotland, for example, regularly provides responses to Scottish Government consultations as well as evidence to committees in Holyrood (Howard League Scotland 2019a, 2019b). Although some London-based groups such as the Howard League for Penal Reform and the Prison Reform Trust have, on occasion, made welcome interventions on important issues in the Welsh criminal justice system (e.g. Howard League for Penal Reform 2019; Prison Reform Trust 2019), their work is very largely focused on Whitehall and Westminster and not the Senedd and Cathays Park.[22] Perhaps the only exception to this pattern was the role played by the justice trades unions in Wales during the fourth Assembly (2011–16), who contributed to debates on prison reform and changes to probation services in Wales. The National Association of Probation Officers (NAPO) has also played an active role in producing briefings for Members of the Senedd and officials (see NAPO 2018).

But this is the exception that proves the rule: those interested in criminal justice-related matters tend not to focus their attention on the Senedd. Moreover, it seems unlikely that they ever will as long as the current constitutional dispensation persists. Yet, by the same token, given that it also seems highly unlikely that those institutions responsible for scrutiny at the England and Wales level will change their approach to the Welsh criminal justice system, lack of engagement at the devolved level by pressure groups and civil society actors reduces the likelihood that anyone will even try to hold that system to proper account in future.

Scrutiny to what ends?

A final, related reason adduced by our interviewees when seeking to explain the barriers to devolved scrutiny of the Welsh criminal justice system is that, quite simply, Senedd members tend to feel that they are more likely to have a positive impact by focusing their time and energy on matters that are clearly within devolved competence. Although there are some issues that fall very clearly on the devolved side of the jagged edge – for example, voting rights for prisoners in devolved and local elections in Wales – this is not usually the case. Rather, as discussed at length in previous chapters, most issues straddle the line of devolved and non-devolved responsibilities. Given the blurred lines of accountability that is the inevitable result, there is a wholly understandable tendency for the Senedd to focus its efforts on those other issues where its responsibilities as a scrutiny body are less ambiguous.

> **Ffion:** Which I think leads back sometimes to why Assembly committees may choose subjects where they know they're more likely to get traction and impact. Ultimately they are limited in

their time – in terms of committee time but also in terms of their tenure. They have five years and they want to make an impact, and if there is a subject where they know they'll be able to get Welsh Government ministers in, there's an evidence base, there is a stakeholder network of people who can come and help shape that, who are lobbying them, [then] that's the subject that will take priority.

**Ffion:** Somebody scoped a paper for the committee in the last Assembly. It all got a bit complicated because the north Wales prison was being built, and the north Walians [members from north Wales] wanted to have a look at that. But then there was a feeling of, 'Oh, but, you know, what impact can we actually have?' And then something more direct, more . . . devolved, frankly, came up, and it took the attention.

**Claire:** People were asked as part of their forward work planning whether they thought that they should be looking at that. And obviously they went back to them and said, well actually, where Spice [a psychoactive drug] is probably the biggest problem is in prisons. Obviously, you've got quite a lot of prison data showing the use of Spice and how it's getting in, and then the implications of that for rehabilitation. But it was just one of those things where . . . even though they [Assembly Members] thought it was an important issue, the committee also had another twelve subjects. And for them, they didn't want to prioritise a subject that they felt was non-devolved. So they thought it was important, but as more prominent issues came to the table, it slid down and then it came off. I think that tends to be the pattern.

Those of us interested in the operation of the Welsh criminal justice system may find this regrettable. We may even wish to challenge the notion that the decision to build western Europe's second largest prison in Wrexham is somehow not the 'core business' of Wales's democratic legislature. Yet it must also be admitted that the ability of that legislature to influence the decision was very limited indeed; and that, in more general terms, the tendency of members to prioritise other matters is perfectly understandable and reasonable. Especially when we recall that the Senedd is a relatively small legislature by comparative international standards, and as a result its time and its resources are at a premium (Expert Panel on Assembly Electoral Reform 2017). All of which means that there are significant opportunity costs involved in devoting scarce resources to criminal justice-related matters at the inevitable expense of other, also urgent, matters that are clearly within the remit of the devolved level and which therefore do not involve the same frustration of rubbing up against a jagged edge of divided powers and responsibilities. But it also, of course, means that the Senedd is not filling the scrutiny gap that is being left at the England and Wales level.

Can matters be improved? Clearly the decision to change the name and the remit of what is now the Legislation, Justice and Constitution Committee is intended to provide more of a focus in the Senedd. But this is unlikely in itself to improve the flow of data from the England and Wales level, let alone significantly improve devolved access to officials and policy makers in the Home Office and Ministry of Justice. There will also remain the fundamental question of whom members of the committee are hoping to sway or influence in making any recommendations, given that the most important powers and responsibilities in the Welsh criminal justice system continue to reside at the England and Wales level.

A related proposal is that the Welsh Government does more to concentrate police and criminal justice-related functions to provide more of a focus for its activities in this area; a context in which the Thomas Commission has recently suggested that it is currently 'difficult to discern a coherent leadership structure' (2019: 457). Providing more of a focus for criminal justice matters within the executive might in turn give more for the legislature to focus on.

But as we have already noted, there is an obvious catch-22 situation here that cannot simply be wished away. While justice is formally reserved and most of the important levers retained at the England and Wales level, establishing (for example) the equivalent of a justice ministry in the Welsh Government would be an almost entirely symbolic move. For reasons explored in the previous chapter, opportunities for effective devolved policy-making in the Welsh criminal justice system are very limited. It is, of course, the case that symbolic moves have their place in politics and there may come a time in which a Welsh Government might wish to pursue this option, if only as a means of shining a light on the UK level's stewardship of the Welsh criminal system. But from a purely functional perspective, there is currently no compelling case. Nor – relatedly – can much more be reasonably expected from the Senedd in this policy area as long as the current constitutional dispensation is maintained. Especially given the opportunity costs in a context of a legislature that is, according to every serious account, already too small to undertake all its scrutiny responsibilities in those areas in which it can reasonably hope to make a difference.

All of which is to say that the 'in principle' problems that we identified in the introduction to this chapter are also the problems we find when we examine the practice of the devolved level's efforts to hold the Welsh criminal justice system properly accountable. At the devolved level, as at the England and Wales level, it is clear that 'nobody really gets under the skin of what's happening in Wales'. Or in the words of another interviewee: 'I think what tends to happen is Westminster will think, "Well, most of those things are devolved", and Cardiff will think, "Well that's not devolved", and these things just fall in the gaps.'[23]

## CONCLUSION

Ensuring effective scrutiny and democratic accountability of any criminal justice system is difficult even at the best of times. In the context of the operation of England and Wales institutions, a pervasive lack of transparency, chronic delays in sharing relevant information and a deep reluctance to hold either individual staff members or the institutions they work for responsible, even in the case of behaviours deemed unlawful in the courts, all serve to undermine the possibility (a point made powerfully in Coles 2006; also House of Commons Justice Committee 2019b: Q388). The stress on performative toughness (as previously discussed in Chapter 3) has also served to render almost entirely marginal any concern with democratic or even legal accountability (Sim 2002; also Scraton 1985). A situation that is brought into stark relief at the time of writing as the UK Home Office publicly attacks efforts to uphold the rule of law as the meddling of 'activist lawyers' (BBC News 2020). But in the case of the Welsh criminal justice system the barriers to scrutiny and accountability are arguably even steeper and more difficult to surmount, in that they are not only cultural and conjunctural but are also – fundamentally – constitutional in nature. The decision to abandon the orthodox pattern of institutional alignment means that the very constitutional underpinnings of the criminal justice system militate against accountability. Quite simply, across the jagged edge of powers and responsibility that characterises and defines it, it does not appear that anyone can hold the Welsh criminal justice system properly accountable.

As we have seen, the main vehicles for ensuring the accountability of England and Wales criminal justice institutions – the inspectorates and the two key select committees – tend to shy away from engaging with the complexities of the Welsh context; other matters that are regarded as enjoying higher salience are given priority. But on those occasions when they do seek to engage they are liable to run into real difficulties. Not least because by crossing over to the devolved side of the jagged edge they are intruding on the scrutiny and accountability functions of devolved institutions themselves. That it is the non-specialist Welsh Affairs Committee that has taken over the task of providing parliamentary scrutiny is perhaps inevitable given both the low salience of Wales among those whose responsibility it is to hold England and Wales criminal justice institutions to account and that committee's search for a meaningful post-devolution role. Yet it also serves as another indicator that whatever the formal constitutional status – Wales as part of the single England and Wales justice system and legal jurisdiction – the position of Wales is, nonetheless, anomalous and indeed incongruous.

Wales's devolved legislature has been no more successful in ensuring that the Welsh criminal justice system is held democratically accountable. This because it is not its job to do so. The Senedd's responsibility is to hold the Welsh Government to account, and as the latter's powers and responsibilities within the Welsh criminal justice system are widely scattered across various policy portfolios, and its policy autonomy – in particular, its meaningful policy autonomy – in this area so constrained, it is fanciful to expect the Senedd to devote much of its scarce time and resources to the task of scrutinising the Welsh Government's justice-related activities. Moreover when, on occasion, the legislature has tried to reach over the jagged edge to the England and Wales side of the constitutional fence, it finds itself intruding on the territory of other, non-devolved accountability mechanisms. The difference, of course, is that this territory is formally reserved to the UK level, leaving the devolved level as even more obviously an interloper. As we have noted, this is a fundamental fact that cannot be wished away. There are clearly many working in the Welsh criminal justice system who wish it could be otherwise, who feel ignored or overlooked in the current dispensation, and who would like to see the devolved level taking a more active interest in their work (see Jones and Wyn Jones 2019: 76–8); but under the terms of this dispensation, it would appear that to be ignored or overlooked is their constitutionally predetermined fate.

The absence of effective scrutiny of and accountability for the Welsh criminal justice system is not some abstract, seminar-room concern. As we saw in Chapter 2, the Welsh criminal justice system functions particularly poorly. This is therefore a context in which scrutiny and accountability is or should be at a particular premium. People living in communities the length and breadth of Wales require advocates with the power to ask difficult questions on their behalf and to demand answers to those questions. They require advocates who, if they remain unsatisfied with the answers they receive, are in a position to demand and enforce action. At present, this not the case. Nor will the situation change as long as the current set of constitutional arrangements persist.

# 7
# THE FUTURE OF THE WELSH CRIMINAL JUSTICE SYSTEM

WHILE KEY ARGUMENTS presented in this book are likely to have been unfamiliar, they are relatively straightforward and easily adumbrated. To recap: even though Wales remains part of what is in formal, constitutional terms a single England and Wales criminal justice system and legal jurisdiction, there exists nonetheless a distinctive Welsh criminal justice system. It is a system shaped and defined by the unique constitutional architecture of Welsh devolution. Defying centuries of practice in 'Westminster-model' polities wherein the alignment of executive, legislature and judiciary is regarded as the *sine qua non* of mature, effective governance and – more recently – democratic accountability, Wales has a powerful devolved parliament and government located within an England and Wales jurisdiction and justice system. There is no meaningful way in which this jurisdiction and justice system can be considered to be 'shared', at least in the sense familiar to scholars of federalism. They are rather the 'reserved' and the jealously guarded preserve of the UK level of government acting, in this case, in its England and Wales capacity.

Given, however, that criminal justice policy and the institutions primarily involved in upholding justice are inevitably embedded in, and umbilically linked to, a raft of other public institutions and related social policies, the Welsh criminal justice system straddles a jagged edge of devolved and non-devolved responsibilities. Whitehall and Westminster are, without doubt, the dominant powers within this system; yet also inevitably, they remain dependent on the sustained input (and one is tempted to add, forbearance) of the devolved level to ensure that the system functions. On the other side of this jagged edge, while the devolved level has extensive responsibilities throughout the Welsh criminal justice system, its meaningful policy autonomy is very limited indeed.

The respective roles of the England and Wales and devolved levels in the Welsh criminal justice system were mapped and explored in a pair of linked chapters, chapters 3 and 4. The first of these focused on the role of England and Wales institutions; institutions that are, as we saw, nigh-on exclusively headquartered in the English capital, with London or its immediate environs also the location of almost all their policy-making capacity. Indeed, even in the context of what remains one of the most highly centralised polities in the developed world, the England and Wales criminal justice system is unusually centralised.

Notwithstanding the constant that is the concentration of command and control functions in London, since the mid-1990s it is also a system that has been characterised by almost incessant organisational churn and policy change. Successive UK governments have piled 'new initiatives' on 'reforms' on profile-grabbing 'crack downs' and 'transformations', with very few of the policies introduced having been properly evidence-based. All of which serves to underline the extent to which performative 'toughness' has become an end in itself in criminal justice policy.

And what of Wales in all of this? The problems it faces in the area of criminal justice are clearly serious and significant when viewed, as in Chapter 2, through a Welsh lens. Yet as we saw very clearly in the subsequent chapter and as has been confirmed throughout the rest of the book, when seen from the apex of the England and Wales criminal justice system, these problems appear far less consequential. Compared to the priority accorded violent crime in major English cities, for example, the problems of Wales appear neither particularly serious nor salient. As such, it should perhaps come as little surprise that there has only been very limited organisational adjustment to the reality of democratic devolution since 1999. Indeed, further underlining Wales's lack of salience is that most of the organisational adaptation that has taken place appears to have been driven not by specifically Welsh considerations but by wider attempts to regionalise administration (though not policy-making) across parts of the England and Wales criminal justice system. While the result has been a degree of administrative devolution within England and Wales institutions active in Wales that, in turn, facilitates communication and cooperation with Wales's devolved institutions, this is more an unintended consequence of changes instituted for other reasons rather than a deliberate attempt to accommodate Welsh devolution.

Chapter 4 mapped the responsibilities of the devolved level in the Welsh criminal justice system. As became clear, they are extensive. They not only encompass responsibilities that bolster the activities of criminal justice institutions 'proper', for example around crime-prevention activities. But underlining the extent to which the conventional portrayal of the criminal justice system in Wales as being simply 'reserved' is – at best – insufficient to capture a much more nuanced reality, they extend into the heart of the police and probation services, the courts, youth justice and the prison estate.

This chapter also explored how the Welsh Government has carried out those various responsibilities. The existing academic literature has tended to focus on those policy areas where there has been a deliberate attempt to do things differently via what is sometimes termed 'dragonisation' or the 'Welsh experiment'. In these cases, the Welsh Government has developed policy interventions that are evidence-based and deliberately progressive in intent. Our own analysis offered a different perspective. We pointed out that claims to a progressive or 'dragonised' policy approach is only part of the story; there are multiple other areas where the Welsh Government finds itself having little choice but to act, in effect, as an agent on behalf of England and Wales institutions. Not only that, but there is also ample evidence that efforts to implement evidence-based, progressive policies end up being hampered or even rolled-back because of the way that the devolution dispensation leaves the devolved level with 'responsibility without power'. In other words, the Welsh Government simply does not control enough of the key policy levers to follow through on its otherwise commendable objectives.

The arguments outlined in chapters 3 and 4 were developed further in Chapter 5, which explores two case studies focusing on different aspects of the operation of the Welsh criminal justice system. The first focused on housing provision for those being released from prison. This is an area of policy with enormous significance for preventing homelessness and reducing the risk of future offending. It is also the subject of (ostensibly) extensive devolved control, and one in which the Welsh Government developed what was arguably once its most celebrated criminal justice-related intervention. The second case study focused on policing; on a part of the criminal justice system that is formally reserved, yet one where the devolved level has extensive responsibilities, in particular in relation to funding. Both cases in their different ways served to make clear that the anomaly represented by the constitutional arrangements for criminal justice in Wales – namely the lack of institutional alignment highlighted in the introduction to this book – is not some abstract concern. Rather, it has negative practical consequences for the operation of the country's criminal justice system. The lack of alignment means that practitioners find themselves not only forced to navigate a needlessly complex and cumbersome system, but also to negotiate between the different (and sometimes competing) priorities of the England and Wales and Welsh tiers of government.

It is important to underline that these difficulties are structural in nature – the outworking of basic contradictions in the constitutional design rather than of deliberate intention. In the context of the prevailing constitutional arrangements, both the UK Government in its England and Wales guise and the Welsh Government have every right to adopt differing positions and priorities. Both have democratic mandates; both have perfectly reasonable and legitimate interests to pursue. This does not negate the fact, however, that the difficulties this creates for practitioners are both real and intractable. Abandoning institutional alignment – that is one of the fundamental tenets of the Westminster model – has universally negative consequences for policy on both sides of the jagged edge.

For effective policy-making, read also effective scrutiny and accountability. Chapter 6 explored the extent to which the Welsh criminal justice system is scrutinised and held properly to account. As we saw, not only have those mechanisms designed to scrutinise and hold the England and Wales system to account tended to ignore the Welsh context, but neither has there been much by the way of scrutiny emanating from the Senedd. It is equally clear, however, that the fundamental problem is again structural. Successful scrutiny and meaningful accountability inevitably require traversing the jagged edge of powers and responsibilities that defines the Welsh criminal justice system. Yet the basic model of democratic accountability deployed in the UK makes this more or less impossible. Thus, for quite understandable reasons, there would be significant resistance if, say, the Commons' Justice Select Committee or even the inspectorates sought in any sustained way to scrutinise and hold to account the Welsh Government for its actions in relation to the Welsh criminal justice system. Likewise, one does not require the gift of prophecy to anticipate the consternation that would greet any attempt by a Senedd committee to take upon itself the role of scrutinising and holding to account the UK Home Office or the Ministry of Justice for their actions in Wales.[1] In terms of scrutiny and accountability at least, the Welsh criminal justice system does not so much straddle a jagged edge of devolved and non-devolved powers and responsibilities, but fall into the gap between them.

Overall, we cannot avoid the conclusion that the way that the Welsh criminal justice system is organised is structurally and endemically dysfunctional. Comparatively speaking it is a system that performs very poorly. It is also a system in which effective policy-making is rendered extremely difficult; this even by the standards of a policy area that is notoriously complex and intractable. Moreover, it is a system that is poorly scrutinised and, at best, only weakly accountable.

At this point it is perhaps tempting to link the poor outcomes highlighted in Chapter 2 to the constitutional underpinnings of the Welsh criminal justice system explored in the remainder of the book. That is, to argue that these undeniably poor outcomes are the *result* of the unorthodox constitutional arrangements that underpin the Welsh criminal justice system. For the sake of clarity it is important, therefore, to underline that that is *not* an argument that we are seeking to advance here. If indeed it exists, to demonstrate the existence of such a causal link would require a very different kind of book from the one that we have written.

What seems irrefutable, however, is that criminal justice outcomes are unlikely to show any systematic improvement in Wales while the current constitutional structure remains in place. They are simply too dysfunctional to allow for any hope in this regard. Absent any change, Wales is almost certain to continue to shadow England's performance (albeit performing worse on many key indicators). All of which leads directly to the question of the future of the Welsh criminal justice system. The remainder of this chapter considers this future in three further steps.

First, we examine the arguments so strongly supported by the UK Government, the Conservative Party and, it would appear, most Welsh Labour MPs, namely that the current constitutional arrangements actually work well for Wales; or certainly well enough that any significant change would be a mistake. Secondly, we examine the case for the devolution of the criminal justice system as recommended in the 2019 report of the Thomas Commission. This is an argument that is also supported by the Welsh Government and – more fitfully – the wider Labour Party, as well as Plaid Cymru. Even if this argument is intellectually compelling, there also appears to be little prospect of any such development in the short to medium term, at least. The final section, therefore, focuses on what steps Welsh civil society – including, in particular, academia – might take in the interim to ensure that the problems of our criminal justice system are not overlooked simply because that is the most convenient outcome for those with the power to introduce the required reforms.

## ARGUING FOR THE STATUS QUO

What is to be done about the Welsh criminal justice system? The answer from both Whitehall and Westminster is easily summarised: a resounding 'nothing'. There is, apparently, no specific issue with the design or structure of the Welsh system that requires any reform beyond the most minor tweaking. To the extent that Wales has problems they are the same problems as the England and Wales system as a whole. Here we will examine the various ways in which this argument is articulated.

The first point to make, however, is that all of this is unfamiliar territory. While a debate about the merits of establishing a Welsh legal jurisdiction has flickered into existence – if only wanly – at various points since the national revival of the late nineteenth century, arguments that Wales is poorly served by the England and Wales criminal justice system and requires an alternative are of much more recent vintage. As such, until equally recently, there has never been any real need for supporters of the status quo to mobilise arguments in its favour. In the field of criminal justice, at least, England and Wales has just been the taken-for-granted, common-sense order of things. But now that debate has been joined, while defenders of the status quo may well hold the whip hand constitutionally speaking, it is equally clear that constructing an intellectually respectable justification for their position is far from straightforward. This is for the simple reason that since democratic devolution, Wales has been the obvious outlier.

We have repeatedly noted that Wales is an anomaly in terms of the Westminster model. As such, justifying the lack of institutional alignment that defines the criminal justice system in Wales also involves justifying why the basic assumptions of that model are, uniquely, somehow not applicable in the Welsh case. Moreover, this – once again – is no mere abstract debating point: the fact that Wales is an obvious outlier when compared to the other devolved territories of the UK, Scotland and Northern Ireland, serves as a constant reminder that, here, normal Westminster-model rules do not apply.

But in fact, supporters of the status quo are on even shakier ground than even this might imply. For within the England and Wales unit, recent UK governments have been enthusiastic about granting devolved control over aspects of the criminal justice system to the mayors of Greater Manchester and London. This enthusiasm stands in stark contrast to their approach to Wales, despite the fact that Wales's devolved institutions have far more extensive powers and responsibilities. Moreover, the justifications provided for devolving criminal justice powers to these large English conurbations also apply – but with much greater force – to Wales. In Manchester, for example, the decision to abolish the role of police and crime commissioner and hand these powers to its elected mayor was explained by the Home Office as an attempt at 'joining up oversight of key public services, to promote further and deeper collaboration within the area' (Home Office 2020i). Also cited was an explicit desire to integrate 'blue light services, ensuring that services are delivered in a more effective and efficient way' (Greater Manchester Combined Authority 2016: 30). There was even explicit recognition of the way that devolving control of aspects of the criminal justice system would allow 'Greater Manchester Combined Authority to better align their local health, education and accommodation services with agencies including the police, Crown Prosecution Service, HMCTS and probation to coordinate their services more effectively to drive rehabilitation and justice outcomes' (HM Treasury 2015: 3). Within England, therefore, the (partial) transfer of criminal justice functions to some metropolitan mayors is championed as a way of avoiding some of the jagged-edge problems described in this book.

Providing a comprehensive defence of the status quo in Wales thus entails not only finding some way of justifying why Westminster-model rules should not apply when Wales is now home to a powerful devolved government and legislature. It also requires justifying why even the rationale for devolving some criminal justice powers within England somehow does not apply in the case of Wales. In short, this is the quintessential 'tough sell'. It is perhaps unsurprising therefore that there has as yet been no comprehensive, intellectually coherent attempt to justify the status quo in relation to Wales.

Despite the absence of a coherent 'anti-reform' argument, it is possible to identify and even classify elements of a wider case in the various speeches and statements of those who champion the current constitutional arrangements for the Welsh criminal justice system. Once defence of the status quo moves beyond the mere assertion that it not only works well, but is 'hugely beneficial' to Wales (per former Secretary of State for Wales, David Jones (2013)) justifications typically involve one or more of the following elements: decrying devolution, deflection and trivialisation. Let us briefly examine these arguments in turn.

Decrying devolution

Even if Wales is the outlier in Westminster-model terms – and even in the context of the (limited) devolution of criminal justice functions to English conurbations – defenders of the status quo are quick to argue that devolving justice functions to Wales presents too many practical challenges and would represent a serious mistake. There are various versions of why this might be the case.

Responding on behalf of the UK Government to a Westminster Hall debate on the Thomas Commission report, Parliamentary Under-Secretary of State for Justice, Chris Philp MP, claimed that devolution would be too costly. Citing the 2014 report of the Silk Commission, he claimed that the 'extra incremental cost' of a devolved justice system (including criminal justice) and legal jurisdiction would amount to some £100m per annum; money that could otherwise 'be spent on more probation officers, more police', and so on (Philp 2020). Should justice be devolved, he claimed that Wales would suffer, as it would no longer be able to benefit from 'economies of scale' such as those which accrue as the Ministry of Justice upgrades its IT systems.

Given the notorious levels of overspend and delay that have tended to accompany UK Government IT procurement exercises (Cellan-Jones 2016; UK Infrastructure and Projects Authority 2018; Savage 2010), it is perhaps kinder to gloss over the latter assertion. In terms of the likely costs of devolving justice, Philp's claim that additional running costs would amount to £100m per annum is not even consistent with the evidence that was provided by the UK Government itself to the Silk Commission. At that point, the UK Government's estimate was that the initial set-up costs associated with devolving justice would amount to some £120–130m, with subsequent additional costs of some £38.5m per annum (Ifan 2019b). Focusing on the additional financial costs involved for devolved government, the Welsh Government estimated set-up costs of £13m, with a £10m per annum of additional costs to follow. In other words, excluding set-up cost, the 'extra incremental cost' of devolving justice would amount to less than half of the amount claimed by the minister; this in the context of a total annual spend on justice functions in Wales of some £1.2bn (Ifan 2019b).

Moreover, while there would clearly be some additional costs involved in devolving justice, there are also potential financial benefits that the minister chose to completely overlook. First, because per capita spend on justice is currently lower in Wales than in England, if justice were devolved then the operation of the Barnett formula would over time ensure that the amount in the Welsh budget derived from UK Government spending on justice in England would equalise on the English per capita level (indeed, would end up slightly exceeding it – for a full explanation see Ifan 2019b: 9–12, 17–18). While it would ultimately be up to the Welsh Government (with Senedd approval) to decide how to allocate the extra resource, these funds could potentially be available to spend on justice-related functions – such as tackling homelessness amongst prison leavers, substance misuse and so on – all of which can potentially help reduce reoffending and improve community safety. It is also the case that even a relatively modest improvement in the performance of the Welsh criminal justice system in a way which reduced reoffending and the overall size of the prison population could potentially generate further financial savings (for an illustration, see Ifan 2019b: 19–22; for an international perspective, see also Henrichson and Delaney 2012; Schrantz et al. 2018).

The UK Government's other key argument against devolving justice to Wales and the creation of a Welsh legal jurisdiction is that such a reform would merely substitute one jagged edge with another. To the extent that it is possible to follow the logic of this argument, the proposition would appear to be that, because most laws that apply in Wales are still created by the Westminster parliament acting in its England and Wales guise, devolving justice to Wales would mean the creation of a jagged edge between the justice system and the legal system. Thus, according to Philp: 'Devolving justice in the context of a body of law where the majority of it applies to England and Wales would actually exacerbate or worsen the jagged edge problem' (Philp 2020). But of course, the creation of a Welsh devolved justice system and a separate legal jurisdiction would lead to the transfer of the (then current) England and Wales criminal statute book to Wales as the basis of Welsh criminal law. From that point on, law and justice policy would become aligned in a way that, as we have seen in the preceding chapters, is simply not possible under current arrangements. It bears repeating that the UK Government's position not only ignores standard practice across those dozens of Westminster-model democracies that its predecessors have propagated around the world, but even its own rationale for devolving criminal justice functions in England.

Other arguments against devolving justice functions tend to focus on the impact on the legal system rather than the wider justice system, namely the courts and legal profession and not the police, prisons, probation services and youth justice. Thus, according to David Jones MP, a Welsh legal jurisdiction would be so small that there is a danger that legal talent would be lost to England, where career opportunities would be much greater (Jones 2013). As it happens, the evidence suggests that Wales's legal industry currently underperforms within the England and Wales legal system, reflecting the overwhelming degree of centralisation in London (see Ifan 2019a). Jones's position also begs the question of how other jurisdictions that are much, much smaller than a putative Welsh jurisdiction are able to manage. Even more fundamentally, however, given the very poor outcomes that characterise the Welsh criminal justice system as currently structured, there is the question of priorities. Do we continue with that structure because it ostensibly benefits Wales's (in reality) rather small and underpowered, if politically influential, legal profession? Or do we prioritise the creation of a system that has the potential to improve on those outcomes for the benefit of society as a whole?

## Deflection

For Welsh Labour MPs, in particular, debates over the future of the Welsh criminal justice system are clearly the source of some discomfort. While many appear to be privately strongly supportive of the continuation of the constitutional status quo, public opposition has been made more difficult by the Welsh Labour Government's explicit support for the devolution of justice and the backing given to this position by the UK party in its 2017 general election manifesto (to which we return in the next section). The response has been to seek to deflect discussion of the manifest inadequacies of the Welsh criminal justice system away from the problematic nature of the constitutional underpinnings of that system and towards a focus on funding and/or delivery instead.

Chris Bryant MP, for example, seeks to link the problems of the criminal justice system in Wales – among which he lists court closures, the distances at which prisoners are kept from their families and the privatisation of probation – with the swingeing cuts to the Ministry of Justice's budget imposed by the Conservative UK governments since 2010. Not only would the devolution of justice not resolve those issues, he claims, but it might even serve to exacerbate them: because the UK Government cannot be trusted to 'devolve the right amount of funding to go with it' (Bryant 2020).

This is a deeply unconvincing argument at many levels. The serious issues that arise because of the distances at which prisoners are held from their home areas are directly linked to the existence of a single England and Wales prison system, and the Ministry of Justice's determination to use all available prison spaces across it (House of Commons Justice Committee 2012: Ev26; Jones 2017). It is also difficult to envisage any devolved Welsh Government deciding to close quite as many courts across Wales, let alone privatise the country's probation service. One also wonders at the logic of a position that is willing to entrust the UK Government with the task of improving the Welsh criminal justice system while simultaneously arguing that the same government would inevitably act in bad faith were it ever to be required to agree a funding formula in the context of devolution. But such is the convoluted nature of the pro-status-quo argument.

Another Welsh Labour MP, Chris Evans, argues that 'the priority for Wales is not constitutional change or more devolution; it is tackling the problem of the prison population and reoffending rates' (Evans 2020). This was also in response to the publication of the Thomas Commission report, which emphatically recommended the devolution of justice as a necessary, though not sufficient, condition for dealing with the myriad problems besetting the Welsh criminal justice system. Ignoring the commissioners' key arguments, Evans's view is that 'in Wales we have tied ourselves up in constitutional knots for too long; we now have to deliver'. Beyond this exhortation, however, it is not clear how the problems of the Welsh criminal justice system – which on Evans's reading include precisely such jagged-edge issues as housing for prison leavers and mental-health provision – can be properly addressed without removing the constitutional anomalies that shape its very character. As such, Evans's standpoint is a paradigmatic case of willing the ends while denying the means.[2]

Trivialisation

Evidence that the Welsh criminal justice system performs poorly is, of course, the source of considerable embarrassment for proponents of the status quo. Not least because of the way that it serves to undermine the blithe assertion that current arrangements serve Wales well. In particular, the revelation that Wales has the highest imprisonment rate in western Europe has become symbolic of wider failings. Thus far, however, the response of those responsible for the England and Wales system has been to argue that poor performance in Wales has been exaggerated. So, for Philp, the imprisonment rate is only 'fractionally higher in Wales' than in England, with the clear implication that there is no particular cause for concern (Philp 2020). Giving evidence to the Thomas Commission, the then Chief Executive of HMPPS, Michael Spurr, claimed that Wales should not be considered as having western Europe's highest imprisonment rate as that (dubious) honour rightly belonged to Guernsey (Spurr 2019). We cannot know the intentions of the official concerned, of course, but given that the population of Guernsey is in fact smaller than that of Ynys Môn/Anglesey – or, more to the point perhaps, smaller than the county borough of Wrexham, home to what will eventually become western Europe's second largest prison – one can only interpret these comments as an attempt to trivialise the failings of the Welsh criminal justice system. Indeed, it remains genuinely striking – and surely instructive – that the ministers and officials responsible for the institutions of the England and Wales legal and justice system seem more concerned with denigrating the overwhelming evidence on the poor performance of the Welsh criminal justice system than acting upon it.

## DEVOLVING JUSTICE

Given that what we have termed institutional alignment is so fundamental to the Westminster tradition, it might have been thought that demands for a separate justice system and legal jurisdiction would have featured centrally in the various calls for home rule or devolution for Wales heard since the late 1880s. After all, no one could ever doubt that modern Welsh politics is other than thoroughly saturated with the assumptions of the Westminster way. Yet while it may be true that the most ambitious schemes for devolution, like the private members' bills presented in 1914 and 1955, contained within them plans for a Welsh jurisdiction and related justice system, in truth they were never a key feature of the rhetoric that accompanied them. Rather the focus was on the need for a *parliament* for Wales – the judiciary and indeed executive followed as a natural corollary of the establishment of a legislature. Campaigns for home rule have been nothing if not thoroughly democratic. Indeed, perhaps the most effective campaign for a Welsh legal jurisdiction (recall that these things are relative), namely the push that accompanied the Speaker's Conference of 1919–20, appears to have been inspired at least as much by economic calculation as it was by national-constitutional considerations (see Evans 2016). Specifically, the belief in at least some senior legal circles in Wales that the legal profession would benefit from a jurisdiction as its establishment would ensure that more of the legal business generated in Wales was transacted in Wales, rather than being transferred to English practices and English (especially London) courts.

From the mid-1960s onwards, supporters of devolution largely focused their arguments on the need to democratise the already-existing layer of administrative devolution in Wales, with the Welsh Office (established after 1964) naturally providing the main focus for their attentions (see Wyn Jones and Scully 2012: 26–56). Given that justice functions were not part of the remit of the Welsh Office and that it functioned entirely within the context of the England and Wales legal framework, this served to ensure that justice and jurisdiction remained very largely out of focus and, indeed, distant from the preoccupations of home rulers. And so it persisted after the establishment of the National Assembly for Wales in 1999; not least because injecting a dose of constitutional orthodoxy into the arrangements for a devolved legislature and executive appeared to be much the more important priority for the nascent Assembly.

Things only began to change – and then, initially at least, only relatively slowly – in the aftermath of the move to what might be termed a full-fat version of legislative devolution following the result of the 2011 referendum. This shifted Welsh devolution from a timid, tightly constrained legislative settlement to a more comprehensive version of the so-called 'conferred powers' model of primary law-making, with that model being preferred over the alternative 'reserved powers' model already in use in Scotland and Northern Ireland. The possibility of creating a reserved powers model for Wales was rejected on the explicit basis that the Labour Government responsible for the relevant legislation – the Government of Wales Act 2006 – was opposed to the establishment of a Welsh legal jurisdiction (see Wyn Jones and Scully 2012: 172–5). As the UK Government of the time considered that (for reasons never adequately elucidated) a reserved powers model would necessarily entail the creation of such a jurisdiction, a conferred powers model was regarded to be the only acceptable route to further legislative empowerment. What this position ignored was that a previous iteration of the very same government had concluded only a few years earlier that a conferred powers model of devolution was in fact an inadequate basis on which to establish a Scottish parliament. A determination arrived at because a conferred powers model could not provide adequate 'legal clarity on the scope of devolution', to quote the assessment of the Scottish Law Commission (cited in Wyn Jones and Scully 2012: 173).

Even if it was ultimately in the context of Wales rather than Scotland, these words were to prove prophetic. Once the conferred powers model was put to work in 2011, three Supreme Court cases were to follow in relatively short order, each to consider whether resulting pieces of Senedd legislation were, in fact, *intra vires* (for details, see Rawlings 2018). In the event, the UK Government was to lose two of those cases comprehensively, leading to concerns in Whitehall that the powers of Welsh legislature might in fact be far more extensive than had ever been intended or desired. Despite having been so recently and so adamantly opposed to a reserved powers model of devolution for Wales, it transpired that it might after all suit its purposes by providing a means of corralling the powers of the devolved level. Not only that, but in another complete reversal of its previous position, central government was now of the view that moving to a reserved powers model did not after all necessarily entail establishing a Welsh legal jurisdiction.

For very different reasons, supporters of devolution in Wales (including the Welsh Government) were themselves firmly supportive of the introduction of a reserved powers model – in their case, because it was regarded as a way of attaining (at last) some much needed clarity and stability in the Welsh devolution dispensation (see, for example, The UK's Changing Union Partnership 2013). Given this confluence of interests between London and Cardiff, it might have been thought that legislating for yet another devolution dispensation for Wales would have proven relatively straightforward; yet this was far from the case. By the time the Wales Act 2017 finally reached the statute book, the legislative process had triggered a fundamental shift in thinking at the devolved level, including the realisation that, ultimately, the country's status as a constitutional outlier was untenable. A lasting devolution settlement for Wales – that is, a settlement worthy of the name – would inevitably require the establishment of a devolved justice system that would underpin a Welsh legal jurisdiction.

This is not the place to provide a detailed account of constitutional developments in Wales in the period between the 2011 referendum and 2017 Act. Not least because it is a complex, multifaceted story that encompasses, inter alia, the Silk Commission process (2012–14), the so-called St David's Day process (2014–15), the production of and response to the Draft Wales Bill, and the passage of the revised Wales Act 2017 (the best account so far is in Rawlings 2018). For present purposes, the pivotal moment was the publication in autumn 2015 of the Draft Wales Bill, whose drafting – apparently at the behest of the Ministry of Justice – revealed for the first time (in public at least) the extent to which Whitehall was determined to constrain Welsh devolved legislative competence in order to maintain control of what it clearly regarded as *its* legal jurisdiction. This was made manifest through the inclusion in the draft Bill of far-reaching 'necessity tests', which would mean that the National Assembly (as it then was) could only legislate to change the criminal law, private law or law relating to reserved matters (such as the England and Wales legal jurisdiction) if the changes were ancillary to a devolved purpose and went no further than necessary to fulfil that purpose (Lewis 2015; Thomas 2015b). It would only take the UK Government's assessment of necessity to differ from the

Assembly's own for the legislation to be challenged in the Supreme Court. Furthermore, even if there were no such challenge, the suggested provisions could have led to chaos in the administration of justice, with defendants raising the question of necessity as a defence in any proceedings relating to an offence created by the Welsh legislature.

Unsurprisingly, these elements of the proposals were roundly condemned, with senior judicial figures also adding their own not-so-subtle warnings that the tests were a recipe for legal uncertainty and conflict (see National Assembly for Wales Constitutional and Legislative Affairs Committee 2015; Thomas 2015c; Rawlings 2018). The most widely discussed proposed remedy was a suggestion from a group of academics (including one of the current authors) and senior practitioners that a 'distinct' rather than separate Welsh legal jurisdiction be established, to allow the Welsh devolved legislature to legislate in a less encumbered fashion (Wales Governance Centre and Constitution Unit 2015). This was a deliberately minimalist proposal that would have left the wider justice system un-devolved and even the judiciary effectively untouched. Notwithstanding this, it was still a step too far for the UK Government. But with even the House of Commons Welsh Affairs Committee (2016) joining in the chorus of criticism aimed at the necessity tests, it was equally clear that they could not stand in their proposed form. In the event, after announcing a pause in the legislative process to allow for reconsideration, the legislation was presented to parliament with the scope of the tests having been moderated. The UK Government performed a partial U-turn – better that, apparently, than having to grapple seriously with the possibility of establishing a Welsh legal jurisdiction.

The revised Bill was subsequently to reach the statute book in uneventful fashion. Nonetheless, this episode has left a legacy that has shaped and will, doubtless, continue to shape subsequent debates over the future of Wales's devolution dispensation, and most significantly the thinking of the Welsh Government. There are at least, two inter-related dimensions to this. First, at its broadest, the very fact that the UK Government could so crudely and – in devolutionist eyes – unreasonably attempt to impose necessity tests in order to police the devolved legislature has prompted the realisation that a stable and sustainable devolution settlement is, ultimately, unobtainable without finally grasping the nettle of justice system and legal jurisdiction. Absent this, Welsh devolution is always likely to be subject to a capricious and, frankly, controlling Whitehall, and destined also to enjoy a distinctly lower status than its Scottish and Northern Irish equivalents.

The second point relates to the relationship between establishing a Welsh legal jurisdiction and devolving justice functions to Wales. Notwithstanding the efforts of the Wales Governance Centre and Constitution Unit (2015, 2016) to separate out the two issues, the Welsh Government has concluded that it is neither desirable nor, in fact, practically feasible to do so. In part, this appears to reflect its desire to arrive at a stable endpoint to the devolution journey; a point where, turning Ron Davies's famous dictum on its head, constitutionally at least, devolution can be regarded to be an event rather than a permanently on-going process. As such a prospect must surely remain fanciful without both devolving justice and establishing a Welsh legal jurisdiction, why not 'just get on with it', so to speak, and do both? But in addition, while academics may well be able to imagine carving up, and indeed carving out, the question of a legal jurisdiction from wider issues relating to the justice system as a whole, the Welsh Government would seem to have concluded that they are, in reality, inextricably linked and must follow in tandem with each other.

This is the thinking that underpinned the drafting of the Welsh Government's Government and Laws of Wales Bill (Welsh Government 2016e); a title that clearly alludes to the so-called Acts of Union (more correctly, the Laws in Wales Acts of 1536 and 1542), which formally abolished Welsh law. The Bill provides a legislative blueprint for a devolution settlement that, to quote the words of the accompanying explanatory summary, the Welsh Government regards as 'clear, stable and long-lasting' (Welsh Government 2016a: 1), and which was published in the summer of 2016 as an obvious counterpoint and contrast to what was to become the Wales Act 2017. Whereas the Whitehall vision of the future Welsh devolution rejected any changes to the status quo with regards the legal or justice systems, the Cathays Park vision – later endorsed by the Senedd – foresaw the devolution of justice after a suitable transition period. It would also divide the current England and Wales legal jurisdiction into two distinct English and Welsh jurisdictions. All this in the context of a comprehensive and, it should be said, admirably comprehensible statute that would serve as Wales's devolved constitution.

There were two subsequent developments that demonstrated the seriousness of the Welsh Government's commitment to this vision of the future. First, it ensured that the Labour Party manifesto for the 2017 general election contained a clear and unambiguous commitment to 'bring forward legislation to make the devolution settlement more sustainable as set out by the Welsh Labour government in its Alternative Wales Bill', that is the Government and Laws of Wales Bill (Labour Party 2017: 105). Secondly, following an election that had seen a much weakened Conservative government return to power in London, First Minister Carwyn Jones announced in September 2017 the establishment of a commission to 'review the operation of the justice system in Wales and set a long-term vision for its future' (Thomas Commission 2019: 30).

Chaired by the former Lord Chief Justice of England and Wales, Lord Thomas of Cwmgiedd, the Thomas Commission (as it inevitably became known) undertook what it described as the first review of the operation of the criminal justice system in Wales in over two hundred years (Thomas Commission 2019: 8). It will come as no surprise to readers of this volume that its conclusions, published in October 2019, were damning. As a result of the evidence collated, the commissioners 'unanimously concluded that the people of Wales are being let down by the system in its current state' (Thomas Commission 2019: 8). In response they proposed the devolution of justice responsibilities to (inter alia):

- enable the proper alignment of justice policy and spending with social, health, education and economic development policies in Wales, to underpin practical long-term solutions;
- place justice at the heart of government; [and]
- enable clearer and improved accountability. (Thomas Commission 2019: 16, also 459–69)

They also recommended that 'the law applicable in Wales should be formally identified as the law of Wales, distinct from the law of England', as well as the establishment of a separate Welsh judiciary (Thomas Commission 2019: 16, 497–500). That is, the Commission endorsed the creation of what has now become customary to describe as a separate rather than a merely distinct Welsh legal jurisdiction (while eschewing the term jurisdiction itself for reasons cogently set out in Thomas Commission 2019: 452–3). In short, the Welsh Government and Senedd's preferred outcome had not only been vindicated, but powerfully supported.

The subsequent months were, however, to underline in brutal fashion that evidence of current failings and eminently sensible and, indeed, rather orthodox proposals for reform would appear to count for very little where the Welsh criminal justice system is concerned. That the UK Government was so contemptuously dismissive of the commission's findings and recommendations (as detailed in the previous section of this chapter) cannot have come as a surprise.[3] What *was* surprising was the fact that Welsh Labour MPs were able to use their influence within their party to water down the 2017 pledge to implement the Welsh Labour Government's vision of the future of devolution. When Labour's manifesto was published ahead of the snap general election in December 2019, the unequivocal commitment of only two years earlier had been reduced to the following:

> Nine years of Tory cuts have done untold damage and the Thomas Commission on Justice in Wales is clear that the justice system is not working for Wales. Labour governments in Wales and Westminster will work together, using the Commission's report, to put that right. (Labour Party 2019: 84)

'Tory cuts' as the framing of the problem and 'using' rather than 'implementing' the Thomas recommendations as the key pledge for action: one need hardly be an expert in textual analysis to recognise that the Welsh Government and the Welsh Labour group in the Senedd had suffered a significant setback. And that even before an election result that removed any realistic possibility of reform for the foreseeable future.

WHAT'S NEXT?

Given the UK level's refusal to engage seriously with the report of the Thomas Commission, it is hard not to conclude this book on a downbeat note. We shall nonetheless avoid being downcast.

There can be no doubt that the Welsh criminal justice system performs very poorly indeed, and this has hugely negative consequences for individuals, families and communities right across the country. Even for those fortunate enough not to be directly impacted, there can surely be no doubt that all our lives are not only coarsened but materially and, dare we say, spiritually, impoverished by the misery and missed opportunities embodied in the bald statistics set out earlier in our analysis. Yet, as presently structured, not only is the Welsh devolved level denied an opportunity to try to improve on those outcomes, but even if it were interested in doing so (which it demonstrably is not), the England and Wales level cannot either. In this catch-22 situation, it is the people of Wales who are the collective losers.

Moreover, while devolution is itself no panacea, it is equally clearly a necessary step in terms of creating the possibility of engaging more creatively and successfully with the problems of our criminal justice system. To suggest as much is not to posit some wild, utopian alternative, but is rather to propose that the Welsh criminal justice system needs to be structured in accordance with the basic postulates of, and standard practice in, Westminster-model democracies across the world. Such a development has been supported by a clear majority in the Welsh legislature, by the Welsh Government and by the only review of the system to have been conducted in modern times. It is a development that also appears to enjoy widespread support among professionals working in the Welsh criminal justice system (see NAPO 2021; Prison Governors Association 2014; Wales and Chester Circuit 2018). Even so, on the basis of arguments that are at best threadbare, the UK Government – supported by both Conservative and most Labour MPs from Wales – maintains that nothing should change: meaning that, for the moment, nothing will.

Yet while realism is clearly in order in assessing the prospects for the future of the Welsh criminal justice system, we can and should eschew fatalism. A more appropriate stance is rather that embodied in the maxim made famous by Gramsci: 'pessimism of the intellect, optimism of the will'. Yes, we are faced with a situation in which there is no immediate way of forcing Whitehall and Westminster to engage seriously with the deficiencies and structural problems of the Welsh criminal justice system. After all, if an expert report produced by a commission chaired by the former Lord Chief Justice of England and Wales can be dismissed so casually, what hope for the rest of us? Yet there are ways to prevent the current state of, and future prospects of, the Welsh criminal justice system from falling off the political agenda.

Clearly the Welsh Government has an important role to play. Elsewhere we have underlined the critical role that research evidence can play in bringing to light the challenges that Wales faces in this area, as well as potential solutions to those challenges (Jones et al. 2019: 55). Given the significant drain on devolved resources represented by spending on criminal justice, one option is to establish a research unit based on the successful Finnish model, which would bring the best international evidence to bear on the problems of Wales (Jones et al. 2019). But in the context of the current discussion, such a unit would also serve to ensure that policy makers at the devolved level, at least, remain focused on the particular challenges created by the constitutional underpinnings of the Welsh criminal justice system.

Civil society actors also have their role to play, not least because the criminal justice system is indelibly linked to (and plays a key role in reproducing) some of the most intractable social problems facing Wales: homelessness, mental health, substance misuse, poverty, social exclusion and racial inequality. In these circumstances, policy makers clearly cannot hope to engage in any fundamentally transformational way with these problems, unless they are also willing and able to engage with the failings of the Welsh criminal justice system. However, until now, with only some exceptions, that is precisely what has tended to happen as most policy discussions in Wales have sidestepped consideration of the role of the criminal justice system. Yet just as Wales's constitutional dispensation is destined to remain unbalanced absent the devolution of justice functions, debate on public policy in Wales is similarly destined to remain unbalanced without a full consideration of the impact of and interaction with the criminal justice system. To the extent that it is a lack of understanding of an extraordinarily complex system, as well as the general inaccessibility of Wales-level data on outcomes that has hindered engagement, we can only hope that this book – and the wider programme of research of which it forms a part – will play some part in empowering civil society to take a more active interest.

Finally and relatedly, academics could and should do much more. Curriculums need to be reformed to ensure that students understand that the Welsh criminal justice system operates in a distinctive way and learn to think critically about the implications of this. Given the number of students who study criminal justice-related subjects in Wales's universities – many of whom then go on to work in or around the country's criminal justice system – it is astonishing that this is not already happening. But this is partly a reflection of the paucity of academic research into the operation of the criminal justice system in the unique constitutional context that is devolved Wales. This book represents the first systematic attempt to provide an overview of that system. As we made clear in the introduction, as authors we are very much aware that there are almost certainly multiple ways in which our account can be improved upon. Nonetheless, we trust that this book will provide useful data as well as a conceptual vocabulary on which our academic colleagues can draw and build in years ahead. Much more than that, however, our earnest hope is that it will inspire current and especially future colleagues to believe that there is something here worth engaging with. Not only because it is intellectually stimulating to consider the operation of a criminal justice system across a jagged edge of divided competences and responsibilities – though that is undoubtedly the case. Even more significantly, we hope to encourage their engagement because this is a system so obviously in need of fundamental transformation. When those reforms are finally introduced, better data and better understanding will help to ensure that they are successful, and that the multiple failings and failures that have been the subject of this book will in time also come to be regarded as features of a less enlightened and less civilised Wales.

# APPENDIX
## List of research participants

| Name | Sector |
|---|---|
| **Anna** | Scrutiny |
| **Anthony** | Policing and community safety |
| **Carol** | Community safety |
| Claire | Scrutiny |
| **Craig** | Policing and community safety |
| **Emma** | Youth justice |
| **Ffion** | Scrutiny |
| **George** | Policing and community safety |
| **Harry** | Policing and community safety |
| **Helen** | Equalities |
| **Holly** | Housing |
| **Huw** | Scrutiny |
| **Isabelle** | Policing and community safety |
| **Jack** | Health |
| **Jamie** | Substance misuse |
| **Jayne** | Community safety and criminal justice |
| **John** | Policing and community safety |
| **Jonathan** | Community safety and criminal justice |
| **Joshua** | Housing |
| **Kate** | Community safety and criminal justice |
| **Laura** | Scrutiny |
| **Luke** | Mental health |
| **Marc** | Community safety and criminal justice |
| **Michael** | Substance misuse |
| **Oliver** | Substance misuse |
| **Olivia** | Policing and community safety |
| **Rhys** | Mental health |
| **Richard** | Policing and community safety |
| **Ross** | Substance misuse |
| **Sally** | Community safety |
| **Sam** | Community safety and criminal justice |
| **Sarah** | Community safety |
| **Sian** | Policing and community safety |
| **Sion** | Policing and community safety |
| **Sophie** | Equalities |
| **Steven** | Mental health |
| **Sue** | Education |
| **William** | Community safety and criminal justice |
| **Wyn** | Mental health |

# NOTES

CHAPTER 1

1   Note that we confine ourselves to the twentieth century. We do not propose to enter into a historiographical discussion on the extent to which it might be argued that a distinctive criminal justice system existed in Wales in the period between the country's formal annexation into England in the mid-sixteenth century and the abolition of the Court of Great Session in 1830. But see, inter alia, Jones (1998); Ireland (2015); Watkin (2007).
2   On the use of the Welsh language in courts see, inter alia, Andrews and Henshaw (1984); Jones (1998); Lewis (1998); Watkin (2007).
3   To the point that Russell and Serban (2021) argue that it no longer has enough intellectual coherence to be analytically useful. One suspects, however, that the authors are themselves aware that their plea that the term Westminster model therefore be 'retired' is destined to fall on deaf ears.
4   Both Scotland (since before 1707) and Northern Ireland (since its formation in 1921) are discrete legal jurisdictions with their own court systems and systems of professional regulation. Policing and justice were among the powers transferred to Scotland's devolved institutions in 1999 while powers over policing and justice were devolved to the Northern Ireland Assembly in April 2010. On the criminal justice system in Northern Ireland both pre- and post-devolution see, inter alia, McAlinden and Dwyer (2015); McEvoy (2001); McGarry and O'Leary (1999); O'Mahony (2012). Prior to democratic devolution in 1999, all laws relating to criminal justice in Scotland were created by the UK Parliament although there remained considerable divergence from the criminal justice systems in England and

Wales and, indeed, Northern Ireland: see Brangan (2019); McAra (2006, 2008); Mooney et al. (2015) and Morrison (2011). For detailed accounts of post-devolution criminal justice policy in Scotland see Buchan and Morrison (2020); Croall et al. (2010, 2015); McAra (2008); and McAra and McVie (2015).

5 Throughout the following, except in the case of direct quotations or when the context might render it particularly jarring, we have tended to refer to the devolved Welsh legislature and executive alike by their current titles, namely Senedd (Welsh Parliament) and Welsh Government respectively. We have done so in order to simplify the narrative. But for the record, what was previously known as the Welsh Assembly Government was renamed the Welsh Government in May 2011 (a development formally confirmed in the Wales Act 2014), while the previous National Assembly for Wales was renamed Senedd Cymru or Welsh Parliament in May 2020.

6 Some aspects of administrative justice provide the exception. There are currently seven devolved tribunals that are the responsibility of the Welsh Government. Yet even here, however, the formal link to the England and Wales jurisdiction is maintained with the president of the Welsh Tribunals being appointed by the Lord Chief Justice for England and Wales, and with section 60 of the Wales Act 2017 making explicitly clear that this is a non-devolved function. On administrative justice, see the pioneering work of David Gardner, Sarah Nason and Huw Pritchard: Gardner (2016); Nason (2017, 2018, 2019); Nason and Pritchard (2020); Pritchard (2017).

7 Relatedly, we are unaware of any study of – or indeed, any publicly available information about – how the UK Government acting in its England and Wales guise responds to Welsh devolved requests to create additional legal duties and responsibilities within the single England and Wales legal jurisdiction. This represents a serious gap in our knowledge about the operation of the current Welsh devolution dispensation.

8 For a helpful overview of some of the issues, see Wales Governance Centre and Constitution Unit (2016: 42–3).

9 The benefits system being the major and significant exception. On the 'social policy Assembly', see Chaney and Drakeford (2004).

10 The mutual reliance of the core institutions of the criminal justice system and those institutions responsible for other aspects of social policy is explicitly recognised by the UK Government (in contexts other than that of Welsh devolution, at least). See, for example, the Crime and Disorder Act 1998, which placed a statutory duty on local authorities and health boards to work alongside criminal justice agencies to reduce crime. The Home Office's (2004a: 3) *Reducing Re-offending National Action Plan* also formally

identified several resettlement pathway areas that were key to delivering a 'seamless' system of support to offenders across England and Wales. These pathways included the provision of support to people who have offended in areas such as healthcare, housing, education and tackling substance misuse. For insightful commentaries see Garland (1996, 2001), Rodger (2008).
11 Although Wales only moved to the reserved powers model of devolution in 2017, to simplify the narrative we have again tended to use the current terminology of devolved and reserved throughout the text.
12 This is not the first use of jagged edge in the context of Welsh devolution. Most prominently, perhaps, it is used on at least six occasions in the report of the Richard Commission to describe the boundary between devolved and non-devolved/reserved powers and responsibilities (Richard Commission 2004: 26, 110, 116, 118, 119, 185).
13 The analysis produced by University College London's Constitution Unit at around the same time was almost equally scathing in its implications, if not perhaps as elegantly wrought (Constitution Unit 1996).
14 Also relevant here are the various contributions to Chaney et al. (2001).
15 '[T]o the extent that it is seriously interested in addressing the problems of the criminal justice system': the caveat is important here. Criminologists have long noted the performative function of government responses to crime. Indeed, Michael Tonry – building on the work of David Garland (2001) – has argued that Tony Blair's New Labour government introduced 'primarily expressive policies without concern for their iatrogenic effects' (2007: 1). More recent examples of performative, 'tough-on-crime' policies that end up exacerbating rather than ameliorating the problems they were ostensibly designed to tackle might include the Ministry of Justice's failed attempt to 'transform' probation services or the same ministry's decision to build super-prisons (both of which we return to below).
16 All available at *https://gov.wales/commission-justice-wales*.
17 See also Watkin (2012) for a fascinating account of earlier and differently motivated debates about the establishment of a Welsh jurisdiction.

## CHAPTER 2

1 In 1955 the then Lord Chief Justice of England (Lord Goddard) objected to a suggestion that Wales should be added to his official title on the basis that even acknowledging the existence of Wales represented a concession to nationalism: 'I can only say that I should hate to have the style of my office altered and I hope it will not be necessary to make any concession to nationalist feeling in Wales in this respect.' This letter was obtained through

research at the National Archives by Manon George in 2016. We are grateful to her for sight of it.
2   The title was changed in 1998 when Lord Bingham took over the role. While this may have been in preparation for the then imminent advent of Welsh devolution, it seems likely that Thomas Bingham's strong links to Boughrood in Powys (after his death he was interred in the grounds of the village's St Cynog's Church) predisposed him to taking Wales more seriously than some of his predecessors. It is also striking that the decision to grant even this most elementary form of recognition seems to have been a personal one rather than the result of any wider political and/or judicial consideration or process (Thomas, 2001; Thomas Commission 2019: 63).
3   Lord Woolf's 1991 report into the disturbances describes a series of incidents at HMP Cardiff on 8 April 1990, including clashes which caused extensive damage to the prison and left five staff members and one prisoner injured (Woolf 1991).
4   The Wales and Berwick Act 1746 created a statutory definition of England as including Wales. The provisions included in the Act were not repealed until the Welsh Language Act 1967.
5   The Welsh Centre for Crime and Social Justice (WCCSJ) provided a partial if honourable exception, although we note that for some years now the WCCSJ appears to have been largely inactive.
6   They are the following universities: Aberystwyth, Bangor, Cardiff, Open, South Wales, Swansea, Trinity Saint David, and Wrexham Glyndŵr. Note also that Cardiff Metropolitan University offers a BA in professional policing.
7   The absence of Welsh data was lamented by the Thomas Commission (2019: 427) in the following terms: 'a recurring issue in our inquiries and work has been the lack of Wales-only statistics in the field of justice ... The lack of specific data has inevitably contributed to a major deficiency in Wales specific research.' Meanwhile a recent report on prison health provision by the Senedd's Health, Social Care and Sport Committee, while thanking one of the current authors for his assistance, makes clear that: 'the lack of Wales-specific data makes it challenging to assess the scale of the impact in prisons in Wales' (2021: 94).
8   HMPPS told the Thomas Commission in February 2019 that a 'working group has been established to look at disaggregating data in our part of the system' (Rees 2019:10). As of June 2021, however, Welsh-only prison data remains available solely to researchers via the provisions of the Freedom of Information Act 2000, while the Welsh Government appears to be still in discussions with the Ministry of Justice about the matter (see Hutt 2021).
9   To give a sense of the absolute numbers involved, in the year ending December 2019, there were 263,447 criminal offences (excluding fraud) recorded in Wales; an average of 721 offences a day (Office for National Statistics 2020b).

10 An average for 2016, 2017, 2018 and 2019 was calculated using quarterly readings. The total for 2015 was calculated using three readings as data for March 2015 are unavailable.
11 In 2019/20, almost 6 in 10 crimes in England and Wales were not reported to police (Office for National Statistics 2020c). We are unable to compare the situation in Wales to that which pertains in England in this regard.
12 In 2004, the Welsh Government's Community Safety Unit Research Team published a Wales-focused analysis of the 2001/2 British Crime Survey. This report was described by the Home Office's Regional Crime Reduction director in Wales as setting a 'precedent and baseline for future reports', indicating that future analyses of the survey would be carried out at the Welsh level and 'become a regular source of monitoring the public's experience of crime and the Criminal Justice System in Wales' (A'Herne 2004: ii). In fact, it proved to be the first and last of its kind.
13 This includes fraud and computer misuse.
14 Local area deprivation is measured using the Welsh Index of Deprivation (see Welsh Government 2019a: 12). For more on the relationship between victimisation and poverty, see Carlen (1988), Dekeseredy et al. (2003), Hope (2001), Lea and Young (1984), Smith and Jarjoura (1988).
15 Adults are defined as aged 16 and over. Children are defined here as being aged 10 to 15.
16 We note that there are other outcomes to be considered when analysing the rate at which crimes are solved. These include cases where a prosecution is prevented or not deemed to be in the public interest, cases where an out-of-court (informal and formal) outcome is reached, cases that remain unsolved because of evidential difficulties (including instances where the victim does not support action), as well as cases where a diversionary activity has been undertaken.
17 As with so many other areas covered in this chapter, further research is needed to understand levels of police recorded crime. This may well include research into the relationship between changing police officer numbers and the number of crimes recorded by police or reported by victims of crime in Wales.
18 The National Crime Agency is not listed as a 'public authority' in Schedule 1 of the Freedom of Information Act 2000 and is not obliged to respond to Freedom of Information requests, hence the element of doubt.
19 A notifiable offence is a crime deemed serious enough by police that it must be recorded.
20 Data in the year ending March 2020 is included in 2019/20. These data are, therefore, largely unaffected by the lockdown measures introduced by the UK prime minister on 23 March 2020.

21 In England data from 2019/20 shows that there were 6 stops and searches per 1,000 White people. The comparable numbers for individuals from other ethnic backgrounds were 53 per 1,000 Black people, 15 per 1,000 mixed ethnic people and 15 per 1,000 Asian people (Home Office 2020f).
22 This total includes all incidents including where a Conducted Energy Device is drawn, aimed, arced, red-dot, drive-stun, fired and angle drive-stun.
23 This in addition to the ten magistrates' courts closed in Wales between 2001 and 2010 (Thomas Commission 2019).
24 The total spent on criminal legal aid in Wales fell from £48,440,000 in 2011/12 to £36,100,000 (Thomas Commission 2019: 125).
25 The sex of 39 of the 5,777 were classed as 'not known' in 2019.
26 All data relating to the 'home address' of prisoners is based on a prisoner's origin address (home address on reception into custody). The Ministry of Justice state that around 97 per cent of prisoners have an origin location, i.e. addresses that are recorded on its central IT system. If no address is given, an offender's committal court address is used as a proxy for the area in which they are resident. Those with no recorded origin are typically foreign nationals or those recently received into custody. No address has been recorded and no court information is available for around 3 per cent of all offenders; these are excluded from the tables included in this book.
27 The average Welsh prison population for each year is calculated using data from March, June, September and December.
28 The average custody rate was higher at magistrates' courts in Wales in eleven out twelve offence groups in 2019. The rate was higher in nine offence groups at the Crown court (Jones 2020b: 76–8).
29 The average for each country has been calculated using the twelve editions of the World Prison Population List published between 1999 and 2018.
30 The team visited HMP Cardiff, Cardiff Crown Court and Cardiff Probation Service.
31 The Equality and Human Rights Commission has its own office in Wales. The Equality Act 2006 established a Wales Committee to advise the Welsh Government and Senedd on matters relating to equality and human rights in Wales. The Act also required that a commissioner 'who knows about conditions in Wales' be appointed to the commission, with this appointment subject to approval by the Senedd.
32 The Lammy Review concluded in 2017 that there remains a lack of 'transparency' over the way in which applications from BAME prisoners are handled and treated by the parole board in England and Wales (Lammy Review 2017: 52).

33  Black prisoners from England served a higher proportion of their determinate sentences in prison (67 per cent), followed by mixed (66 per cent), White (62 per cent) and Asian (58 per cent) prisoners between 2015 and 2018 (Ministry of Justice 2020h).
34  We return to the role of 'resettlement prisons' later in this book.
35  For research on the Welsh language and probation practice, see Madoc-Jones and Buchanan (2003).
36  A 2018 review by the Welsh Language Commissioner recommended that HMPPS make changes to the way in which data on the language needs of prisoners are collected and used, as well as underlining the need for HMPPS to improve opportunities for prisoners to use the Welsh language (Welsh Language Commissioner 2018). The formal response is provided in HMPPS (2020).
37  It was with the establishment of National Offender Management Service (NOMS) in 2004 that the reduction of reoffending became, for the first time, a 'stated objective' of the correctional service in England and Wales 'as a whole' (Nacro 2004: 1). NOMS was replaced by HMPPS in 2017.
38  In 2019, the average custodial sentence length for women sentenced in Wales was 10.3 months compared to 18.3 months for men (Ministry of Justice 2020a).
39  For more on the impact of short-term sentences on women, see Baldwin and Epstein (2017); HM Inspectorate of Prisons (2019a).
40  The period between 2013 and 2019 saw a small decline (of 2 per cent) in the female prison population across both England and Wales from 3,884 to 3,794 (Ministry of Justice 2014a, 2020i).
41  When measured as a rate per 100,000 of the total population (men and women), the Welsh female imprisonment rate in 2017 would have ranked third highest in western Europe (Walmsley 2017). Only the rate recorded in Spain (9.6 per 100,000) and Portugal (8.5 per 100,000) exceeded the female imprisonment rate in Wales (8.3 per 100,000) in 2017.
42  It should be noted that concerns remain over 'serious flaws' in the learning process following deaths in prison custody (INQUEST 2014: 3).
43  In 2016 a record twelve self-inflicted deaths were recorded across the female prison estate in England and Wales (Ministry of Justice 2020v).
44  A request for information on the number of Welsh mothers in prison was sent to the Ministry of Justice but refused on the basis that this information exceeded the cost limit to retrieve.
45  Home Office data provided to the Welsh Affairs Committee in 2006 show that the average 'distance from home' for female Welsh prisoners was 101 miles. Although described as 'distance from home', the figures provided by the

Home Office were calculated on the basis of the distance between the court where women were sentenced and the prison they were being held in at the end of September 2006 (see House of Commons Welsh Affairs Committee 2007: Ev 97).

46 The average custodial sentence length for women in Wales has increased from 8.8 months in 2013 to 10.3 months in 2019 (Ministry of Justice 2020a).

47 The Welsh Government has based its approach on the United Nations Convention on the Rights of the Child. The Rights of Children and Young Persons (Wales) Measure 2011, for example, attempted to provide some legislative teeth to the UNCRC in Wales. Welsh ministers are under a statutory duty 'when exercising any of their functions, [to] have due regard to the requirements of' part 1 of the UNCRC and certain paragraphs of 2 Optional Protocols. In Wales, Welsh ministers must take account of UNCRC rights in exercising their functions, and are vulnerable to judicial review if they do not. The UK Government has not incorporated the UNCRC into its own domestic legislation.

48 See Evans et al. (2021) and Thomas (2015a) for more detailed and critical discussions of the claims being made about distinct approach to youth justice in Wales.

49 From 254 custodial sentences in 2010 to fifty-two in 2019 (Ministry of Justice 2020a).

50 There are nine Adverse Childhood Experiences included in the study: sexual abuse, physical abuse, verbal abuse, domestic violence, parental separation, mental illness, alcohol abuse, drug abuse, incarceration (Bellis et al. 2015).

51 Hillside Secure Children's Home provides accommodation for children (of any gender) aged 12 to 17. In April 2016, the Youth Justice Board (YJB) reduced the number of beds contracted at Hillside from ten to six. The Young Persons' Unit at HMYOI Parc is a facility managed by G4S on the same site as HMP Parc in Bridgend. The unit holds boys between 15 and 18 and has a Certified Normal Accommodation of sixty-four. HMYOI Werrington in Staffordshire is now the closest YOI for boys from north Wales. The number of children from Wales held at HMYOI Werrington has increased since the YJB decided to decommission HMYOI Hindley in Greater Manchester in 2014 (House of Commons Welsh Affairs Committee 2015). There is no YOI accommodation for girls in England and Wales; girls are held either in secure children's homes or secure training centres. In the year ending March 2019, there were (on average) two girls from Wales in youth custody (Youth Justice Board 2021a). For a detailed account of the problems facing girls from north Wales, see Hughes et al. (2012).

52 For an England- and Wales-wide view, see Pitts (2015).

## CHAPTER 3

1. We return to the role of Westminster in Chapter 6 below.
2. See the new Schedule 7A to the Government of Wales Act 2006.
3. The tendency to treat Wales as an afterthought is already well attested in wider debates on devolution. See, for example, Hazell 2015; House of Commons Justice Committee 2009; House of Commons Welsh Affairs Committee 2010a; House of Lords Select Committee on the Constitution 2016; Thomas 2017; Rycroft 2019.
4. Infamously, New Labour created over 3,000 new criminal offences in its first decade in power (Morris 2011).
5. While the Home Office was established in the eighteenth century, the Ministry of Justice post-dates the advent of democratic devolution. It was established only in 2007 when some of the previous functions of the Home Office and those executive functions (i.e. non-judicial functions) traditionally invested in the office of the Lord Chancellor (after 2003, the Department of Constitutional Affairs) were combined in a new department of state.
6. Those organisations included here are derived from the list of departments, agencies and bodies included on the UK Government's website in 2020, *https://www.gov.uk/government/organisations*.
7. In preparing this table we asked the Ministry of Justice and Home Office to provide us with a list of those organisations that have 'a specific Welsh unit or a Welsh directorate' (e.g. a form of administrative devolution). The Independent Office for Police Conduct was listed by the Home Office as one of the 'agencies and bodies' that does not have a Welsh unit or directorate. Yet the Independent Office for Police Conduct itself lists a 'Director for Wales' (see *https://www.policeconduct.gov.uk/who-we-are/our-people*).
8. The Judicial Appointments Commission has one 'Lay Commissioner with special knowledge of Wales'. Dr Barry Morgan, the former archbishop of Wales, was appointed as a lay commissioner in July 2020 (see *https://judicialappointments.gov.uk/the-rt-rev-dr-barry-morgan/*).
9. The Law Commission has a Wales Advisory Committee and now undertakes projects at the instigation of the Welsh Government (because of a recent change in the law), so bypasses Whitehall.
10. Territorial representation on the UK Supreme Court raises a number of significant questions which we can only touch upon in the present context. Justices of the Court have always included members of the Scottish and Northern Irish judiciaries or eminent lawyers from those jurisdictions. Over the past decade a convention appears to have developed ensuring that a Welsh judge participates in devolution-related cases. The appointment of Lord

David Lloyd-Jones as a Justice of the Court in 2017 appeared to confirm the direction of travel towards the explicit recognition of what we might term Welsh distinctiveness, especially given that the court has regularly chosen to highlight his credentials as both Welsh and a Welsh speaker. The Thomas Commission recommended that 'Wales should be put in a similar position to Scotland and Northern Ireland regarding the appointment of a judge to the Supreme Court' (Thomas Commission 2019: 15).

11  The 8.3 per cent figure for the Home Office equates to 100 minus a comparability factor of 91.7 per cent. For Northern Ireland, the equivalent figures are, again, 8.3 per cent for the Home Office and 0.1 per cent for the Ministry of Justice (HM Treasury 2019). Attentive readers may well ask how it is that the Ministry of Justice sponsored Criminal Injuries Compensation Authority operates in Scotland without, it appears, spending any money there? The explanation is that any schemes it is responsible for in Scotland are in fact funded by the Scottish Government.

12  Our key interest here is the division between those with policy making functions and those with operational roles. But as civil service grades tend to be determined by levels of responsibility rather than functions, these do not map onto grades in any straightforward way. There are SCS staff undertaking operational roles and Grade 6/7s in policy roles. For the purposes of this discussion, therefore, we include both. But it's worth noting that in our experience, few in the senior echelons of the civil service (whatever their grade) would challenge the view that most policy roles are based in London.

13  We note that in February 2022, the Ministry of Justice announced that it is planning to open seven new regional offices outside of London, including one in Cardiff. The proposals will see around 2,000 Ministry of Justice staff leave London by 2030, with a commitment to transferring 500 roles to Wales (Ministry of Justice 2022a).

14  The Home Office were unable to provide a separate breakdown for SCS staff and those at G6 and G7 level.

15  'CPS Direct' operates as a fifteenth 'virtual' area and provides charging decisions on cases considered a priority all year round (Crown Prosecution Service 2021b).

16  Youth Justice Board (YJB) Cymru was established around 2008 in order to recognise the growing distinctiveness of youth justice arrangements in Wales. However, the UK Government's decision to transfer responsibility for custodial services from the YJB in September 2017 to the newly formed Youth Custody Service (which forms a distinct part of HM Prison and Probation Service) means that the YJB now plays a more limited or 'refined'

role (Allars and Taylor 2018: 6). In Wales, these changes have served to limit the role that a distinct YJB Cymru can play in shaping youth justice services.
17  Petty France is a street in central London that is home to one of the Ministry of Justice's three main bases in that city. The other is in Leeds.
18  Within its Serious and Organised Crime Strategy the Home Office draws a clear distinction between the role played by other UK Government departments and the devolved governments in shaping the policy. While 'major contributions' were made to the strategy by other UK Government departments, the Home Office claims to have worked 'in close partnership with the devolved administrations' (Home Office 2018c: 9).
19  Stevens (2011) found that high levels of turnover within the UK civil service are often caused by a desire amongst officials to develop an expertise in a wide range of subjects by experiencing many different departments. In 2017/18, 14 per cent of staff left the Ministry of Justice (Sasse and Norris 2019).
20  Tom Sasse and colleagues neatly sum up the resulting dysfunction: 'This means that on complex decisions of great importance to the public, inexperienced ministers are advised by similarly inexperienced officials' (Sasse et al. 2020: 12).
21  The Welsh Government has four main directorates: Office of the First Minister and Brexit; Health and Social Services; Education and Public Services; Economy, Skills and Natural Resources (see Table 4.1).
22  During this period 17 per cent of recorded crimes were in London. Almost a third (31 per cent) of police-recorded crimes in England and Wales were in London and north-west England in the year ending June 2019.
23  The nation or region with the next highest number was north-east England with 281,662 recorded crimes in the year ending December 2019 (Office for National Statistics 2020b).

## CHAPTER 4

1  It might reasonably be countered that control of the relevant policy levers does not guarantee positive outcomes. But a related problem with the current constitutional dispensation is that lack of proper accountability makes it much more difficult to identify, diagnose and address problems. We discuss this issue at length in Chapter 6.
2  Is it worth noting that Welsh ministers and the Senedd can legislate to create criminal offences within areas of competence and can legislate for certain limited criminal justice matters 'around' those crimes, including 'making provision about responsibility for the prosecution of devolved offences' (as per Schedule 7A para 8(2) of the Government of Wales Act 2006).

Coronavirus regulations are arguably the most high-profile example of this, which have included creating a new category of enforcement officers with wide-ranging powers under those same regulations.

3   Schedule 7A (Section B5 Exception) of the Government of Wales Act 2006 allows the Senedd to give the police 'Powers of entry, search and seizure relating to the detection or investigation of an offence of a kind provision for the creation of which is within the Senedd's legislative competence.'

4   The National Police Chiefs' Council brings together and is funded by police forces in England, Wales and Northern Ireland, as well as the armed services and a number of British Overseas Territories. It replaced the Association of Chief Police Officers in April 2015.

5   HM Inspectorate of Prisons found in 2015 that each court custody suite in Wales has access to healthcare advice from a specialist health adviser, Taylormade Medical Services (HMI Prisons 2016b).

6   The total cost of prison healthcare in prisons in south Wales exceeds the amount provided by the UK Government through the block grant. In 2017/18, prison healthcare in Wales (excluding HMP Berwyn) cost local health boards £3.879m, while just £2.544m was allocated in the block grant (Senedd Health, Social Care and Sport Committee 2021). The difference is met by the Welsh Government and the devolved budget. Prison healthcare at HMP Berwyn is fully funded by HM Prison and Probation Service (HMPPS). In 2017/18, Betsi Cadwaladr University Health Board received £10,066,230 from HMPPS for the provision of healthcare at HMP Berwyn (Jones 2019c).

7   The findings of the *Prisoner ACE Survey* found that more than a quarter (28 per cent) of prisoners in Wales reported that they had experienced mental illness before reaching the age of 18 (Ford et al. 2019).

8   For the uninitiated, 'Measure' was the formal title given to legislation produced by the then National Assembly of Wales under the terms of Part Three of the Government of Wales Act 2006, which, between 2007 and 2011, set out the constitutional framework within which the Assembly could create primary legislation. This was superseded when the procedure for creating primary legislation set out under Part Four of the 2006 Act was enacted following an affirmative vote in the March 2011 referendum. After this, primary legislation produced by the National Assembly became known as an 'Act'. Acts and Measures have the same legal status.

9   The Justice Policy Division draws together and centralises a number of pre-existing functions in Welsh Government – including a previous justice policy team – bolstered by a small expansion in overall staff numbers: it remains a modest undertaking.

10  The contract to deliver provision for education and skills at HMP Berwyn was awarded to Novus Cambria in 2016. The contact was worth £18.7m and is due to last five years (Novus Cambria 2016).
11  In fairness, we should note that in the wake of the publication of the aforementioned Hanson (2019) report, a draft policy is currently being produced, a process that is likely to have been delayed by the pandemic. It remains to be seen what (substantively) emerges from this process.
12  Confirming this point, one of Welsh Labour's key pledges in the manifesto that underpinned its successful campaign at the 2021 devolved election was to fund another 100 police and community support officers in addition to the 500 it already supports (Welsh Labour 2021: 62).
13  A civil servant informed the authors that in relation to court closures, following the announcement by the UK Government of its proposals to 'rationalise' HMCTS, on 8 December 2014 the first minister, Carwyn Jones AM, wrote to Lord Chancellor and Secretary of State for Justice, Chris Grayling MP, to set out concerns raised by Professor Sir Adrian Webb as the chair of the Committee for Administrative Justice and Tribunals Wales, about likely impacts of the proposed cuts to the HMCTS estate in Wales. In January 2016, Minister for Public Services, Leighton Andrews AM, wrote to the Parliamentary Under-Secretary for State, Shailesh Vara MP, reiterating the significant concerns that had been expressed in the consultation response about the likely negative impact of the proposed reforms on access to justice in Wales.
14  For the avoidance of doubt, we stress that this is not the only issue that has impacted on the ability of Welsh Government to successfully deliver on an alternative approach. The academic literature is helpful here: the research on prison leavers and housing services in Wales (to which we will return in the next chapter) also highlights the impact of austerity (Ifan and Siôn 2019), the operation of the welfare benefit system and how policies have been implemented by housing services (Mackie 2015). That said, there is a consensus across a range of specific policy areas that the impact of UK Government policies on the England and Welsh criminal justice system have regularly frustrated the Welsh Government's policy intentions. This is also the view – indeed, the lived experience – of many of our interviewees.
15  Which may be regarded as a response to a thematic review of substance misuse provision across the prison estate in England and Wales in 2015. The review raised concern over the absence of an Integrated Drug Treatment System (IDTS) in Wales leading to 'poorer outcomes' for some prisoners (HMI Prisons 2015b: 14).

16  It should be noted that, in this particular case at least, the current Scottish devolution dispensation also stands as a barrier to more enlightened policy developments. In April 2018, Members of the Scottish Parliament voted 79–27 in support of a Scottish Government motion calling on the UK Government to allow a safe drug injecting facility to be established in Glasgow. Despite this, the Home Office has consistently refused to sanction such a development. Addressing a UK drugs summit (also in Glasgow) in February 2020, the UK police and crime minister, Kit Malthouse, described drug consumption rooms as a 'distraction' from tackling the underlying problems (Barrie 2020). Faced, however, with a further rise in drug-related deaths in Scotland, in August 2021 the Scottish Government made clear that it would seek to establish these facilities 'irrespective of the ... constitutional constraints that we face' (McGivern 2021). It remains to be seen what this might mean in practice.

17  It is worth underlining that Michael is referring here to the original substance misuse strategy published in 2008 (Welsh Government 2008b). Subsequently, more – though far-from-all – legislative levers did become available at the devolved level following the affirmative vote in the 2011 referendum. It was on the basis of these powers that the Public Health (Minimum Price for Alcohol) (Wales) Act 2018 became law.

18  Although it is important to stress again that the Welsh Government has not been consistently progressive across all of its criminal justice-related policy responsibilities. We have already noted some areas where Welsh variation from English approaches have been minimal, but we might also cite the Welsh Government's decision to sell the land that allowed the Wrexham super prison, HMP Berwyn, to be built.

## CHAPTER 5

1  The inspectors did not include Wales as part of their research. We return to the extent to which the various England and Wales inspectorates (including HMI Probation) engage with Wales in the next chapter.

2  Note that prisoners released from Welsh prisons with no Welsh connections were not covered by the Welsh Government's policy (as noted in HMI Prisons 2008: 87).

3  HMP Altcourse operated as the 'local' prison for north Wales prior to the opening of HMP Berwyn in 2017. The Welsh Government invested £100,000 in 2007 to develop a North Wales Resettlement Unit at HMP Altcourse. The unit was set up to provide a base for Welsh service providers visiting the prison to deliver resettlement support to Welsh prisoners (Jones 2017).

4   A review of priority need in Wales published in 2019 found that the definition of vulnerability was deeply problematic. The research found that the threshold for vulnerability was too high and that the test used to establish vulnerability was inconsistent and often 'traumatic for individuals' forced to prove that they were vulnerable in order to qualify for priority need status (Mackie et al. 2020: 34).
5   It was only in 2013 that the Ministry of Justice introduced designated resettlement prisons which might have helped mitigate this problem (Ministry of Justice 2013b). We touch on the effectiveness of this policy below.
6   In June 2022 the Ministry of Justice announced their intention to end the practice of automatically releasing prisoners on a Friday as part of their plan to 'reduce reoffending and cut crime'. It remains to be seen what impact this policy will have if/when it is introduced (Ministry of Justice 2022b).
7   From 66,300 in 2001 to 83,540 in 2013 (Home Office 2003b; Ministry of Justice 2014a).
8   The Prison Link service is run by Shelter Cymru.
9   In 2019, 62 per cent of all people sentenced to prison in Wales were sentenced to fewer than 12 months (Jones 2020b).
10  It is important to note that there is no female prison in Wales or any capacity to hold male Category A prisoners, which means that these prisoners currently *have* to be held in institutions outside Wales. In December 2019, this amounted to 249 Welsh women and a total of thirty-two male Category A prisoners (Ministry Justice 2020q; 2020ziv).
11  A point that does not seem to have been fully appreciated in Johnston and Politowski (2016).
12  A matter to which we return in Chapter 7 below.
13  The England and Wales criminal justice system has been particularly badly hit by the austerity policies of successive UK governments. Indeed, the Ministry of Justice's budget saw 'the deepest cuts' of all UK Government departments (Ifan 2019c: 9)
14  Dyfed-Powys Police introduced a mental health triage service in January 2015, which is jointly funded by Dyfed-Powys Police and the Hywel Dda University Health Board (Jones and Wyn Jones 2019). A three-person mental health triage team was introduced by Gwent Police in September 2018 and is jointly funded by the health service (Office of the Police and Crime Commissioner for Gwent 2019). North Wales Police introduced its own triage system in 2020 having received funding from the Welsh Government (Betsi Cadwaladr University Health Board 2019; North Wales Police 2021).

15  TARIAN is a regional organised crime unit, part funded by the Home Office, Welsh Government and the three police forces in south Wales. The unit is focused on tackling organised crime across south Wales. See *https://www.tarianrocu.org.uk*.

## CHAPTER 6

1  For the avoidance of doubt, we are not seeking to claim that institutional alignment of the kind that is standard in Westminster-model systems somehow guarantees effective scrutiny and accountability. The challenges faced by Westminster in holding the UK Government to account underline the extent to which democratic accountability is much simpler in broad-brush theory than it is in everyday practice. For reasons that will become clearer by the end of this chapter, our point is rather that, without such alignment, even the basic prerequisites that might allow for effective scrutiny and accountability are absent.
2  In addition, Her Majesty's Crown Prosecution Service Inspectorate (HMCPSI) has a statutory duty to inspect the operation of both the Crown Prosecution Service (CPS) and the Serious Fraud Office. We have omitted consideration of its role in relation to Wales from this discussion as, in its case, there is substantially less overlap with the role of the Welsh Government.
3  Scrutiny of the criminal justice system is also provided by a range of other organisations and bodies including the Prison and Probation Ombudsman, the Independent Office for Police Conduct, Independent Monitoring Boards, Lay Observers and the Independent Advisory Panel on Deaths in Custody.
4  Health Inspectorate Wales also works alongside the Prison and Probation Ombudsman for England and Wales. All deaths in prison custody in Wales are subject to a clinical review by Health Inspectorate Wales as part of a review completed on behalf of the Prisons and Probation Ombudsman.
5  HMI Probation's annual report for 2017 referred to the Welsh Government on just one occasion where it incorrectly stated that 'the Welsh government has devolved responsibility for youth justice' (HMI Probation 2017: 93).
6  HM Inspectorate of Prisons' 2015 review of patterns of substance misuse concluded that the Welsh Government's decision not to introduce an Integrated Drug Treatment System (IDTS) had led to 'poorer outcomes' for prisoners held in Wales compared with England (HMI Prisons 2015b: 14). In a written response to the National Assembly for Wales Health and Social Care Committee's inquiry into alcohol and substance misuse in 2015, HM Inspectorate of Prisons (2015c: 6) also told members that the absence of an integrated drug service in local prisons meant that both HMP Cardiff

and HMP Swansea were 'lagging behind' their counterparts in England. Of particular concern to inspectors was that those remanded or held in Welsh local prisons were subject to a rapid detoxification (regardless of their own wishes or determination to desist from substance misuse) only to then be released into the community. For opiate-dependent prisoners who have been detoxified in custody, the policy increased the risk of 'accidental overdose' for those reusing opiates upon release (HMI Prisons 2015b: 14). A 'key driver' behind the introduction of IDTS in England was to reduce the number of drug overdoses on release; HM Inspectorate of Prisons (2015b: 24) recommended that IDTS be rolled out across Welsh prisons.

7   Interestingly and perhaps revealingly, following a subsequent inspection of HMP Parc (carried out in November 2019), HM Inspectorate of Prisons made the same recommendation on housing support for prison leavers but this time it was directed at HMPPS and not the Welsh Government (HMI Prisons 2020c: 54).

8   Benton and Russell (2013: 793) argue that one of the most significant levers in the hands of select committees is the threat of further evidence sessions and inquiries.

9   In 2013, the House of Commons Home Affairs Committee began an inquiry into the powers given to police and crime commissioners to remove chief constables. The committee heard evidence from the former chief constable of Gwent Police, Carmel Napier, who had been 'persuaded to retire voluntarily' by the police and crime commissioner, Ian Johnston (House of Commons Home Affairs Committee 2013: 4).

10  This even before the Parliamentary Constituency Act 2020, which will see the number of Welsh MPs being reduced by a fifth from 40 to 32, has taken effect. This will compare to England's 543.

11  Other areas of recent interest for the committee include nuclear power, Brexit and broadcasting. The latter case is particularly instructive in the current context in that Welsh Affairs has taken the lead role in scrutinising the operation of the (reserved) Welsh language television channel, S4C. Apparently because the members of the 'correct' specialist select committee in Westminster, the Digital, Culture, Media and Sport committee, are not interested in undertaking the work themselves.

12  The reduction in the number of Welsh MPs is surely likely to exacerbate this problem over the longer term.

13  We note in this context that the Welsh Affairs Committee conducted a one-off evidence session on policing in Wales in March 2022. No report was produced but a transcription of the evidence session is available (House of Commons Welsh Affairs Committee 2022).

14  Interview with Sian.
15  This is of course an oversimplification in as much as there are a number of other committees – for example, the petitions committee – that do not fit neatly into this schema. Nonetheless, the seven principal legislation and policy committees of the Senedd's sixth term (i.e. from May 2021) have mirrored ministerial portfolios. Whilst this is not mandated by the standing orders it was also the pattern in the previous term.
16  Since 2011 the responsibility for 'justice' has been held by the Minister for Local Government and Communities (May 2011 to March 2013); Minister for Local Government and Government Business (March 2013 to September 2014); Minister for Public Services (September 2014 to May 2016); Cabinet Secretary for Communities and Children (May 2016 to November 2017); Cabinet Secretary for Local Government and Public Services (November 2017 to December 2018); first minister supported by the deputy minister and chief whip (December 2018 to May 2021); and the Minister for Social Justice (2021–present).
17  Thus far, the Legislation, Justice and Constitution (LJC) Committee has focused its attentions on the impact of the pandemic, the report of the Thomas Commission and the likely effects of the UK Government's Internal Market Bill. This reflects the fact that its remit is, to quote the Senedd's Business Committee, 'high-level justice policy matters, such as the devolution of justice and policing, and any matters which relate to law-making'. What the Business Committee terms the 'practical application of justice policy' will continue to be scrutinised by the appropriate policy and legislation committees (see minutes of the Senedd Business Committee, 13 July 2021). Hence our scepticism that the addition of justice to the title of the LJC Committee presages any fundamental change in the extent to which the Senedd engages with or scrutinises the Welsh Government's current roles in the Welsh criminal justice system (as analysed in the remainder of this chapter).
18  When Senedd committees require criminal justice-related data from the UK/England and Wales level the request is made by a letter from the committee chair to the relevant minister/Secretary of State. Should it be necessary then this is followed up by official (clerk) to official (civil servant) communication.
19  New psychoactive substances; the National Assembly for Wales Health and Social Care Committee carried out an inquiry into the growth of new psychoactive substances in Wales during the fourth Assembly (2011–16). The committee's final report was published in March 2015.
20  See Eisner (2018) and Morris (2019). For examples of the work done by journalists based in Wales, see Will Hayward (2019) and Jenny Rees (2020).

It is a matter of regret that in September 2021, the position of BBC Wales home affairs correspondent that had been established only three years previously was restructured out of existence.
21  Media reports on the impact of the COVID-19 pandemic on prison health in the UK regularly failed to distinguish between the different territorial, and therefore institutional, contexts (e.g. Allison and Pegg 2020; Shearer 2020; Smith 2020; White 2020).
22  Examples of such engagement include providing written and oral evidence submissions to the House of Commons Welsh Affairs Committee inquiries and public opposition to the Ministry of Justice's plans to build 'super' prisons in Wales. See BBC News 2017b; Prison Reform Trust 2014.
23  Interview with Ffion.

## CHAPTER 7

1  Albeit welcome in itself, the then Lord Chancellor's willingness to give evidence to Senedd's Legislation, Justice and Constitution Committee in February 2021 does not negate this fundamental point (see *https://record.senedd.wales/Committee/11065*). That appearance is rather better understood as a courtesy than an opportunity for detailed scrutiny of the kind we might expect when standard Westminster-model lines of accountability apply. It remains to be seen whether his successors will even be willing to extend even this minimal level of recognition.
2  It is also worth recalling the words of the then prime minister, Gordon Brown, when addressing the Northern Ireland Assembly on the issue of devolving justice powers to Northern Ireland:
> There is something more vital at stake for your entire society, something that only the completion of devolution can deliver. How can you, as an Assembly, address common criminality, low-level crime and youth disorder when you are responsible for only some of the levers for change, and when you have responsibility for education, health and social development but have to rely on Westminster for policing and justice? (Brown 2008)
3  Even if we disregard the poor intellectual quality of the UK Government's reaction to the Thomas Commission report, it is striking that it was left to a lowly Parliamentary Under-Secretary of State for Justice, namely Chris Philp, to lead its response; this despite Lord Thomas's exalted status as the former Lord Chief Justice of England and Wales. For the avoidance of doubt, this was itself a clear and carefully calibrated signal of the government's lack of interest in or respect for the commission's work.

# BIBLIOGRAPHY

A'Herne, David (2004), 'Foreword', in Andy Aitchison and Jocelyn Kynch (eds), *Crime and Victimisation in Wales: Results from the British Crime Survey 2001/02*. March 2004. Cardiff: RDS Research Team, Community Safety Unit, Welsh Assembly, *https://gov.wales/sites/default/files/statistics-and-research/2019-06/040301-crime-victimisation-2001-02-en.pdf* (accessed 6 May 2020).

Allars, Colin and Charlie Taylor (2018), 'Foreword', in Youth Justice Board (2018), *Annual Report and Accounts 2017/18*. July 2018. London: The Youth Justice Board for England and Wales, pp. 6–7, *https://assets.publishing.service.gov.uk/government/uploads/system/uploads/attachment_data/file/726302/YJB_Annual_Report_and_Accounts_2017-18.pdf* (accessed 19 October 2019).

Allen, Grahame (2019), *How our local police forces are funded*. House of Commons Library Briefing, December 2019. London: House of Commons, *https://commonslibrary.parliament.uk/insights/how-our-local-police-forces-are-funded/* (accessed 9 September 2020).

Allen, Rob (2006), 'Being honest about criminal justice', in Richard Garside and Will McMahon (eds), *Does criminal justice work? The 'Right for the wrong reasons' debate.* London: Crime and Society Foundation, pp. 57–64, *https://www.crimeandjustice.org.uk/sites/crimeandjustice.org.uk/files/right%20for%20wrong.pdf* (accessed 8 April 2020).

Allison, Eric and David Pegg (2020), 'Discharged UK prisoners with Covid-19 symptoms given travel warrants', *The Guardian*. 7 April 2020, https://www.theguardian.com/world/2020/apr/07/discharged-uk-prisoners-with-covid-19-symptoms-given-travel-warrants (accessed 12 May 2020).

Anderson, Sarah (2019), 'Rethinking adverse childhood experiences'. *Howard League for Penal Reform, Early Career Academics Network Bulletin*, 41 (April 2019): 5–10, https://howardleague.org/wp-content/uploads/2019/04/ECAN-bulletin-Spring-2019.pdf (accessed 22 November 2019).

Andrews, John and Lesley Henshaw (1984), *The Welsh language in the courts*. Aberystwyth: University College of Wales.

Annison, Harry (2019), 'Transforming Rehabilitation as "policy disaster": Unbalanced policy-making and probation reform'. *Probation Journal*, 66(1): 43–59.

Ashworth, Andrew and Julian V. Roberts (2013), *Sentencing Guidelines: Exploring the English Model*. Oxford: Oxford University Press.

Bache, Ian and Matthew Flinders (2004), 'Multi-Level Governance and the Study of the British State'. *Public Policy and Administration*, 19(1): 31–51.

Baldwin, Lucy and Rona Epstein (2017), 'Short but not Sweet: a study of the impact of short custodial sentences on mothers and their children'. July 2017. Leicester: De Montfort University, https://dora.dmu.ac.uk/bitstream/handle/2086/14301/Final%20 3%20Research%20report%20LB%20RE.doc?sequence=3&isAllowed=y (accessed 15 December 2020).

Barrie, Douglas (2020), 'UK crime minister mulls cross-border police talks to tackle drugs trade'. *The Belfast Telegraph*, 27 February 2020, https://www.belfasttelegraph.co.uk/news/uk/uk-crime-minister-mulls-cross-border-police-talks-to-tackle-drugs-trade-38996812.html (accessed 15 October 2020).

Bates, Stephen, Mark Goodwin and Stephen McKay (2017), 'Do UK MPs engage more with Select Committees since the Wright Reforms? An Interrupted Time Series Analysis, 1979–2016'. *Parliamentary Affairs*, 70(4): 780–800.

BBC News (2011), 'Home Office anger as AMs vote down Welsh police changes'. BBC News, 9 February 2011, http://www.bbc.co.uk/news/mobile/uk-wales-politics-12402552 (accessed 7 January 2020).

BBC News (2017a), '"Not practical" for Met Police to investigate all crime'. BBC News, 16 October 2017, https://www.bbc.co.uk/news/uk-england-london-41633205 (accessed 6 April 2020).

BBC News (2017b), 'Wales 21st Century "Botany Bay" with new prison plan'. BBC Wales News, 26 September 2017, https://www.bbc.co.uk/news/uk-wales-politics-41400023 (accessed 28 November 2019).

BBC News (2018), 'AMs back calls for legal medicinal cannabis for patients'. BBC Wales News, 17 January 2018, https://www.bbc.co.uk/news/uk-wales-politics-42709244 (accessed 6 January 2021).

BBC News (2020), 'Home Office scraps "activist migrant lawyers" clip'. BBC News, 28 August 2020, https://www.bbc.co.uk/news/uk-politics-53937593 (accessed 10 September 2020).

Belknap, Joanne (2020), *The Invisible Woman: Gender, Crime, and Justice*. *Thousand Oaks*, California: Sage.

Bellis, Mark, Kathryn Ashton, Karen Hughes, Katherine Ford, Julie Bishop and Shantini Paranjothy (2015), *Adverse Childhood Experiences and their impact on health-harming behaviours in the Welsh adult population*. Cardiff: Public Health Wales, https://www.basw.co.uk/system/files/resources/basw_114245-2_0.pdf (accessed 23 June 2020).

Bennett, Trevor and Katy Holloway (2011), *Evaluation of the Take Home Naloxone Demonstration Project*. Cardiff: Welsh Government, https://gov.wales/sites/default/files/statistics-and-research/2019-08/110627naloxonefinalreporten.pdf (accessed 2 July 2020).

Benton, Meghan and Meg Russell (2013), 'Assessing the Impact of Parliamentary Oversight Committees: The Select Committees in the British House of Commons'. *Parliamentary Affairs*, 66(4): 772–97.

Betsi Cadwaladr University Health Board (2019), Written evidence to the National Assembly for Wales Health, Social Care and Sport Committee's Inquiry into Mental Health in Policing and Police Custody. Bangor: Betsi Cadwaladr University Health Board, https://business.senedd.wales/documents/s86811/MHP21%20-%20 Betsi%20Cadwaladr%20University%20Health%20Board.pdf (accessed 7 May 2020).

Bevan, Aneurin (1952), *In Place of Fear*. London: William Heinemann.

Boivin, Rémi and Gilbert Cordeau (2011), 'Measuring the Impact of Police Discretion on Official Crime Statistics: A Research Note'. *Police Quarterly*, 14(2): 186–203.

Bosworth, Mary (2000), 'Confining Femininity: A History of Gender, Power and Imprisonment'. *Theoretical Criminology*, 4(3): 265–84.

Bowcott, Owen (2019), 'Jump in unrepresented defendants as legal aid cuts continue to bite'. *The Guardian*, 24 November 2019, https://www.theguardian.com/law/2019/nov/24/legal-aid-cuts-prompt-rise-in-unrepresented-defendants (accessed 11 February 2020).

Brangan, Louise (2019), 'Civilizing imprisonment: The limits of Scottish penal exceptionalism'. *British Journal of Criminology*, 59(4): 780–99.

Brewster, David (2017), 'Culture(s) of control: Political dynamics in cannabis policy in England & Wales and the Netherlands'. *European Journal of Criminology*, 14(5): 566–85.

Brewster, David and Robert Jones (2019), 'Distinctly Divergent or Hanging onto English Coat Tails? Drug Policy in Post-Devolution Wales'. *Criminology and Criminal Justice*, 19(3): 364–81.

Bridges, Andrew (2010), 'Foreword,' in HMI Probation (2010), *History of HMI Probation*. Manchester: HMI Probation, https://www.justiceinspectorates.gov.uk/probation/wp-content/uploads/sites/5/2014/03/history-hmi-probation.pdf (accessed 6 October 2020).

British Transport Police (2021), *Premises in Wales*. Data obtained from British Transport Police via the Freedom of Information Act 2000.

Broome, Laura and Jason Davies (2020), *South Wales PSC Mental Health Triage: Second Evaluation*. May 2020. Swansea: Swansea University, https://cronfa.swan.ac.uk/Record/cronfa54387/Download/54387__17426__8a19f2ebb6fd4e05b20cd6bd6dcd09eb.pdf (accessed 21 October 2020).

Brown, Aaron (2020), *A Rights-Based Analysis of Youth Justice in the United Kingdom*. London: UNICEF.

Brown, Aaron and Anthony Charles (2021), 'The Minimum Age of Criminal Responsibility: The Need for a Holistic Approach'. *Youth Justice*, 21(2): 153–71.

Brown, Gordon (2008), *Address by The Prime Minister to the Northern Ireland Assembly*. The Rt Hon Gordon Brown MP. 18 September 2008. Stormont: Northern Ireland Assembly, http://archive.niassembly.gov.uk/Speakers_Office/reports/gordon_brown.htm (accessed 13 November 2019).

Brunton-Smith, Ian and Kathryn Hopkins (2013), *The factors associated with proven reoffending following release from prison: findings from Waves 1 to 3 of SPCR. Results from the Surveying Prisoner Crime Reduction (SPCR) longitudinal cohort study of prisoners*. Ministry of Justice Analytical Series. London: Ministry of Justice.

Bryant, Chris (2020), *During a debate on the Commission on Justice in Wales*. Vol. 670: debated on Wednesday 22 January 2020. Column 145WH. London: House of Commons, https://hansard.parliament.uk/commons/2020-01-22/debates/45A32F4F-4FD7-4AE5-99B6-2780FD13082B/CommissionOnJusticeInWales (accessed 28 January 2020).

Buchan, Jamie and Katrina Morrison (2020), 'Compromise, partnership, control: Community justice authorities in Scotland'. *Criminology and Criminal Justice*, 20(2): 226–43.

Buil-Gil, David, Juanjo Medina and Natalie Schlomo (2021), 'Measuring the Dark Figure of Crime in Geographic Areas: Small Area Estimation from the Crime Survey for England and Wales'. *The British Journal of Criminology*, 61(2): 364–88.

Bunting, Lisa, Lorna Montgomery, Suzanne Mooney, Mandi MacDonald, Stephen Coulter, Gavin Davidson, Trisha Forbes and David Hayes (2019), *Evidence Review-Developing Trauma-informed practice in Northern Ireland*. April 2019. Belfast: Queens University Belfast, https://pureadmin.qub.ac.uk/ws/portalfiles/portal/168311525/ACEs_Report_A4_Feb_2019_Developing_a_Trauma_Informed_Approach_Full_Evidence_Review.pdf (accessed 20 May 2020).

Burrows, John, Roger Tarling, Alan Mackie, Rachel Lewis and Geoff Taylor (2000), *Review of police forces' crime recording practices*. Home Office Research Study 204. London: Home Office.

Cardiff University, Swansea University and ARCS Ltd (2009), *Evaluation of the Effectiveness of the Safer Communities Fund 2006–2009*. Final Research Report Submitted to the Welsh Assembly Government by Cardiff University, Swansea University and ARCS Ltd. July 2009.

Care Inspectorate Wales, Her Majesty's Inspectorate of Constabulary and Fire & Rescue Services, Healthcare Inspectorate Wales, Her Majesty's Inspectorate of Probation and Estyn (2020), *Joint Inspection of Child Protection Arrangements (JICPA): Newport, December 2019.* April 2020, https://careinspectorate.wales/sites/default/files/2020-09/200902-JICPA-Newport-December19-en.pdf (accessed 6 July 2020).

Carlen, Pat (1988), *Women, Crime and Poverty.* Milton Keynes: Open University Press.

Caro, Robert (2019), *The Power Broker: Robert Moses and the Fall of New York.* London: The Bodley Head.

Case, Stephen, Samantha Clutton and Kevin Haines (2005), 'Extending entitlement: A Welsh policy for children'. *Wales Journal of Law and Policy*, 4(2): 187–202.

Cellan-Jones, Rory (2016), 'Government IT – has the war on waste stalled?'. BBC News, 31 October 2016, https://www.bbc.co.uk/news/technology-37822750 (accessed 21 April 2021).

Centre for Justice Innovation (2018), *The changing use of pre-sentence reports.* July 2018. London: Centre for Justice Innovation, https://justiceinnovation.org/sites/default/files/media/documents/2019-04/cji-changing-use-psr-briefing_wip-1.pdf (accessed 18 March 2020).

Chaney, Paul and Mark Drakeford (2004), 'The Primacy of Ideology: Social Policy and the First Term of the National Assembly for Wales'. *Social Policy Review*, 16: 121–42.

Chaney, Paul, Tom Hall and Andrew Pithouse (2001), *New Governance – New Democracy? Post-devolution Wales.* Cardiff: University of Wales Press.

Charman, Sarah and Stephen Savage (2007), 'Controlling crime and disorder: the Labour legacy', in Martin Powell (ed.), *Modernising the welfare state: The Blair Legacy.* Bristol: Bristol University Press and Policy Press, pp. 105–24.

Chesney-Lind, Meda and Lisa Pasko (2004), *The female offender: Girls, women, and crime.* Thousand Oaks, CA: Sage.

Civil Nuclear Constabulary (2021), *Police in Wales.* Data obtained from Civil Nuclear Constabulary via the Freedom of Information Act 2000.

Clinks (2018), *Under Represented, Under Pressure, Under Resourced: The voluntary sector in Transforming Rehabilitation.* April 2018. TrackTR, a partnership project of Clinks, NCVO and TSRC, monitors voluntary sector involvement in Transforming Rehabilitation London: Clinks, *https://www.clinks.org/sites/default/files/2018-10/clinks_track-tr_ under_final-web.pdf* (accessed 11 February 2020).

Coates, Dame Sally (2016), *Unlocking Potential: A review of education in prison.* May 2016. London: Ministry of Justice, *https://assets.publishing.service.gov.uk/government/uploads/system/ uploads/attachment_data/file/524013/education-review-report.pdf* (accessed 12 August 2020).

Codd, Helen (2008), *In the Shadow of Prison: Families, Imprisonment and Criminal Justice.* Oxford: Routledge.

Cohen-Ennis, Ciara (2021), 'Claims cuts to legal aid has led to "broken" criminal justice system'. ITV News Wales, 11 March 2021, *https://www.itv.com/news/wales/2021-03-11/claims-cuts-to-legal-aid- has-led-to-broken-criminal-justice-system* (accessed 6 April 2021).

Cohen, Jean L. and Andrew Arato (1992), *Civil Society in Political Theory*, Boston. Ma: MIT Press.

Coker, Richard (2020), *Expert Report: Covid-19 and prisons in England and Wales.* April 2020. London: Howard League for Penal Reform, *https://howardleague.org/wp-content/uploads/2020/04/2020_04_01_ COKER_Report_HL_PRT.pdf* (accessed 17 June 2020).

Coles, Deborah (2006), 'Deaths in custody: State violence denied'. *Criminal Justice Matters*, 66: 30–2.

Constitution Unit (1996), *An Assembly for Wales.* London: Constitution Unit, University College London, *https://www.ucl.ac.uk/constitution-unit/sites/constitution-unit/ files/4_1.pdf* (accessed 4 August 2020).

Conteh, Charles (2013), *Policy Governance in Multi-level Systems: Economic Development and Policy Implementation in Canada.* Montreal: McGill-Queen's University Press.

Cornock, David (2017), 'Committee roles for Davies, Davies, Davies (and Davies)'. BBC Wales News, 11 September 2017, *https://www.bbc.co.uk/news/uk-wales-politics-41227347* (accessed 21 July 2020).

Corston, Baroness (2007), *The Corston Report*. London: Home Office, https://webarchive.nationalarchives.gov.uk/20130206102659/http:/www.justice.gov.uk/publications/docs/corston-report-march-2007.pdf (accessed 13 May 2020).

Cosgrove, Faye and Pauline Ramshaw (2015), 'It is what you do as well as the way that you do it: the value and deployment of PCSOs in achieving public engagement'. *Policing and Society*, 25(1): 77–96.

Criminal Justice Alliance (2012), *Crowded Out? The impact of prison overcrowding on rehabilitation*. March 2012. London: Criminal Justice Alliance.

Criminal Justice Joint Inspection (2021a), *Impact of the pandemic on the Criminal Justice System: A joint view of the Criminal Justice Chief Inspectors on the Criminal Justice System's response to Covid-19*. January 2021. London: HM Inspectorate of Prisons, https://www.justiceinspectorates.gov.uk/cjji/wp-content/uploads/sites/2/2021/01/2021-01-13-State-of-nation.pdf (accessed 2 March 2021).

Criminal Justice Joint Inspection (2021b), *About CJJI*. London: Criminal Justice Joint Inspection, https://www.justiceinspectorates.gov.uk/cjji/about-cjji/ (accessed 11 January 2021).

Croall, Hazel, Gerry Mooney and Mary Munro (2010), *Criminal Justice in Scotland*. Abingdon: Willan Publishing.

Croall, Hazel, Gerry Mooney and Mary Munro (2015), *Crime, Justice and Society in Scotland*. London: Routledge.

Croke, Rhian and Jane Williams (2015), *Wales UNCRC Monitoring Group: Report to the United Nations Committee on the Rights of the Child*. Cardiff: Children in Wales. July 2015.

Cross, Sir Rupert and Ashworth, Andrew (1981), *The English Sentencing System*. London: Butterworth & Co Publishers.

Crown Prosecution Service (2011), *Annual Report and Accounts 2010–11*. HC 1000. London: Crown Prosecution Service, https://assets.publishing.service.gov.uk/government/uploads/system/uploads/attachment_data/file/229133/1000.pdf (accessed 1 December 2020).

Crown Prosecution Service (2021a), 'Cymru-Wales'. London: Crown Prosecution Service. https://www.cps.gov.uk/cymruwales (accessed 18 November 2020).

Crown Prosecution Service (2021b), 'The CPS Areas, CPS Direct, CPS Central Casework Divisions and CPS Proceeds of Crime'. London: Crown Prosecution Service, https://www.cps.gov.uk/about-cps/cps-areas-cps-direct-cps-central-casework-divisions-and-cps-proceeds-crime (accessed 8 July 2020).

Cymorth Cymru (2013), *A consultation response from Cymorth Cymru. Consultation on the proposal to amend the duty of a local authority to accommodate a former prisoner as a result of their priority need status*. October 2013. Cardiff: Cymorth Cymru, https://www.cymorthcymru.org.uk/files/7214/3318/8935/Cymorth_Cymru_response_-_removal_of_priority_need_for_ex-offenders.pdf (accessed 25 September 2019).

Davies, Alun (2018a), *Written statement: Policing Board*. Written statement by the Cabinet Secretary for Local Government and Public Services. November 2018. Cardiff: Welsh Government, https://gov.wales/written-statement-policing-board (accessed 6 August 2020).

Davies, Alun (2018b), *Towards a Welsh Justice Policy*. Cabinet Paper. CAB(17-18)44. Cabinet Secretary for Local Government and Public Services. March 2018. Cardiff: Welsh Government, https://www.webarchive.org.uk/wayback/en/archive/20210615102418/https://gov.wales/cabinet-meeting-21-march-2018 (accessed 8 October 2020).

Davies, Darren and Nicholas Williams (2009), *Clear Red Water: Welsh Devolution and Socialist Politics*. London: Francis Boutle.

Deering, John and Jonathan Evans (2021), 'Lost in Translation or a Work in Progress? Developing Desistance-Informed Youth Justice Practice in the Welsh Context'. *British Journal of Social Work*, 51(8) 3172–89.

Deering, John and Martina Feilzer (2015), *Privatising Probation: Is Transforming Rehabilitation the end of the probation ideal?* Bristol: Policy Press.

de Smith, Stanley Alexander (1961), 'Westminster's Export Models: The Legal Framework of Responsible Government'. *Journal of Commonwealth Political Studies*, 1(1): 2–16.

Dehaghani, Roxanna and Daniel Newman (2021), 'The crisis in legally aided criminal defence in Wales: bringing Wales into discussions of England and Wales'. *Legal Studies*, 41(2): 234–51.

Dekeseredy, Walter, Shahid Alvi, Martin Schwartz and Andreas Tomaszewski (2003), *Under Siege: Poverty and Crime in a Public Housing Community*. Maryland: Lexington Books.

Dick, Cressida (2019), 'Policing and trust in the digital age'. John Harris Memorial Lecture 2019. Cressida Dick CBE QPM, Commissioner of the Metropolitan Police. The Police Foundation Annual Lecture. June 2019, https://www.police-foundation.org.uk/past-event/2019-cressida-dick-cbe-qpm-commissioner-of-the-metropolitan-police/ (accessed 6 March 2020).

Drakeford, Mark (2007), 'Devolution and Social Justice in the Welsh Context'. *Benefits*, 19(2): 173–80.

Drakeford, Mark (2009), 'Children first, offenders second: youth justice in a devolved Wales'. *Criminal Justice Matters*, 78: 8–9.

Drakeford, Mark (2010), 'Devolution and youth justice'. *Criminology and Criminal Justice: An International Journal*, 10(2): 137–54.

Drakeford, Mark (2018), *Written Statement – Removal of the Sanction of Imprisonment for the Non-Payment of Council Tax*. Mark Drakeford, Cabinet Secretary for Finance. November 2018, https://gov.wales/written-statement-removal-sanction-imprisonment-non-payment-council-tax (accessed 12 January 2021).

Dunleavy, Patrick and Dominic Muir (2013), *Parliament bounces back – how Select Committees have become a power in the land*. Democratic Audit UK. July 2013, https://www.democraticaudit.com/2013/07/18/parliament-bounces-back-how-select-committees-have-become-a-power-in-the-land/ (accessed 9 February 2021).

Eisner, Chiara (2018), 'Welsh prisons are much harsher than England's on opioid treatment'. *The Economist*, 14 July 2018, https://www.economist.com/britain/2018/07/12/welsh-prisons-are-much-harsher-than-englands-on-opioid-treatment (accessed 24 July 2019).

Edwards, Adam (2002), 'Learning from diversity: the strategic dilemmas of community-based crime control', in Adam Edwards and Gordon Hughes (eds), *Crime control and community: The new politics of public safety*. London: Willan, pp. 140–66.

Elazar, Daniel (1987), *Exploring Federalism*. Tuscaloosa, AL: University of Alabama Press.

Elfleet, Helen (2017), 'Empowered to be Resilient: Neo-Liberal Penal Rhetoric and The Corston Report (2007)'. *Prison Service Journal*, 230: 33–8.

Emsley, Clive (1991), *The English Police: A Political and Social History*. London: Longman.

Emsley, Clive (2007), 'Community Policing/Policing and Communities: Some Historical Perspectives'. *Policing: A Journal of Policy and Practice*, 1 (2): 235–43.

Essex, Sue, Robert Smith and Peter Williams (2008), *Affordable Housing Task and Finish Group*. Report to the Deputy Minister for Housing. June 2008. Cardiff: Welsh Government, https://gov.wales/sites/default/files/publications/2019-05/the-essex-review-supply-of-affordable-housing.pdf (accessed 9 November 2020).

Evans, Adam (2016), 'Wales as nation or region? The Conference on Devolution's Judiciary sub-committee, 1919–20'. *Welsh History Review*, 28(1): 146–73.

Evans, Chris (2020), *During a debate on the Commission on Justice in Wales*. Vol. 670: debated on Wednesday 22 January 2020. Column 148WH. London: House of Commons, https://hansard.parliament.uk/commons/2020-01-22/debates/45A32F4F-4FD7-4AE5-99B6-2780FD13082B/CommissionOnJusticeInWales (accessed 28 January 2020).

Evans, Jonathan, Dusty Kennedy, Tricia Skuse and Jonny Matthew (2020), 'Trauma-informed practice and desistance theories: Competing or complementary approaches to working with children in conflict with the law?'. *Salus Journal – A Journal of Law Enforcement, National Security, and Emergency Management*, 8(2): 55–76.

Evans, Jonathan, Robert Jones and Nerys Musgrove (2021), 'Dragonisation Revisited: A Progressive Criminal Justice Policy in Wales'. *Criminology and Criminal Justice*, 22(4): 636–53.

Expert Panel on Assembly Electoral Reform (2017), *A Parliament that works for Wales*. November 2017. Expert Panel on Assembly Electoral Reform. Cardiff: National Assembly for Wales, https://senedd.wales/media/eqbesxl2/a-parliament-that-works-for-wales.pdf (accessed 28 April 2020).

Explanatory Memorandum to the Welsh Ministers (Transfer of Functions) Order 2009. No. 703, https://www.legislation.gov.uk/uksi/2009/703/pdfs/uksiem_20090703_en.pdf (accessed 15 June 2020).

Field, Stuart (2015), 'Developing local cultures in criminal justice policy-making: The case of youth justice in Wales', in Martin Wasik and Sotirios Santatzoglou (eds), *The Management of Change in Criminal Justice: Who Knows Best?* Basingstoke: Palgrave Macmillan, pp. 170–85.

Finnane, Mark (2016), 'The origins of modern policing', in Alison Liebling, Shadd Maruna and Lesley McAra (eds), *The Oxford Handbook of the History of Crime and Criminal Justice*. Oxford: Oxford University Press, pp. 456–73.

Ford, Kat, Emma Barton, Annemarie Newbury, Karen Hughes, Zoe Bezeczky, Janine Roderick and Mark Bellis (2019), *Understanding the prevalence of adverse childhood experiences (ACEs) in a male offender population in Wales: The Prisoner ACE Survey*. Wrexham: Public Health Collaborating Unit, https://phw.nhs.wales/files/aces/the-prisoner-ace-survey/ (accessed 20 July 2021).

Ford, Matt (2017), 'Trends in criminal justice spending, staffing and populations'. *UK Justice Policy Review FOCUS: Issue 2*. December 2017. London: Centre for Crime and Justice Studies, https://www.crimeandjustice.org.uk/sites/crimeandjustice.org.uk/files/Trends%20in%20criminal%20justice%20spending%2C%20staffing%20and%20populations%2C%20Dec%202017_0.pdf (accessed 3 November 2021).

Freeguard, Gavin, Lucy Campbell, Aron Cheung, Alice Lilly and Charlotte Baker (2018), *Whitehall Monitor 2018: The General Election, Brexit and Beyond*. London: Institute for Government, https://www.instituteforgovernment.org.uk/sites/default/files/publications/5890%20IFG%20-%20Whitehall%20Monitor%202018%20web.pdf (accessed 8 January 2021).

Gardner, David C. (2016), *Administrative Law and the Administrative Court in Wales*. Cardiff: University of Wales Press.

Garland, David (1996), 'Limits of the Sovereign State: Strategies of Crime Control in Contemporary Society'. *British Journal of Criminology*, 36(4): 445–71.

Garland, David (2001), *The Culture of Control*. Oxford: Oxford University Press.

Garside, Richard, Roger Grimshaw, Matt Ford, Neala Hickey and Helen Mills (2020), *UK Justice Policy Review*. Vol. 9. London: Centre for Crime and Justice Studies.

Gauke, David (2019), 'Smarter sentences, safer streets: David Gauke speech'. 18 July 2019. London: Ministry of Justice, *https://www.gov.uk/government/speeches/smarter-sentences-safer-streets* (accessed 13 May 2020).

Geddes, Marc (2018), 'Committee Hearings of the UK Parliament: Who gives Evidence and does this Matter?'. *Parliamentary Affairs*, 71(2): 283–304.

Gofal (2014), *Gofal evidence: Housing (Wales) Bill*. Written evidence submitted to the National Assembly for Wales Communities, Equality and Local Government Committee, Housing (Wales) Bill: Stage 1, *https://business.senedd.wales/documents/s23407/HB%2044%20-%20 Gofal.pdf* (accessed 4 June 2020).

Goffman, Erving (1961), *Asylums: Essays on the Social Situation of Mental Patients and Other Inmates*. London: Penguin.

Goldson, Barry (2010), 'The sleep of (criminological) reason: Knowledge – policy rupture and New Labour's youth justice legacy'. *Criminology and Criminal Justice*, 10(1) 155–78.

Goldson, Barry and Damon Briggs (2021), *Making Youth Justice: Local penal cultures and differential outcomes: lessons and prospects for policy and practice*. London: Howard League for Penal Reform, *https://howardleague.org/wp-content/uploads/2021/03/Making-Youth-Justice.pdf* (accessed 2 December 2021).

Goudriaan, Heike, Karin Wittebrood and Paul Nieuwbeerta (2006), 'Neighbourhood Characteristics and Reporting Crime: Effects of Social Cohesion, Confidence in Police Effectiveness and Socio-Economic Disadvantage'. *British Journal of Criminology*, 46(4): 719–42.

Greater Manchester Combined Authority (2016), *Report of Tony Lloyd, GM Interim Mayor and Liz Treacy, GMCA Monitoring Officer*. Data obtained from the Greater Manchester Combined Authority via the Freedom of Information Act 2000.

Griffiths, Lesley (2014), 'Written submitted by Lesley Griffiths AM, Minister for Local Government and Government Business'. Written evidence submitted to the House of Commons Welsh Affairs Committee's Inquiry on Prisons in Wales and the treatment of Welsh offenders. July 2014, http://data.parliament.uk/WrittenEvidence/CommitteeEvidence.svc/EvidenceDocument/Welsh%20Affairs/Prisons%20in%20Wales%20and%20treatment%20of%20Welsh%20offenders/written/11111.html (accessed 19 August 2021).

Haines, Kevin (2009), 'The Dragonisation of Youth Justice', in Wayne Taylor, Rod Earle and Richard Hester (eds), *Youth Justice Handbook: Theory, Policy and Practice*. Cullompton: Willan Publishing, pp. 231–42.

Haines, Kevin and Stephen Case (2015), *Positive Youth Justice: Children First, Offenders Second*. Bristol: Policy Press.

Haines, Kevin, Stephen Case, Eddie Isles, Ian Rees and Amy Hancock (2004), *Extending Entitlement: Making It Real*. Cardiff: Youth Policy Team, Welsh Assembly Government.

Haines, Kevin, Stephen Case, Katie Davies and Anthony Charles (2013), 'The Swansea Bureau: A model of diversion from the Youth Justice System'. *International Journal of Law, Crime and Justice*, 41(2): 167–87.

Hales, Gavin and Andy Higgins (2016), *Prioritisation in a changing world: seven challenges for policing*. Paper 2. September 2016. London: The Police Foundation, https://www.police-foundation.org.uk/2017/wp-content/uploads/2017/06/changing_world_paper_2.pdf (accessed 17 January 2021).

Hall-Williams, John Eryl (1970), *The English Penal System in Transition*. London: Butterworths.

Hanson, David (2019), *Reforming Outcomes: A review of Offender Education in Wales*. March 2019. Cardiff: Welsh Government, https://gov.wales/sites/default/files/publications/2019-03/reforming-outcomes-a-review-of-offender-education-in-wales_0.pdf (accessed 16 July 2020).

Hawton, Keith, Louise Linsell, Tunde Adeniji, Amir Sariaslan and Seena Fazel (2014), 'Self-harm in prisons in England and Wales: an epidemiological study of prevalence, risk factors, clustering, and subsequent suicide'. *The Lancet*, 383(9923): 1147–54.

Hayward, Will (2019), 'The reality of life inside Wales' prisons'. *Wales Online*, 8 September 2019, https://www.walesonline.co.uk/news/wales-news/parc-prison-jail-inmate-drugs-16722178 (accessed 1 December 2019).

Hazell, Robert (2015), *Devolution and the Future of the Union*. April 2015. London: The Constitution Unit at University College London, https://www.ucl.ac.uk/constitution-unit/sites/constitution-unit/files/4fd7c881.pdf (accessed 4 February 2021).

Health Inspectorate Wales and HM Inspectorate of Prisons (2014), *Memorandum of Understanding between Healthcare Inspectorate Wales (HIW) and Her Majesty's Inspectorate of Prisons (HMIP)*. Caerphilly: Health Inspectorate Wales, https://www.justiceinspectorates.gov.uk/prisons/wp-content/uploads/sites/4/2014/02/mem-understanding-health-wales-hmip.pdf (accessed 4 May 2021).

Henderson, Ailsa and Richard Wyn Jones (2021), *Englishness: The Political Force Transforming Britain*. Oxford: Oxford University Press.

Henrichson, Christian and Ruth Delaney (2012), *The Price of Prisons What Incarceration Costs Taxpayers*. January 2012. New York: Vera Institute of Justice.

Hetherington, Katy (2020), *Ending childhood adversity: a public health approach*. Edinburgh: Public Health Scotland, http://www.healthscotland.scot/media/3107/ending-childhood-adversity-a-public-health-approach.pdf (accessed 6 November 2020).

HM Courts and Tribunals Service (2019), 'Providing a service to Welsh speakers'. 1 March 2019. London: HM Courts and Tribunals Service, https://www.gov.uk/government/news/providing-a-service-to-welsh-speakers (accessed 9 March 2020).

HM Inspectorate of Constabulary Fire & Rescue Services (2018), *Policing and Mental Health: Picking Up the Pieces*. London: HMICFRS, https://www.justiceinspectorates.gov.uk/hmicfrs/wp-content/uploads/policing-and-mental-health-picking-up-the-pieces.pdf (accessed 24 February 2021).

HM Inspectorate of Constabulary and Fire & Rescue Services (2021), *2021/22 PEEL assessment*. London: HMICFRS,

https://www.justiceinspectorates.gov.uk/hmicfrs/peel-assessments/
how-we-inspect/2018-19-peel-assessment/#effectiveness (accessed
24 February 2021).

HM Inspectorate of Constabulary and Fire & Rescue Services, College of
Policing and Independent Office for Police Conduct (2021), *A duty
to protect: Police use of protective measures in cases involving violence
against women and girls*. August 2021. London: HMICFRS.
https://www.justiceinspectorates.gov.uk/hmicfrs/publications/police-
super-complaints-police-use-of-protective-measures-in-cases-of-violence-
against-women-and-girls/ (accessed 22 February 2022).

HM Inspectorate of Prisons (2007), *The mental health of prisoners: a
thematic review of the care and support of prisoners with mental health
needs*. October 2007. London: HM Inspectorate of Prisons,
https://www.justiceinspectorates.gov.uk/hmiprisons/wp-content/uploads/
sites/4/2014/07/Mental-Health.pdf (accessed 6 July 2020).

HM Inspectorate of Prisons (2008), *Report on an unannounced full
follow-up inspection of HMP & YOI Parc*. 7–11 July 2008. London:
HM Inspectorate of Prisons,
https://webarchive.nationalarchives.gov.uk/20130207003519/https:/
www.justice.gov.uk/downloads/publications/inspectorate-reports/hmipris/
prison-and-yoi-inspections/parc/Parc_2008-rps.pdf (accessed 8 July
2020).

HM Inspectorate of Prisons (2010), *Report on a full unannounced
Inspection of HMP Altcourse*. 15–22 January 2010. London:
HM Inspectorate of Prisons,
https://www.justiceinspectorates.gov.uk/prisons/wp-content/uploads/
sites/4/2014/03/Altcourse_2010_rps.pdf (accessed 8 July 2020).

HM Inspectorate of Prisons (2014), *Report on a full unannounced
Inspection of HMP Altcourse*. 9–20 June 2014. London: HM
Inspectorate of Prisons,
https://www.justiceinspectorates.gov.uk/hmiprisons/wp-content/uploads/
sites/4/2014/10/Altcourse-2014-web.pdf (accessed 8 July 2020).

HM Inspectorate of Prisons (2015a), *Report on an unannounced
Inspection of HMP & YOI Stoke Heath*. 13–23 April 2015. London:
HM Inspectorate of Prisons,
https://www.justiceinspectorates.gov.uk/hmiprisons/wp-content/uploads/
sites/4/2015/08/Stoke-Heath-web-2015.pdf (accessed 8 July 2020).

HM Inspectorate of Prisons (2015b), *Changing patterns of substance misuse in adult prisons and service responses: A thematic review.* December 2015. London: HM Inspectorate of Prisons, https://www.justiceinspectorates.gov.uk/hmiprisons/wp-content/uploads/sites/4/2015/12/Substance-misuse-web-2015.pdf (accessed 6 July 2020).

HM Inspectorate of Prisons (2015c), *Written evidence to the National Assembly for Wales' Health and Social Care Committee inquiry into alcohol and substance misuse.* London: HM Inspectorate of Prisons, https://business.senedd.wales/documents/s35735/ASM%2022%20Her%20Majestys%20Chief%20Inspector%20of%20Prisons.pdf (accessed 6 July 2020).

HM Inspectorate of Prisons (2016a), *The impact of distance from home on children in custody: A thematic review by HM Inspectorate of Prisons.* October 2016. London: HM Inspectorate of Prisons, https://www.justiceinspectorates.gov.uk/hmiprisons/wp-content/uploads/sites/4/2016/09/The-impact-of-distance-from-home-on-children-in-custody-Web-2016.pdf (accessed 12 August 2020).

HM Inspectorate of Prisons (2016b), *Report on an inspection visit to court custody facilities in Wales.* 6–31 July. London: HM Inspectorate of Prisons, https://www.justiceinspectorates.gov.uk/hmiprisons/wp-content/uploads/sites/4/2016/02/Wales-court-custody-web-2015.pdf (accessed 11 August 2020).

HM Inspectorate of Prisons (2017), *Annual report 2016/17.* 17 July 2017. London: HM Inspectorate of Prisons, https://www.justiceinspectorates.gov.uk/hmiprisons/wp-content/uploads/sites/4/2017/07/HMIP-AR_2016-17_CONTENT_201017_WEB.pdf (accessed 10 August 2020).

HM Inspectorate of Prisons (2019a), *Report on an unannounced Inspection of HMP Eastwood Park.* 3–17 May 2019. London: HM Inspectorate of Prisons, https://www.justiceinspectorates.gov.uk/hmiprisons/wp-content/uploads/sites/4/2019/08/Eastwood-Park-Web-2019.pdf (accessed 8 July 2020).

HM Inspectorate of Prisons (2019b), *Report on an unannounced inspection of HMP Cardiff by HM Chief Inspector of Prisons.* 15–26 July 2019. London: HM Inspectorate of Prisons, https://www.justiceinspectorates.gov.uk/hmiprisons/wp-content/uploads/sites/4/2019/11/Cardiff-Web-2019.pdf (accessed 8 July 2020).

HM Inspectorate of Prisons (2020a), *Report on a scrutiny visit to HMP Swansea. 25 August and 2–3 September 2020*. London: HM Inspectorate of Prisons, https://www.justiceinspectorates.gov.uk/hmiprisons/wp-content/uploads/sites/4/2020/10/Swansea-SV-web-2020.pdf (accessed 8 July 2020).

HM Inspectorate of Prisons (2020b), *Report on an unannounced inspection of HMYOI Parc. 11–22 November 2019*. London: HM Inspectorate of Prisons, https://www.justiceinspectorates.gov.uk/hmiprisons/wp-content/uploads/sites/4/2020/02/Parc-CYP-web-2019.pdf (accessed 8 July 2020).

HM Inspectorate of Prisons (2020c), *Report on an unannounced inspection of HMP Parc by HM Chief Inspector of Prisons. 11–22 November 2019*. London: HM Inspectorate of Prisons, https://www.justiceinspectorates.gov.uk/hmiprisons/wp-content/uploads/sites/4/2020/03/Parc-web-2019.pdf (accessed 8 July 2020).

HM Inspectorate of Prisons (2021), *What we do*. London: HM Inspectorate of Prisons, https://www.justiceinspectorates.gov.uk/hmiprisons/about-hmi-prisons/ (accessed 18 August 2020).

HM Inspectorate of Probation (2016a), *Transforming Rehabilitation: Early Implementation 4. An independent inspection of the arrangements for offender supervision*. January 2016. Manchester: HM Inspectorate of Probation, https://www.justiceinspectorates.gov.uk/hmiprobation/wp-content/uploads/sites/5/2016/01/TransformingRehabilitation4.pdf (accessed 18 November 2019).

HM Inspectorate of Probation (2016b), *Transforming Rehabilitation: Early Implementation 5. An independent inspection of the arrangements for offender supervision*. May 2016. Manchester: HM Inspectorate of Probation, https://www.justiceinspectorates.gov.uk/hmiprobation/wp-content/uploads/sites/5/2016/05/Transforming-Rehabilitation-5.pdf (accessed 18 November 2019).

HM Inspectorate of Probation (2016c), *A thematic inspection of the provision and quality of services in the community for women who offend*. September 2016. Manchester: HM Inspectorate of Probation, https://www.justiceinspectorates.gov.uk/hmiprobation/wp-content/uploads/sites/5/2016/09/A-thematic-inspection-of-the-provision-and-quality-of-services-in-the-community-for-women-who-offend.pdf (accessed 12 February 2020).

HM Inspectorate of Probation (2017), *2017 Annual Report*. Manchester: HM Inspectorate of Probation, https://www.justiceinspectorates.gov.uk/hmiprobation/wp-content/uploads/sites/5/2017/12/HMI-Probation-Annual-Report-2017lowres-1.pdf (accessed 24 June 2019).

HM Inspectorate of Probation (2018), *Domestic abuse: the work undertaken by Community Rehabilitation Companies (CRCs)*. September 2018. Manchester: HM Inspectorate of Probation, https://www.justiceinspectorates.gov.uk/hmiprobation/wp-content/uploads/sites/5/2018/09/Report-Domestic-Abuse-the-work-undertaken-by-CRCs.pdf (accessed 18 November 2019).

HM Inspectorate of Probation (2019a), *Report of the Chief Inspector of Probation*. March 2019. Manchester: HM Inspectorate of Probation, https://www.justiceinspectorates.gov.uk/hmiprobation/wp-content/uploads/sites/5/2019/03/HMI-Probation-Chief-Inspectors-Report.pdf (accessed 9 January 2020).

HM Inspectorate of Probation (2019b), *An inspection of probation services in the Wales division of Kent, Surrey and Sussex Community Rehabilitation Company*. July 2019. Manchester: HM Inspectorate of Probation, https://www.justiceinspectorates.gov.uk/hmiprobation/wp-content/uploads/sites/5/2019/06/Wales-division-of-KSS-CRC-English-version.pdf (accessed 12 August 2020).

HM Inspectorate of Probation (2020), *Accommodation and support for adult offenders in the community and on release from prison in England*. July 2020. Manchester: HM Inspectorate of Probation, https://www.justiceinspectorates.gov.uk/hmiprobation/wp-content/uploads/sites/5/2020/07/FINAL-Accomodation-Thematic-inspection-report-v1.0.pdf (accessed 14 April 2021).

HM Prison and Probation Service (2020), *The Welsh Language in Prisons: An Overview of the rights and experiences of Welsh speaking prisoners: HMPPS' response to the Welsh Language Commissioner*. September 2020. London: HM Prison and Probation Service, *https://assets.publishing.service.gov.uk/government/uploads/system/uploads/attachment_data/file/927534/The_Welsh_Lanaguage_in_Prisons_-_07-09-20.odt* (accessed 12 March 2021).

HM Prison and Probation Service in Wales (2018), *Written evidence submission to the Senedd's inquiry into Rough Sleeping in Wales.* Cardiff: HM Prison and Probation Service in Wales, *https://business.senedd.wales/documents/s71914/RS09%20-%20Her%20Majestys%20Prison%20and%20Probation%20Service.pdf* (accessed 14 December 2020).

HM Treasury (2015), *Further Devolution to Greater Manchester Combined Authority.* London: HM Treasury, *https://assets.publishing.service.gov.uk/government/uploads/system/uploads/attachment_data/file/508116/Further_Devolution_to_Greater_Manchester_Combined_Authority_FINAL.pdf* (accessed 21 January 2021).

HM Treasury (2019), *Spending Round 2019. Table C.1: Comparability factors applied in this Spending Round.* September 2019. London: HM Treasury, *https://www.gov.uk/government/publications/spending-round-2019-document/spending-round-2019#statistical-annex* (accessed 16 June 2020).

Holloway, Katy and Fiona Brookman (2010), *An Evaluation of the Women's Turnaround Project. Final report prepared for NOMS Cymru.* April 2010. Treforest: University of Glamorgan, *https://pure.southwales.ac.uk/files/1345742/report.pdf* (accessed 15 September 2021).

Holloway, Katy, Kate Williams and Jo Brayford (2017), *Evaluation of the Pan-Wales Women's Triage (The Diversion Scheme).* September 2017. Treforest: University of South Wales.

Holzinger, Owen (2018), *Assembly to debate Police Settlement 2018–19. National Assembly for Wales Research Service.* February 2018. Cardiff: National Assembly for Wales, *https://research.senedd.wales/research-articles/assembly-to-debate-police-settlement-2018-19/* (accessed 18 December 2020).

Home Office (1998), *Tackling drugs to build a better Bri*tain: The Government's ten year strategy for tackling drugs misuse. London: Home Office, *https://assets.publishing.service.gov.uk/government/uploads/system/ uploads/attachment_data/file/259785/3945.pdf* (accessed 16 March 2020).

Home Office (2001a), *Criminal justice: The way ahead*. London: Home Office, *https://assets.publishing.service.gov.uk/government/uploads/system/ uploads/attachment_data/file/250876/5074.pdf* (accessed 16 March 2020).

Home Office (2001b), *Policing a new century: A blueprint for reform*. London: Home Office. *https://assets.publishing.service.gov.uk/government/uploads/system/ uploads/attachment_data/file/250905/policing_survey.pdf* (accessed 16 March 2020).

Home Office (2003a), *Respect and responsibility: Taking a stand against anti-social behaviour*. London: Home Office.

Home Office (2003b), *Prison statistics: England and Wales: 2001*. Presented to Parliament by the Secretary of State for the Home Department by Command of Her Majesty. February 2003. Cm 5743. London: Home Office, *https://assets.publishing.service.gov.uk/government/uploads/system/ uploads/attachment_data/file/251049/5743.pdf* (accessed 16 March 2020).

Home Office (2004a), *Reducing Re-offending: National Action Plan*. London: Home Office, *https://www.nicco.org.uk/userfiles/downloads/024%20-%20Reducing %20Reoffending%20Action%20Plan%202004.pdf* (accessed 16 March 2020).

Home Office (2004b), *Reducing Crime – Changing Lives: The Government's plans for transforming the management of offenders*. London: Home Office.

Home Office (2004c), *Cutting Crime, Delivering Justice: A Strategic Plan for Criminal Justice 2004–08*. London: Home Office, *https://assets.publishing.service.gov.uk/government/uploads/system/ uploads/attachment_data/file/251064/6288.pdf* (accessed 14 March 2020).

Home Office (2004d), *Confident Communities in a Secure Britain: The Home Office Strategic Plan 2004–08*. London: Home Office, *https://assets.publishing.service.gov.uk/government/uploads/system/uploads/attachment_data/file/251067/6287.pdf* (accessed 14 March 2020).

Home Office (2004e), *Building communities, beating crime.* London: Home Office, *https://assets.publishing.service.gov.uk/government/uploads/system/uploads/attachment_data/file/251058/6360.pdf* (accessed 16 March 2020).

Home Office (2006a), *A Five Year Strategy for Protecting the Public and Reducing Re-Offending.* London: Home Office, *https://assets.publishing.service.gov.uk/government/uploads/system/uploads/attachment_data/file/272221/6717.pdf* (accessed 15 March 2020).

Home Office (2006b), *Rebalancing the criminal justice system in favour of the law-abiding majority.* London: Home Office.

Home Office (2018a), *Serious Violence Strategy.* April 2018. London: Home Office, *https://assets.publishing.service.gov.uk/government/uploads/system/uploads/attachment_data/file/698009/serious-violence-strategy.pdf* (accessed 21 May 2020).

Home Office (2018b), *Action Against Hate: The UK Government's plan for tackling hate crime – 'two years on'.* London: Home Office, *https://assets.publishing.service.gov.uk/government/uploads/system/uploads/attachment_data/file/748175/Hate_crime_refresh_2018_FINAL_WEB.PDF* (accessed 21 May 2020).

Home Office (2018c), *Serious and Organised Crime Strategy.* London: Home Office, *https://assets.publishing.service.gov.uk/government/uploads/system/uploads/attachment_data/file/752850/SOC-2018-web.pdf* (accessed 21 May 2020).

Home Office (2020a), *Police recorded crime and outcomes open data tables.* Outcomes open data year ending March 2020 [various years]. Pivot table. London: Home Office, *https://www.gov.uk/government/statistics/police-recorded-crime-open-data-tables* (accessed 8 March 2021).

Home Office (2020b), *Police workforce England and Wales statistics* [multiple years]. Table H1: Police officers, by police force area [multiple years]. London: Home Office, *https://www.gov.uk/government/collections/police-workforce-england-and-wales* (accessed 8 March 2021).

Home Office (2020c), *Police workforce England and Wales statistics* [multiple years]. Table H11 Police community support officers, by police force area and sex [multiple years]. London: Home Office, *https://www.gov.uk/government/collections/police-workforce-england-and-wales* (accessed 8 March 2021).

Home Office (2020d), *Police powers and procedures England and Wales statistics* [multiple years]. Table A.05: Persons arrested for notifiable offences by sex and Police Force Area [multiple years]. London: Home Office, *https://www.gov.uk/government/collections/police-powers-and-procedures-england-and-wales* (accessed 8 March 2021).

Home Office (2020e), *Police powers and procedures England and Wales statistics* [multiple years]. Table SS.13: Persons and vehicles searched under stop and search powers and resultant arrests, by police force area and population, England and Wales. London: Home Office, *https://www.gov.uk/government/collections/police-powers-and-procedures-england-and-wales* (accessed 8 March 2021).

Home Office (2020f), *Stop and Searches per 1,000 population by ethnicity – Wales-only and England-only.* Data obtained from the Home Office via the Freedom of Information Act 2000. London: Home Office.

Home Office (2020g), *Police use of force statistics, England and Wales: April 2019 to March 2020.* Table 16. Number of times tactics were used, by police force and officer perceived ethnicity of person involved, year ending March 2020. London: Home Office, *https://www.gov.uk/government/statistics/police-use-of-force-statistics-england-and-wales-april-2019-to-march-2020* (accessed 8 March 2021).

Home Office (2020h), *Workforce by Region.* Data obtained from the Home Office via the Freedom of Information Act 2000. London: Home Office.

Home Office (2020i), *Abolition of Police and Crime Commissioner in Greater Manchester.* Data obtained from the Home Office via the Freedom of Information Act 2000. London: Home Office.

Home Office (2021), *From harm to hope: A 10-year drugs plan to cut crime and save lives.* London: Home Office.

https://assets.publishing.service.gov.uk/government/uploads/system/uploads/attachment_data/file/1079147/From_harm_to_hope_PDF.pdf (accessed 16 March 2022).

Home Office and Ministry of Justice (2021), *Police, Crime, Sentencing and Courts Bill*. Introduced to the UK Parliament on 9 March 2021. London: Stationary Office, https://publications.parliament.uk/pa/bills/cbill/58-01/0268/200268.pdf (accessed 23 June 2021).

Hood, Roger (1974), 'Some Fundamental Dilemmas of the English Parole System and a Suggestion for an Alternative Structure', in David Thomas (eds), *Parole: Its Implications for the Criminal Justice and Penal Systems*. Cambridge: Cambridge Institute of Criminology.

Hooghe, Liesbet and Gary Marks (2003), 'Unraveling the Central State, but How? Types of Multi-Level Governance'. *The American Political Science Review*, 97(2): 233–43.

Hope, Tim (2001), 'Crime victimisation and inequality in risk society', in Roger Matthews and John Pitts (eds), *Crime, Disorder and Community Safety*. London: Routledge, pp. 193–218.

Hopkins, Kathryn, Noah Uhrig and Matthew Colahan (2016), *Associations between ethnic background and being sentenced to prison in the Crown Court in England and Wales in 2015*. Ministry of Justice Statistical Publication. November 2016. London: Ministry of Justice, https://www.gov.uk/government/uploads/system/uploads/attachment_data/file/568896/associations-between-ethnic-background-being-sentenced-to-prison-in-the-crown-court-in-england-and-wales-2015.pdf (accessed 6 December 2019).

Hough, Mike, Jessica Jacobson and Andrew Millie (2003), *The Decision to Imprison: Sentencing and the Prison Population*. London: Prison Reform Trust.

House of Commons Home Affairs Committee (2013), *Police and Crime Commissioners: power to remove Chief Constables*. Sixth Report of Session 2013–14. July 2013. London: Stationary Office, https://publications.parliament.uk/pa/cm201314/cmselect/cmhaff/487/487.pdf (accessed 21 April 2021).

House of Commons Home Affairs Committee (2018a), *Domestic Abuse*. Ninth Report of Session 2017–19. October 2018. London: Stationary Office, *https://publications.parliament.uk/pa/cm201719/cmselect/cmhaff/ 1015/1015.pdf* (accessed 8 April 2021).

House of Commons Home Affairs Committee (2018b), *Policing for the future*. Tenth Report of Session 2017–19. October 2018. London: Stationary Office, *https://publications.parliament.uk/pa/cm201719/cmselect/cmhaff/ 515/515.pdf* (accessed 8 April 2021).

House of Commons Justice Committee (2008), *Towards Effective Sentencing*. Fifth Report of Session 2007–08. July 2008. London: Stationary Office, *https://publications.parliament.uk/pa/cm200708/cmselect/cmjust/184/ 184.pdf* (accessed 2 April 2021).

House of Commons Justice Committee (2009), *Devolution: A Decade On*. Fifth Report of Session 2008–09. May 2009. London: Stationary Office, *https://publications.parliament.uk/pa/cm200809/cmselect/ cmjust/529/529i.pdf* (accessed 19 November 2019).

House of Commons Justice Committee (2012), *The budget and Structure of the Ministry of Justice*. House of Commons Second Report of Session 2012–13. August 2012. London: Stationary Office, *https://publications.parliament.uk/pa/cm201213/cmselect/ cmjust/97/97ii.pdf* (accessed 15 July 2020).

House of Commons Justice Committee (2013), *Women offenders: after the Corston Report*. Second Report of Session 2013–14. July 2013. London: Stationary Office, *https://www.parliament.uk/globalassets/documents/commons- committees/Justice/Women-offenders.pdf* (accessed 30 July 2020).

House of Commons Justice Committee (2016), *Prison safety*. Sixth Report of Session 2015–16. May 2013. London: Stationary Office, *https://publications.parliament.uk/pa/cm201516/cmselect/ cmjust/625/625.pdf* (accessed 4 November 2020).

House of Commons Justice Committee (2018), *Transforming Rehabilitation*. Ninth Report of Session 2017–19. June 2018. London: Stationary Office, *https://publications.parliament.uk/pa/cm201719/cmselect/ cmjust/482/482.pdf* (accessed 27 May 2020).

House of Commons Justice Committee (2019a), *Prison population 2022: planning for the future*. Sixteenth Report of Session 2017–19. March 2019. London: Stationary Office, https://publications.parliament.uk/pa/cm201719/cmselect/ cmjust/483/483.pdf (accessed 4 November 2020).

House of Commons Justice Committee (2019b), *Prison Governance*. First report of session 2019. October 2019. London: Stationary Office.

House of Commons Justice Committee (2020a), *Coronavirus (COVID-19): The impact on probation services*. Third Report of Session 2019–21. July 2020. London: Stationary Office, https://committees.parliament.uk/publications/1944/documents/ 18919/default/ (accessed 18 September 2020).

House of Commons Justice Committee (2020b), *Coronavirus (Covid-19): The impact on prisons*. Fourth Report of Session 2019–21. July 2020. London: Stationary Office, https://publications.parliament.uk/pa/cm5801/cmselect/ cmjust/299/299.pdf (accessed 18 September 2020).

House of Commons Justice Committee (2020c), *Ageing prison population*. Fifth Report of Session 2019–21. July 2020. London: Stationary Office, https://committees.parliament.uk/publications/2149/documents/ 19996/default/ (accessed 1 March 2021).

House of Commons Public Accounts Committee (2019), *Transforming rehabilitation: progress review*. Ninety-Fourth Report of Session 2017–19. April 2019. London: Stationary Office, https://publications.parliament.uk/pa/cm201719/cmselect/cmpubacc/1747/1747.pdf (accessed 1 March 2021).

House of Commons Public Administration and Constitutional Affairs Committee (2018), *The Minister and the Official: The Fulcrum of Whitehall Effectiveness*. Fifth Report of Session 2017–19. June 2018. London: Stationary Office, https://publications.parliament.uk/pa/cm201719/cmselect/ cmpubadm/497/497.pdf (accessed 16 December 2020).

House of Commons Welsh Affairs Committee (2005), *Police Service, Crime and Anti-Social Behaviour in Wales*. Fourth Report of Session 2004–05. March 2005. London: Stationary Office, https://publications.parliament.uk/pa/cm200405/cmselect/ cmwelaf/46/46ii.pdf (accessed 7 October 2020).

House of Commons Welsh Affairs Committee (2006a), *Proposed Restructuring of the Police Forces in Wales*. Second Report of Session 2005–06. February 2006. London: Stationary Office.

House of Commons Welsh Affairs Committee (2006b), *Current Restructuring of the Police Forces in Wales*. Fifth Report of Session 2005–06. July 2006. London: Stationary Office, https://publications.parliament.uk/pa/cm200506/cmselect/cmwelaf/1418/1418.pdf (accessed 7 October 2020).

House of Commons Welsh Affairs Committee (2007), *Welsh Prisoners in the Prison Estate*. Third Report of Session 2006–07. May 2007. London: Stationary Office, https://publications.parliament.uk/pa/cm200607/cmselect/cmwelaf/74/74.pdf (accessed 14 October 2019).

House of Commons Welsh Affairs Committee (2010a), *Wales and Whitehall*. Eleventh Report of Session 2009–10. March 2010. London: Stationary Office, https://publications.parliament.uk/pa/cm200910/cmselect/cmwelaf/246/246.pdf (accessed 7 October 2020).

House of Commons Welsh Affairs Committee (2010b), *Welsh prisoners in the prison estate: follow-up*. Ninth Report of Session 2009–10. February 2010. London: Stationary Office, https://publications.parliament.uk/pa/cm200910/cmselect/cmwelaf/143/143.pdf (accessed 14 October 2019).

House of Commons Welsh Affairs Committee (2014), *Work of the Police and Crime Commissioners in Wales*. Oral and written evidence. March 2014. London: Stationary Office, https://publications.parliament.uk/pa/cm201314/cmselect/cmwelaf/532-i/532i.pdf (accessed 7 October 2020).

House of Commons Welsh Affairs Committee (2015), *Prisons in Wales and the Treatment of Welsh Offenders*. Fourth Report of Session 2014–15. March 2015. London: Stationary Office, https://publications.parliament.uk/pa/cm201415/cmselect/cmwelaf/113/113.pdf (accessed 14 October 2019).

House of Commons Welsh Affairs Committee (2016), *Pre-legislative scrutiny of the draft Wales Bill: First Report of Session 2015–16*. February 2016. London: Stationary Office, https://publications.parliament.uk/pa/cm201516/cmselect/cmwelaf/449/449.pdf (accessed 28 October 2019).

House of Commons Welsh Affairs Committee (2019), *Prison provision in Wales*. Fourth Report of Session 2017–19. April 2019. London: Stationary Office, https://publications.parliament.uk/pa/cm201719/cmselect/cmwelaf/742/742.pdf (accessed 11 October 2019).

House of Commons Welsh Affairs Committee (2022), *Oral evidence: One-off session on policing in Wales*. 30 March 2022. London: House of Commons. https://committees.parliament.uk/oralevidence/10051/pdf/ (accessed 18 April 2022).

House of Commons Welsh Affairs Committee (2022), *Oral evidence: One-off session on policing in Wales*. 30 March 2022. London: House of Commons. https://committees.parliament.uk/oralevidence/10051/pdf/ (accessed 18 April 2022).

House of Lords Select Committee on the Constitution (2016), *The Union and Devolution*. 10th Report of Session 2015–16. May 2016. London: House of Lords, https://publications.parliament.uk/pa/ld201516/ldselect/ldconst/149/149.pdf (accessed 4 February 2021).

Howard League for Penal Reform (2019), 'Howard League for Penal Reform response to the National Assembly for Wales Health, Social Care and Sport Committee's inquiry into the provision of health and social care in the adult prison estate'. London: Howard League for Penal Reform, https://business.senedd.wales/documents/s90478/HSP20%20-%20Howard%20League%20for%20Penal%20Reform.pdf (accessed 20 November 2019).

Howard League for Penal Reform (2020), 'Child arrests in England and Wales 2019: Research Briefing'. London: Howard League for Penal Reform, https://howardleague.org/wp-content/uploads/2020/12/Child-Arrests-2019-FINAL-online.pdf (accessed 2 June 2020).

Howard League Scotland (2019a), *Written evidence to the Scottish Parliament's Justice Committee's inquiry into the Presumption Against Short Periods of Imprisonment (Scotland) Order 2019*, https://archive2021.parliament.scot/S5_JusticeCommittee/Inquiries/PASS-HowardLeague.pdf (accessed 17 August 2020).

Howard League Scotland (2019b), *Written evidence to the Scottish Parliament's Standards, Procedures and Public Appointments Committee's scrutiny of the Scottish Elections (Franchise and Representation) Bill*, https://archive2021.parliament.scot/S5_Standards/Inquiries/Howard-LeagueScotland.pdf (accessed 17 August 2020).

Howlett, Michael and Joshua Newman (2010), 'Policy analysis and policy work in federal systems: Policy advice and its contribution to evidence-based policy-making in multi-level governance systems'. *Policy and Society*, 29(2): 123–36.

Hughes, Caroline and Iolo Madoc-Jones (2005), 'Meeting the needs of Welsh speaking young offenders'. *Howard Journal of Criminal Justice*, 44(4): 374–86.

Hughes, Caroline, Sarah Dubberley and Julian Buchanan (2012), 'Girls from Wales in the Secure Estate: Sent to Coventry?' *Social Policy and Society*, 11(4): 519–31.

Humphreys, Caroline and Tamsin Stirling (2008), *Necessary but not sufficient: housing and the reduction of re-offending*. Welsh Local Government Association. June 2008, https://senedd.wales/NAfW%20Documents/cc_3__awe_02_-_wlga_necessary_but_not_sufficient-housing_the_reduction_of_reoffending-3.pdf%20-%2009122009/cc_3__awe_02_-_wlga_necessary_but_not_sufficient-housing_the_reduction_of_reoffending-3-English.pdf (accessed 7 August 2019).

Hutt, Jane (2019), *Statement by the Deputy Minister and Chief Whip on International Women's Day*. Senedd Cymru, Plenary, 5 March 2019. Cardiff: Senedd Cymru, https://record.assembly.wales/Plenary/5565#A49303 (accessed 19 March 2019).

Hutt, Jane (2021), *Questions to the Minister for Social Justice*. Plenary, 30 June 2021. Cardiff: Senedd Cymru, https://record.assembly.wales/Plenary/12320#C371057 (accessed 13 July 2021).

Ifan, Guto (2019a), *The Legal Economy in Wales*. May 2019. Cardiff: Wales Governance Centre at Cardiff University, https://www.cardiff.ac.uk/__data/assets/pdf_file/0008/1699217/Legal-Economy-report-FINAL.pdf (accessed 3 June 2019).

Ifan, Guto (2019b), *Fiscal Implications of Devolving Justice*. August 2019. Cardiff: Wales Governance Centre at Cardiff University, https://www.cardiff.ac.uk/__data/assets/pdf_file/0010/1699219/Fiscal-implications-report-FINAL.pdf (accessed 9 September 2019).

Ifan, Guto (2019c), *Public Spending on Justice System for Wales*. August 2019. Cardiff: Wales Governance Centre at Cardiff University, https://www.cardiff.ac.uk/__data/assets/pdf_file/0005/1549094/Public-spending-on-the-justice-system-for-Wales-Final.pdf (accessed 3 June 2019).

Ifan, Guto and Cian Siôn (2019), *Cut to the Bone? An analysis of Local Government finances in Wales, 2009–10 to 2017–18 and the outlook to 2023–24*. Wales Fiscal Analysis. Cardiff: Wales Governance Centre at Cardiff University, https://www.cardiff.ac.uk/__data/assets/pdf_file/0010/1448920/local_government_finance_report_Feb19_final.pdf (accessed 1 April 2019).

Independent Anti-Slavery Commissioner (2019), *Independent Anti-Slavery Commissioner Strategic Plan 2019–2021*. Presented to Parliament pursuant to Section 42 (10) (a) of the Modern Slavery Act 2015. October 2019. London: Stationary Office, https://www.antislaverycommissioner.co.uk/media/1329/independent-anti-slavery-commissioners-strategic-plan-19-21-screen-readable.pdf (accessed 7 July 2020).

Independent Monitoring Board (2020), *Annual Report of the Independent Monitoring Board at HMP Berwyn for reporting Year 1 March 2019 to 29 February 2020*. September 2020. https://s3-eu-west-2.amazonaws.com/imb-prod-storage-1ocod6bqky0vo/uploads/2020/09/AR-Berwyn-2019-20-for-circulation.pdf (accessed 4 February 2021).

INQUEST (2014), *Preventing the deaths of women in prison: the need for an alternative approach*. January 2014. London: INQUEST, https://www.inquest.org.uk/Handlers/Download.ashx?IDM-F=163ade66-0574-4f07-999b-b9b4fbf7f233 (accessed 28 October 2020).

Institute for Government (2019), *Location of the civil service*. London: Institute for Government, https://www.instituteforgovernment.org.uk/explainers/location-of-civil-service (accessed 8 May 2020).

Ireland, Richard (2015), *Land of White Gloves? A History of Crime and Punishment in Wales*. Abingdon: Routledge.

Jackson, Ceri (2018a), 'Making Murderers'. BBC News, 18 February 2018, https://www.bbc.co.uk/news/resources/idt-sh/Lynette_White_Cardiff_Murder (accessed 2 December 2019).

Jackson, Rebecca (2018b), *Trapped on the Streets: Understanding rough sleeping in Wales.* Swansea: Shelter Cymru, https://sheltercymru.org.uk/wp-content/uploads/2018/09/Trapped-on-the-Streets-Full-Report.pdf (accessed 27 July 2019).

Jahanshahi, Babak, Kath Murray and Susan McVie (2021), 'ACEs, places and inequality: Understanding the effects of adverse childhood experiences and poverty on offending in childhood'. *British Journal of Criminology*, 62(3): 751–72.

James, Julie (2019a), *Access to Justice and Human Rights.* Supplementary evidence of the Welsh Government to the Commission on Justice in Wales. Julie James AM, Leader of the House. Cardiff: Welsh Government, https://gov.wales/sites/default/files/publications/2018-09/Supplementary-evidence-to-the-justice-commission-from-welsh-government-access-to-justice-and-human-rights.pdf (accessed 13 January 2020).

James, Julie (2019b), *Letter from the Welsh Government's Minister for Housing and Local Government to the Chair of the National Assembly Cross Party Group on Faith* (Darren Miller MS). 15 February 2019. Cardiff: Welsh Government.

James, Julie (2020), *Written Statement: Final Police Settlement 2020–21.* January 2020. Cardiff: Welsh Government, https://gov.wales/written-statement-final-police-settlement-2020-21 (accessed 21 February 2020).

Johnston, Neil and Benjamin Politowski (2016), *Police Funding.* House of Commons Library Briefing Paper No. 7259, 25 February 2016. London: House of Commons, https://researchbriefings.files.parliament.uk/documents/CBP-7279/CBP-7279.pdf (accessed 7 October 2020).

Jones, Carwyn (2008), 'The Law in Wales: The Next Ten Years', *The Law Society Annual Lecture*, National Eisteddfod of Wales.

Jones, David (2013), 'Wales in the continuing union'. Speech given by the Wales Secretary at the Wales Governance Centre at Cardiff University's Annual Lecture. June 2013. Cardiff: Wales Governance Centre at Cardiff University, https://www.gov.uk/government/speeches/welsh-secretary-delivers-wales-in-the-continuing-union-speech--2 (accessed 4 January 2019).

Jones, Kathryn and Steve Eaves (2007), *The Provision of Welsh language Choice in the North Wales Criminal Justice Sector*. Carmarthen: Welsh Language Board.

Jones, Mark Ellis (1998), 'An invidious attempt to accelerate the abolition of our language: The abolition of the Court of Great Sessions and the Welsh language'. *Welsh History Review*, 19(2): 226–64.

Jones, Robert (2017), 'The Hybrid System: Imprisonment and Devolution in Wales'. Unpublished thesis. Cardiff: Cardiff University.

Jones, Robert (2018a), *Imprisonment in Wales: A Factfile*. June 2018. Cardiff: Wales Governance Centre at Cardiff University, https://www.cardiff.ac.uk/__data/assets/pdf_file/0008/1195577/Imprisonment-in-Wales-A-Factfile.pdf (accessed 5 March 2019).

Jones, Robert (2018b), *Imprisonment in Wales: A Breakdown by Local Authority*. August 2018. Cardiff: Wales Governance Centre at Cardiff University, https://www.cardiff.ac.uk/__data/assets/pdf_file/0010/1286992/Imprisonment-in-Wales-A-Local-Authority-Breakdown-.pdf (accessed 5 March 2019).

Jones, Robert (2019a), *Sentencing and Immediate Custody in Wales: A Factfile*. January 2019. Cardiff: Wales Governance Centre at Cardiff University, https://www.cardiff.ac.uk/__data/assets/pdf_file/0010/1417339/Sentencing-and-Immediate-Custody-in-Wales-A-Factfile-140119.pdf (accessed 5 March 2019).

Jones, Robert (2019b), *Sentencing and Imprisonment in Wales: 2018 Factfile*. August 2019. Cardiff: Wales Governance Centre at Cardiff University, https://www.cardiff.ac.uk/__data/assets/pdf_file/0004/1547914/WGC-Report-SentencingandImprisonment04.pdf (accessed 10 September 2019).

Jones, Robert (2019c), *Written evidence submitted to the National Assembly's Health, Social Care and Sport Committee's inquiry into the Provision of health and social care in the adult prison estate*. Cardiff: Wales Governance Centre at Cardiff University, https://www.cardiff.ac.uk/__data/assets/pdf_file/0009/1468512/WRITTEN-EVIDENCE-THE-PROVISION-OF-HEALTH-AND-SOCIAL-CARE-IN-THE-ADULT-PRISON-ESTATE.pdf (accessed 10 September 2019).

Jones, Robert (2020a), *Covid-19 and Imprisonment in Wales*. April 2020. Cardiff: Wales Governance Centre at Cardiff University, https://www.cardiff.ac.uk/__data/assets/pdf_file/0012/2205300/Covid-19-and-Imprisonment-in-Wales-April-2020-FINAL.pdf (accessed 1 May 2020).

Jones, Robert (2020b), *Prison, Probation and Sentencing in Wales: 2019 Factfile*. September 2020. Cardiff: Wales Governance Centre at Cardiff University, https://www.cardiff.ac.uk/__data/assets/pdf_file/0010/2446129/Prison,-Probation-and-Sentencing-in-Wales-2019-Factfile.pdf (accessed 23 September 2020).

Jones, Robert (2020c), 'Criminology and criminal justice in post-devolution Wales'. *European Journal of Criminology*. 19(4): 811–29.

Jones, Robert and Richard Wyn Jones (2019), *Justice at the Jagged Edge in Wales*. March 2019. Cardiff: Wales Governance Centre at Cardiff University, https://www.cardiff.ac.uk/__data/assets/pdf_file/0006/1699215/Justice-at-the-Jagged-Edge.pdf (accessed 30 March 2019).

Jones, Robert, Richard Wyn Jones, Huw Pritchard and Luke Nicholas (2019), *International evidence on driving down imprisonment rates: What Wales could be?* September 2019. Cardiff: Wales Governance Centre at Cardiff University, https://www.cardiff.ac.uk/__data/assets/pdf_file/0015/1701402/International-Evidence-on-Driving-Down-Imprisonment-Rates.pdf (accessed 9 October 2019).

Jones, Robert, Jonathan Evans and Kevin Haines (2021), 'The Criminal Justice System in Wales', in Steve Case, Phil Johnson, David Malow, Roger Smith and Kate Williams (eds), *The Oxford Textbook on Criminology*. Second Edition. Oxford: Oxford University Press. [Online].

Jones, Robert, Michael Harrison and Trevor Jones (2022), 'Policing and Devolution in the UK: The 'Special' Case of Wales'. *Policing: A Journal of Policy and Practice*. 1–13. DOI: https://doi.org/10.1093/police/paac063.

Jones, Timothy and Jane Williams (2004), 'Wales as a Jurisdiction'. *Public Law*, 2: 78–101.

Joseph Rowntree Foundation (1996), *The Housing Needs of Ex-Prisoners*. Housing Research 178. April 1996. York: The Joseph Rowntree Foundation.

Jukes, Matt (2018), *Written evidence submission to the Commission on Justice in Wales*. Chief Constable, South Wales Police Chair of the Welsh Chief Officers Group. June 2018. https://gov.wales/sites/default/files/publications/2019-01/Submission%20to%20Commission%20on%20Justice%20in%20Wales%20from%20the%20Welsh%20Chief%20Constables.pdf (accessed 4 February 2020).

Kaleidoscope (2017), 'Why we want to set up drug consumption rooms'. November 2017. St Mellons: Kaleidoscope, http://www.kaleidoscopeproject.org.uk/2017/11/02/want-set-drug-consumption-rooms-dcr/ (accessed 13 July 2020).

Kelly-Irving, Michelle and Cyrille Delpierre (2019), 'A Critique of the Adverse Childhood Experiences Framework in Epidemiology and Public Health: Uses and Misuses'. *Social Policy and Society*, 18(3): 445–56.

Kelso, Alexandra (2009), *Parliamentary Reform at Westminster*. Manchester: Manchester University Press.

Kenny, Michael, Philp Rycroft and Jack Sheldon (2021), 'Union at the Crossroads Can the British state handle the challenges of devolution?' Bennett Institute and The Constitution Society Report, https://consoc.org.uk/publications/union-at-the-crossroads-can-the-british-state-handle-the-challenges-of-devolution-by-michael-kenny-philip-rycroft-and-jack-sheldon/ (accessed 12 October 2021).

Labour Party (2017), *For the Many, Not the Few*. The Labour Party Manifesto 2017. London: The Labour Party, https://labour.org.uk/wp-content/uploads/2017/10/labour-manifesto-2017.pdf (accessed 26 November 2021).

Labour Party (2019), *It's Time for Real Change*. The Labour Party Manifesto 2019. London: The Labour Party, https://labour.org.uk/wp-content/uploads/2019/11/Real-Change-Labour-Manifesto-2019.pdf (accessed 26 November 2021).

Lahman, Maria K. E., Katrina L. Rodriguez, Lindsey Moses, Krista M. Griffin, Bernadette M. Mendoza and Wafa Yacoub (2015), 'A Rose by Any Other Name is Still a Rose? Problematising Pseudonyms in Research'. *Qualitative Inquiry*, 21(5): 445–53.

Lammy, David (2017), *The Lammy Review. An independent review into the treatment of, and outcomes for, Black, Asian and Minority Ethnic individuals in the Criminal Justice System*. September 2017. London: Lammy Review, *https://assets.publishing.service.gov.uk/government/uploads/system/uploads/attachment_data/file/643001/lammy-review-final-report.pdf* (accessed 11 February 2020).

Lea, John and Jock Young (1984), *What is to be Done about Law and Order?* London: Penguin.

Lewer, Dan, Emma King, Glen Bramley, Suzanne Fitzpatrick, Morag Treanor, Nick Maguire, Miriam Bullock, Andrew Hayward and Al Story (2020), 'The ACE Index: mapping childhood adversity in England'. *Journal of Public Health*, 42(4): 487–95.

Lewis, Emyr (2015), *Observations submitted to the Joint Meeting of the Constitutional and Legal Affairs Committee of the National Assembly for Wales and the Welsh Affairs Committee of the House of Commons*. Cardiff: National Assembly for Wales, *https://busnes.senedd.cymru/documents/s45768/DWB%202%20-%20Emyr%20Lewis.pdf* (accessed 23 April 2020).

Lewis, Emyr (2019), 'Bydded cyfiawnder! Ffarwel i "EnglandandWales"', *Transactions of the Honourable Society of Cymmrodorion* (new series), 25: 117–30.

Lewis, Robyn (1998), *Cyfiawnder dwyieithog? Golwg ar yr ieithoedd Cymraeg a Saesneg yn Llysoedd Ynadon Cymru/Bilingual justice? A view of the Welsh and English languages in the Magistrates' Courts of Wales*. Llandysul: Gomer.

Liebling, Alison, David Price and Guy Shefer (2010), *The Prison Officer*. London: Routledge.

Light, Miriam, Eli Grant and Kathryn Hopkins (2013), *Gender differences in substance misuse and mental health amongst prisoners: Results from the Surveying Prisoner Crime Reduction (SPCR) longitudinal cohort study of prisoners*. London: Ministry of Justice, *https://assets.publishing.service.gov.uk/government/uploads/system/uploads/attachment_data/file/220060/gender-substance-misuse-mental-health-prisoners.pdf* (accessed 16 April 2020).

Lijphart, Arend (1984), *Democracies: Patterns of Majoritarian and Consensus Government in Twenty-One Countries*. New Haven, CT: Yale University Press.

Lijphart, Arend (1999), *Patterns of Democracy: Government Forms and Performance in Thirty-Six Countries*. New Haven, CT: Yale University Press.

Loader, Ian (2006), 'Fall of the "Platonic Guardians" Liberalism: Criminology and Political Responses to Crime in England and Wales'. *British Journal of Criminology*, 46(4): 561–86.

Loader, Ian and Aogan Mulcahy (2003), *Politics and the Condition of England: Memory, Politics and Culture*. Oxford: Oxford University Press.

Loveday, Barry and Richard Smith (2015), 'A critical evaluation of current and future roles of police community support officers and neighbourhood wardens within the Metropolitan Police Service and London boroughs: Utilising "low-cost high-value" support services in a period of financial austerity'. *International Journal of Police Science & Management*, 17(2): 74–80.

Lowe, Trudy, Helen Innes, Martin Innes and Daniel Grinnell (2015), *The work of Welsh Government funded Community Support Officers*. February 2015. Merthyr Tydfil: Welsh Government, https://orca.cf.ac.uk/88880/1/150226-wg-funded-community-support-officers-en.pdf (accessed 12 September 2019).

McAlinden, Anne-Marie and Clare Dwyer (2015), *Criminal Justice in Transition: The Northern Ireland Context*. Oxford: Hart Publishing.

McAllister, Laura (2005), 'The Value of Independent Commissions: An Insider's Perspective on the Richard Commission'. *Parliamentary Affairs*, 58(1): 38–52.

McAra, Lesley (2006), 'Welfare in crisis? Youth Justice in Scotland', in John Muncie and Barry Goldson (eds), *Comparative Youth Justice*. London: SAGE, pp. 127–45.

McAra, Lesley (2008), 'Crime, Criminology and Criminal Justice in Scotland'. *European Journal of Criminology*, 5(4): 481–504.

McAra, Lesley and Susan McVie (2015), 'The Scottish juvenile justice system policy and practice', in John Winterdyk (ed.), *Juvenile Justice: International Perspectives, Models and Trends*. Boca Raton, FL: CRC Press, pp. 263–94.

McConville, Seán (1981), *A History of English Prison Administration: Volume I. 1750–1877*. London: Routledge and Kegan Paul.

McEvoy, Kieran (2001), *Paramilitary Imprisonment in Northern Ireland: Resistance, Management and Release*. Oxford: Oxford University Press.

McEwen, Nicola, Michael Kenny, Jack Sheldon and Coree Brown Swan (2020), 'Intergovernmental Relations in the UK: Time for a Radical Overhaul'. *The Political Quarterly*, 9(3): 632–40.

McGarry, John and Brendan O'Leary (1999), *Policing Northern Ireland: Proposals for a New Start*. Belfast: Blackstaff.

McGivern, Mark (2021), 'Scotland will introduce life saving drug consumption rooms and defy UK says minister'. *Daily Record*, 4 August 2021, https://www.dailyrecord.co.uk/news/scottish-news/scotland-introduce-life-saving-drug-24682249 (accessed 2 November 2021).

Mackie, Peter (2015), 'Homelessness Prevention and the Welsh Legal Duty: Lessons for International Policies'. *Housing Studies*, 30(1): 40–59.

Mackie, Peter (2017), *Written evidence to the National Assembly for Wales' Equality, Local Government and Communities Committee's inquiry into Rough Sleeping in Wales*, http://senedd.assembly.wales/documents/s71916/RS11%20-%20Peter%20Mackie.pdf (accessed 5 November 2019).

Mackie, Peter and Simon Hoffman (2011), *Homelessness legislation in Wales: stakeholder perspectives on potential improvements*. Project Report. Cardiff: Welsh Government.

Mackie, Peter, Ian Thomas and Kate Hodgson (2012), *Impact analysis of existing homelessness legislation in Wales: A report to inform the review of homelessness legislation in Wales*. January 2012. Cardiff: Cardiff University, http://www.senedd.assembly.wales/documents/s7352/Impact%20analysis%20of%20existing%20homelessness%20legislation%20in%20Wales.pdf (accessed 5 November 2019).

Mackie, Peter, Tim Gray, Caroline Hughes, Iolo Madoc-Jones, Victoria Mousteri, Hal Pawson, Nick Spyropoulos, Tamsin Stirling, Helen Taylor and Beth Watts (2020), *Review of Priority Need in Wales*. Cardiff: Welsh Government, GSR report number 70/2020, https://gov.wales/sites/default/files/statistics-and-research/2020-10/review-of-priority-need-in-wales.pdf (accessed 7 November 2019).

Mackintosh, John P. (1970), *The Government and Politics of Britain*. London: Hutchinson.

McLaughlin, Eugene, John Muncie and Gordon Hughes (2001), 'The Permanent Revolution: New Labour, New Public Management and the Modernization of Criminal Justice'. *Criminal Justice*, 1(3): 301–18.

Macpherson, Lord (1999), *The Stephen Lawrence Inquiry: Report of an inquiry by Sir William Macpherson of Cluny*. London: Stationary Office, https://assets.publishing.service.gov.uk/government/uploads/system/uploads/attachment_data/file/277111/4262.pdf (accessed 13 May 2020).

McWilliams, William (1986), 'The English Probation System and the Diagnostic Ideal'. *Howard Journal of Criminal Justice*, 25(4): 241–60.

Madoc-Jones, Iolo and Julian Buchanan (2003), 'Welsh language, identity and probation practice: The context for change'. *Probation Journal*, 50(3): 225–38.

Madoc-Jones, Iolo, Caroline Hughes, Sarah Dubberley, Caroline Gorden, Karen Washington-Dyer, Fiona Wilson, Anya Ahmed, Kelly Lockwood and Mark Wilding (2018a), *Evaluation of homelessness services to adults in the secure estate: Main findings report*. June 2018. Cardiff: Welsh Government, https://gov.wales/sites/default/files/statistics-and-research/2019-06/180627-evaluation-homelessness-services-adults-secure-estate-en.pdf (accessed 5 November 2019).

Madoc-Jones, Iolo, Wulf Livingston and Caroline Hughes (2018b), *Written evidence submission to the Commission on Justice in Wales*. June 2018. Wrexham: Glyndŵr University, https://gov.wales/sites/default/files/publications/2018-06/Submission-from-dr-iolo-madoc-jones-and-dr-wulf-livingston-and-dr-caroline-hughes.pdf (accessed 19 February 2020).

Maguire, Mike and Jane Nolan (2007), 'Accommodation and related services for ex-prisoners', in Anthea Hucklesby and Lystra Hagley-Dickinson (eds), *Prisoner Resettlement: Policy and Practice*. Oxford: Willan Publishing, pp. 144–73.

Maguire, Mike, Katy Holloway, Mark Liddle, Fionn Gordon, Paul Gray, Alison Smith and Sam Wright (2010), *Evaluation of the Transitional Support Scheme (TSS)*. Final report to Welsh Assembly Government, https://gov.wales/sites/default/files/statistics-and-research/2019-09/101108-transitional-support-scheme-summary-en.pdf (accessed 4 March 2020).

Marshall, Brandon, Michael J. Milloy, Evan Wood, Julio Montaner and Thomas Kerr (2011), 'Reduction in overdose mortality after the opening of North America's first medically supervised safer injecting facility: a retrospective population-based study'. *Lancet*, 377 (9775): 1429–37.

Mawby, Robert (2004), 'Myth and reality in rural policing: Perceptions of the police in a rural county of England'. *Policing: An International Journal of Police Strategies and Management*, 27(3): 431–46.

May, Josh (2015), 'Frank Field: Committee chairmanship more important than Cabinet post'. *Politics Home*, June 2015.

Mears, Daniel, Joshua Cochran, Sonja Siennick and William Bales (2012), 'Prison Visitation and Recidivism'. *Justice Quarterly*, 29(6): 888–918.

Merritt, Jonathan (2010), 'W(h)ither the PCSO? Police Perceptions of the Police Community Support Officer's Role, Powers and Future Directions'. *Policing: An International Journal of Police Strategies & Management*, 33(4): 731–49.

Millie, Andrew, Jessica Jacobson and Mike Hough (2003), 'Understanding the growth in the prison population in England and Wales'. *Criminal Justice*, 3(4): 369–87.

Milloy, Michael J. and Evan Wood (2009), 'Emerging role of supervised injecting facilities in human immunodeficiency virus prevention'. *Addiction*, 104(4): 620–1.

Ministry of Defence Police (2017), *Police in Wales*. Data obtained from the Ministry of Justice via the Freedom of Information Act 2000.

Ministry of Justice (2013a), *Press Release: 'Modernisation of the Prison Estate'*. 4 September 2013. London: Ministry of Justice, https://www.gov.uk/government/news/modernisation-of-the-prison-estate (accessed 10 January 2019).

Ministry of Justice (2013b), *Transforming Rehabilitation: A Strategy for Reform*. May 2013. London: Ministry of Justice, https://consult.justice.gov.uk/digital-communications/transforming-rehabilitation/results/transforming-rehabilitation-response.pdf (accessed 6 February 2019).

Ministry of Justice (2014a), *Prison population figures: 2013* [multiple months]. London: Ministry of Justice, https://www.gov.uk/government/statistics/prison-population-figures (accessed 2 April 2019).

Ministry of Justice (2014b), *Written evidence submitted by the Ministry of Justice to the House of Commons Welsh Affairs Committee's Inquiry on Prisons in Wales and the Treatment of Welsh Offenders*. July 2014. London: Ministry of Justice, http://data.parliament.uk/WrittenEvidence/CommitteeEvidence.svc/ EvidenceDocument/Welsh%20Affairs/Prisons%20in%20Wales%20 and%20treatment%20of%20Welsh%20offenders/written/11128.html (accessed 11 March 2019).

Ministry of Justice (2014c), *List of Resettlement Prisons*. London: Ministry of Justice, https://assets.publishing.service.gov.uk/government/uploads/system/ uploads/attachment_data/file /387197/resettlement-prison-list.pdf (accessed 6 February 2019).

Ministry of Justice (2016a), *Prison Safety and Reform*. November 2016. London: Ministry of Justice, https://assets.publishing.service.gov.uk/government/uploads/system/ uploads/attachment_data/file/565014/cm-9350-prison-safety-and-reform-_web_.pdf (accessed 4 June 2020).

Ministry of Justice (2016b), *The government response to Charlie Taylor's Review of the Youth Justice System*. December 2016. London: Ministry of Justice, https://assets.publishing.service.gov.uk/government/uploads/system/ uploads/attachment_data/file/576554/youth-justice-review-government-response-print.pdf (accessed 16 June 2020).

Ministry of Justice (2017), *Report of the Justice in Wales Working Group*. September 2017. London: Ministry of Justice.

Ministry of Justice (2018a), *Female Offender Strategy*. June 2018. London: Ministry of Justice, https://assets.publishing.service.gov.uk/government/uploads/system/ uploads/attachment_data/file/719819/female-offender-strategy.pdf (accessed 4 June 2020).

Ministry of Justice (2018b), *Victims Strategy*. September 2018. London: Ministry of Justice, https://assets.publishing.service.gov.uk/government/uploads/system/ uploads/attachment_data/file/746930/victim-strategy.pdf (accessed 4 June 2020).

Ministry of Justice (2018c), *Strengthening Probation, Building Confidence*. Consultation document. July 2018. London: Ministry of Justice, https://consult.justice.gov.uk/hm-prisons-and-probation/strengthening-probation-building-confidence/supporting_documents/strengtheningprobationbuildingconfidence.pdf (accessed 6 February 2019).

Ministry of Justice (2020a), *Criminal Justice System statistics quarterly: December 2019. Principal offence proceedings and outcomes by Home Office offence code data tool*. London: Ministry of Justice, https://assets.publishing.service.gov.uk/government/uploads/system/uploads/attachment_data/file/888344/HO-code-tool-principal-offence-2019.xlsx (accessed 2 March 2021).

Ministry of Justice (2020b), *Welsh people in prison (based on home address prior to entering custody) broken down by sentence length* [multiple years]. Data obtained from the Ministry of Justice via the Freedom of Information Act 2000.

Ministry of Justice (2020c), *Radical sentencing overhaul to cut crime*. 16 September 2020. London: Ministry of Justice, https://www.gov.uk/government/news/radical-sentencing-overhaul-to-cut-crime (accessed 24 October 2020).

Ministry of Justice (2020d), *Welsh people in prison [based on home address prior to entering custody]* [multiple years]. Data obtained from the Ministry of Justice via the Freedom of Information Act 2000.

Ministry of Justice (2020e), *English people in prison [based on home address prior to entering custody]* [multiple years]. Data obtained from the Ministry of Justice via the Freedom of Information Act 2000.

Ministry of Justice (2020f), *Welsh prisoners by ethnicity*. Data obtained from the Ministry of Justice via the Freedom of Information Act 2000.

Ministry of Justice (2020g), *Proportion of sentence served by Welsh prisoners broken down by ethnicity. Welsh prisoners by ethnicity*. Data obtained from the Ministry of Justice via the Freedom of Information Act 2000.

Ministry of Justice (2020h), *Proportion of sentence served by English prisoners broken down by ethnicity. Welsh prisoners by ethnicity*. Data obtained from the Ministry of Justice via the Freedom of Information Act 2000.

Ministry of Justice (2020i), *Prison population figures: 2019* [multiple months]. London: Ministry of Justice, *https://www.gov.uk/government/statistics/prison-population-figures-2019* (accessed 7 March 2020).

Ministry of Justice (2020j), *Criminal Justice System statistics quarterly: December 2019.* Court outcomes by Police Force Area data tool. London: Ministry of Justice, *https://assets.publishing.service.gov.uk/government/uploads/system/uploads/attachment_data/file/938553/court-outcomes-by-PFA-2019.xlsx* (accessed 2 March 2021).

Ministry of Justice (2020k), *Pre-sentence Reports in Wales* [multiple years]. Data obtained from the Ministry of Justice via the Freedom of Information Act 2000.

Ministry of Justice (2020l), *Concordance between sentences proposed and given where a Pre-Sentence Report was prepared, 2019, Wales.* Data obtained from the Ministry of Justice via the Freedom of Information Act 2000.

Ministry of Justice (2020m), *Concordance between sentences proposed and given where a Pre-Sentence Report was prepared, 2019, England.* Data obtained from the Ministry of Justice via the Freedom of Information Act 2000.

Ministry of Justice (2020n), *Probation* [multiple periods]. Table 4.8: Offenders supervised by the Probation Service on 31 December 2019, by National Probation Service region, division and Community Rehabilitation Company, England and Wales, *https://www.gov.uk/government/collections/offender-management-statistics-quarterly* (accessed 2 March 2021).

Ministry of Justice (2020o), *Proven reoffending statistics quarterly bulletin, October 2018 to December 2018.* October 2020. London: Ministry of Justice, *https://assets.publishing.service.gov.uk/government/uploads/system/uploads/attachment_data/file/849200/statistics-on-race-and-the-cjs-2018.pdf* (accessed 2 March 2021).

Ministry of Justice (2020p), *Proven reoffending statistics: October to December 2018.* Proven reoffending geographical data tool. London: Ministry of Justice, *https://assets.publishing.service.gov.uk/government/uploads/system/uploads/attachment_data/file/930450/Geographical_data_tool_jan08_dec18_final.xlsx* (accessed 2 March 2021).

Ministry of Justice (2020q), *Welsh women in prison (based on home address prior to entering custody)* [multiple years]. Data obtained from the Ministry of Justice via the Freedom of Information Act 2000.

Ministry of Justice (2020r), *Probation supervision by sex in Wales.* Data obtained from the Ministry of Justice via the Freedom of Information Act 2000.

Ministry of Justice (2020s), *English women in prison (based on home address prior to entering custody)* [multiple years]. Data obtained from the Ministry of Justice via the Freedom of Information Act 2000.

Ministry of Justice (2020t), *Story of the Prison Population 1993–2020*. London: Ministry of Justice, *https://assets.publishing.service.gov.uk/government/uploads/system/uploads/attachment_data/file/930166/Story_of_the_Prison_Population_1993-2020.pdf* (accessed 4 March 2021).

Ministry of Justice (2020u), *Safety in custody: quarterly update to December 2019*. Table 2.1: Annual self-harm, summary statistics, England and Wales, 2004–2019, *https://www.gov.uk/government/statistics/safety-in-custody-quarterly-update-to-december-2019* (accessed 5 March 2021).

Ministry of Justice (2020v), *Safety in custody quarterly: update to September 2019*. Table 1.5: Self-inflicted deaths in prison custody and rates by gender since 1978, England and Wales, *https://www.gov.uk/government/statistics/safety-in-custody-quarterly-update-to-september-2019* (accessed 5 March 2021).

Ministry of Justice (2020w), *Funding boost to steer more women away from crime*. 4 May 2020. London: Ministry of Justice, *https://www.gov.uk/government/news/funding-boost-to-steer-more-women-away-from-crime* (accessed 9 June 2020).

Ministry of Justice (2020x), *Welsh women in prison (based on home address prior to entering custody) broken down by sentence type.* Data obtained from the Ministry of Justice via the Freedom of Information Act 2000.

Ministry of Justice (2020y), *Incidents at Young Offender Institutions in England and Wale*s [multiple years]. Data obtained from the Ministry of Justice via the Freedom of Information Act 2000.

Ministry of Justice (2020z), *Criminal Justice System statistics quarterly: September 2019.* First Time Entrants Data Tool, *https://www.gov.uk/government/statistics/criminal-justice-system-statistics-quarterly-september-2019* (accessed 2 March 2021).

Ministry of Justice (2020zi), *Workforce – all organisations*. Data obtained from the Ministry of Justice via the Freedom of Information Act 2000.

Ministry of Justice (2020zii), *Justice Devolution Team*. Data obtained from the Ministry of Justice via the Freedom of Information Act 2000.

Ministry of Justice (2020ziii), *Offender management statistics quarterly: October to December 2019*. Table 3.3: Releases from determinate and indeterminate sentences by establishment, and sex. London: Ministry of Justice, https://assets.publishing.service.gov.uk/government/uploads/system/uploads/attachment_data/file/882180/Releases_Q42019.ods (accessed 5 March 2021).

Ministry of Justice (2020ziv), *Welsh prisoners by security category*. Data obtained from the Ministry of Justice via the Freedom of Information Act 2000.

Ministry of Justice (2020zv), *Community Performance Quarterly, update to March 2020 (Accommodation Circumstance Tables)*. Table 9 and Table 10 – Community Performance Quarterly, update to March 2020 (Accommodation Circumstance Tables), https://www.gov.uk/government/statistics/community-performance-quarterly-update-to-march-2020 (accessed 5 March 2021).

Ministry of Justice (2021), *Statistics on Ethnicity and the Criminal Justice System 2020*. December 2021. London: Ministry of Justice. https://assets.publishing.service.gov.uk/government/uploads/system/uploads/attachment_data/file/1037903/Statistics_on_Ethnicity_and_the_Criminal_Justice_Sysytem_2020.pdf (accessed 20 January 2022).

Ministry of Justice (2022a), *MoJ creating more than 2,000 jobs across England and Wales to spread opportunity*. 1 February 2022. London: Ministry of Justice. https://www.gov.uk/government/news/moj-creating-more-than-2-000-jobs-across-england-and-wales-to-spread-opportunity (accessed 2 February 2022).

Ministry of Justice (2022b), *End to Friday releases to cut crime and make streets safer*. 14 June 2022. London: Ministry of Justice. https://www.gov.uk/government/news/end-to-friday-releases-to-cut-crime-and-make-streets-safer (accessed 20 June 2022).

Ministry of Justice and Welsh Government (2018), *Concordat between the Welsh Government and the UK Ministry of Justice*. June 2018. London: Ministry of Justice, *https://www.gov.uk/government/uploads/system/uploads/attachment_ data/file/719350/moj-wg-concordat.pdf* (accessed 13 May 2021).

Mitchell, James (2010), 'The Narcissism of Small Differences: Scotland and Westminster'. *Parliamentary Affairs*, 63(1): 98–116.

Montesquieu [1748] (1989), *The Spirit of the Laws*, trans. and ed. Anne M. Cohler, Basia Carolyn Miller and Harold Samuel Stone. Cambridge: Cambridge University Press.

Mooney, Gerry, Hazel Croall, Mary Munro and Gill Scott (2015), 'Scottish criminal justice: Devolution, divergence and distinctiveness'. *Criminology and Criminal Justice*, 15(2): 205–24.

Morgan, Rod (2009), *Report to the Welsh Assembly Government on the question of devolution of youth justice responsibilities.* Cardiff: Welsh Assembly Government.

Morris, Nigel (2011), 'More than 3,600 new offences under Labour'. *The Independent*, 23 October 2011, *https://www.independent.co.uk/news/uk/home-news/more-than-3-600-new-offences-under-labour-918053.html* (accessed 18 May 2020).

Morris, Steven (2019), 'Wales has highest incarceration rate in western Europe – study'. *The Guardian*, 16 January 2019, *https://www.theguardian.com/uk-news/2019/jan/16/wales-has-highest-incarceration-rate-in-western-europe-prison-population-england* (accessed 24 January 2019).

Morrison, Katrina (2011), 'Penal Transformation in Post-Devolution Scotland: Change and Resistance'. PhD Thesis. Edinburgh: University of Edinburgh.

Nacro (2004), *NOMS: Will it Work?*. June 2004. London: Nacro.

Nason, Sarah (2017), *Administrative Justice in Wales and Comparative Perspectives.* Public Law of Wales. Cardiff: University of Wales Press.

Nason, Sarah (2018), *Administrative Justice: Wales' First Devolved Justice System.* Bangor: Prifysgol Bangor University, *http://adminjustice.bangor.ac.uk/documents/AJWalesReportESRC-Dec18.pdf* (accessed 25 October 2019).

Nason, Sarah (2019), 'The "New Administrative Law" of Wales'. *Public Law*, (4): 703–23.

Nason, Sarah and Huw Pritchard (2020), 'Administrative Justice and the Legacy of Executive Devolution: Establishing a Tribunals System for Wales'. *Australian Journal of Administrative Law*, 26(4): 262–81.

National Assembly for Wales Constitutional and Legislative Affairs Committee (2012), *Inquiry into a Separate Welsh Jurisdiction*. December 2012. Cardiff: National Assembly for Wales, https://senedd.wales/media/p1jd4kha/cr-ld9135-e-english.pdf (accessed 14 October 2019).

National Assembly for Wales Constitutional and Legislative Affairs Committee (2015), *Report on the UK Government's Draft Wales Bill*. December 2015. Cardiff: National Assembly for Wales, https://senedd.wales/laid%20documents/cr-ld10468/cr-ld10468-e.pdf (accessed 14 October 2019).

National Assembly for Wales Debate, Plenary, 14 December 2016, http://record.assembly.wales/Plenary/4013 (accessed 13 April 2019).

National Assembly for Wales Debate, Plenary, 22 January 2019, http://record.assembly.wales/Plenary/5419#C158045 (accessed 28 January 2019).

National Assembly for Wales Economy, Infrastructure and Skills Committee (2017), *Inquiry into the Apprenticeship Levy*. March 2017. Cardiff: National Assembly for Wales, https://senedd.wales/laid%20documents/cr-ld10999/cr-ld10999-e.pdf (accessed 10 November 2020).

National Assembly for Wales Economy, Infrastructure and Skills Committee (2018), *Apprenticeship Levy: one year on*. August 2018. Cardiff: National Assembly for Wales, https://senedd.wales/laid%20documents/cr-ld11718/cr-ld11718-e.pdf (accessed 10 November 2020).

National Assembly for Wales Equality, Local Government and Communities Committee (2018), *Life on the streets: Preventing and tackling rough sleeping in Wales*. Cardiff: National Assembly for Wales, http://www.assembly.wales/laid%20documents/cr-ld11517/cr-ld11517-e.pdf (accessed 5 November 2019).

National Assembly for Wales Health and Social Care Committee (2015), *Inquiry into New Psychoactive Substances*. Cardiff: National Assembly for Wales, https://senedd.wales/media/03qie2so/cr-ld10147-e.pdf (accessed 7 October 2021).

National Assembly for Wales (Transfer of Functions) Order 1999 (1999), https://www.legislation.gov.uk/uksi/1999/672/made (accessed 3 June 2020).

National Association of Probation Officers (2018), *Welsh Assembly Briefing: How do you solve a Problem like Probation?*. February 2018. London: National Association of Probation Officers, https://www.napo.org.uk/sites/default/files/BR03%20-%20Welsh%20Assembly%20Briefing%20draft%20DR.pdf (accessed 10 April 2021).

National Association of Probation Officers (2021), *Notice of Proposed Motions and Constitutional Amendments*. Annual General Meeting, 14–16 October 2021. London: National Association of Probation Officers, https://www.napo.org.uk/sites/default/files/AGM02- 2021%20Notice%20of%20Motions%20for%20AGM%20Final_2.pdf (accessed 22 November 2021).

National Audit Office (2012), *Restructuring of the National Offender Management Service*. September 2012. HC 593 London: National Audit Office, https://www.nao.org.uk/wp-content/uploads/2012/09/1213593.pdf (accessed 8 December 2020).

National Audit Office (2019), *Transforming Rehabilitation: Progress Review*. Report by the Comptroller and Auditor General. March 2019. London: National Audit Office, https://www.nao.org.uk/wp-content/uploads/2019/02/Transforming-Rehabilitation-Progress-review.pdf (accessed 16 November 2020).

National Offender Management Service (2016), *Annual Report and Accounts 2015–2016*. July 2016. London: National Offender Management Service, https://assets.publishing.service.gov.uk/government/uploads/system/uploads/attachment_data/file/535810/NOMS_AR_2015-16_FINAL_WEB__2_.pdf (accessed 30 August 2019).

National Offender Management Service Cymru, Welsh Government and Youth Justice Board (2006), *Joining Together in Wales: An Adult and Young People's Strategy to Reduce Reoffending*. January 2006. London: National Offender Management Service.

Neil, Robert (2020), 'We must help our prisons in the fight against coronavirus'. *The House*, 19 March 2020, https://www.politicshome.com/thehouse/article/bob-neill-mp-we-must-help-our-prisons-in-the-fight-against-coronavirus (accessed 25 May 2020).

Nellis, Mike (2004), 'Into the field of corrections: the end of English probation in the early 21st century?' *Cambrian Law Review*, 35: 115–33.

Newman, Daniel (2019), Evidence to the Commission on Justice in Wales. Cardiff: Cardiff University, *https://gov.wales/sites/default/files/publications/2018-12/Submission%20to%20Justice%20Commission%20from%20Daniel%20Newman.pdf* (accessed 29 October 2019).

Newman, Daniel and Roxanna Dehaghani (2022), *Experiences of Criminal Justice*. Bristol: Bristol University Press.

Niven, Stephen and Duncan Stewart (2005), *Resettlement Outcomes on Release from Prison in 2003*. Home Office Research Findings, 248.

North Wales Police (2018), *Written evidence submission to the National Assembly's inquiry into Rough Sleeping in Wales*, *https://business.senedd.wales/documents/s72685/RS21a%20-%20North%20Wales%20Police.pdf* (accessed 5 November 2019).

North Wales Police (2021), *Mental Health Triage*. North Wales Police response to a Freedom of Information request. March 2021, *https://www.northwales.police.uk/cy-GB/SysSiteAssets/foi-media/north-wales/disclosure-2021/2021-167-mental-health-triage.pdf* (accessed 18 May 2020).

Novus Cambria (2016), *Novus Cambria Awarded Learning and Skills Contract for HMP Berwyn*, *http://www.novuscambria.ac.uk/news_articles/11* (accessed 17 December 2020).

Obinger, Herbert, Stephan Leibfried and Francis G. Castles (2005), *Federalism and the Welfare State: World and European Experiences*. Cambridge: Cambridge University Press.

O'Connor, Sarah and Cynthia O'Murchu (2019), 'What went wrong at Britain's prison of the future?', *Financial Times*, 7 March 2019, *https://www.ft.com/content/e8454c86-3f9d-11e9-9bee-efab61506f44* (accessed 17 December 2020).

Office for National Statistics (2020a), *Crime in England and Wales: Police Force Area data tables: [Multiple Years]. Table P3: Police recorded crime by offence group and police force area, English regions and Wales, rate of offences, [Multiple Years]*. *https://www.ons.gov.uk/peoplepopulationandcommunity/crimeandjustice/datasets/policeforceareadatatables* (accessed 25 June 2021).

Office for National Statistics (2020b), *Crime in England and Wales: Police Force Area data tables: [Multiple Years]. Table P1: Police recorded crime by offence group and police force area, English regions and Wales, number of offences, [Multiple Years]*, https://www.ons.gov.uk/peoplepopulationandcommunity/crimeandjustice/datasets/policeforceareadatatables (accessed 25 June 2021).

Office for National Statistics (2020c), *Crime in England and Wales: year ending March 2020 – Annual trend and demographic tables. Table D10: Percentage of CSEW incidents reported to the police or Action Fraud, year ending December 1981 to year ending March 2020*, https://www.ons.gov.uk/file?uri=%2fpeoplepopulationandcommunity%2fcrimeandjustice%2fdatasets%2fcrimeinenglandandwalesannualtrendanddemographictables%2fcurrent/annualtrendanddemographictables201920.xlsx (accessed 25 June 2021).

Office for National Statistics (2020d), *Crime in England and Wales: year ending March 2020 – Annual trend and demographic tables. Table D2: Proportion of adults who were victims of all CSEW crime and personal crime (including fraud and computer misuse), and proportion of households who were victims of household crime, by household and area characteristics, year ending March 2020*, https://www.ons.gov.uk/file?uri=%2fpeoplepopulationandcommunity%2fcrimeandjustice%2fdatasets%2fcrimeinenglandandwalesannualtrendanddemographictables%2fcurrent/annualtrendanddemographictables201920.xlsx (accessed 25 June 2021).

Office for National Statistics (2020e), *Crime in England and Wales: year ending March 2020 – Annual trend and demographic tables. Table D15: Experience of anti-social behaviour in local area, by household and area characteristics, year ending March 2020*, https://www.ons.gov.uk/file?uri=%2fpeoplepopulationandcommunity%2fcrimeandjustice%2fdatasets%2fcrimeinenglandandwalesannualtrendanddemographictables%2fcurrent/annualtrendanddemographictables201920.xlsx (accessed 25 June 2021).

Office for National Statistics (2020f), *Crime in England and Wales: year ending March 2020 – Annual trend and demographic tables. Table D6: Proportion of children aged 10 to 15 who experienced victimisation in the last year (preferred measure), by household and area characteristics, year ending March 2020*, https://www.ons.gov.uk/file?uri=%2fpeoplepopulationandcommunity%2fcrimeandjustice%2fdatasets%2fcrimeinenglandandwalesannualtrendanddemographictables%2fcurrent/annualtrendanddemographictables201920.xlsx (accessed 25 June 2021).

Office for National Statistics (2020g), *Wales population mid-year estimate* [multiple years], https://www.ons.gov.uk/peoplepopulationandcommunity/populationandmigration/populationestimates (accessed 25 June 2021).

Office for National Statistics (2020h), *England population mid-year estimate* [multiple years], https://www.ons.gov.uk/peoplepopulationandcommunity/populationandmigration/populationestimates (accessed 25 June 2021).

Office for National Statistics (2020i), *Crime in England and Wales: Annual supplementary tables*. Table S12: Visibility of police foot patrols, by household and area characteristics, year ending March 2020 CSEW, https://www.ons.gov.uk/peoplepopulationandcommunity/crimeandjustice/datasets/crimeinenglandandwalesannualsupplementarytables (accessed 25 June 2021).

Office for National Statistics (2020j), *Crime in England and Wales: Annual supplementary tables*. Table S6: Perceptions of the local police, by household and area characteristics, year ending March 2020 CSEW, https://www.ons.gov.uk/peoplepopulationandcommunity/crimeandjustice/datasets/crimeinenglandandwalesannualsupplementarytables (accessed 25 June 2021).

Office of the Police and Crime Commissioner for Gwent (2019), *Gwent Police & Crime Plan: Delivering a Safer Gwent 2017–2021 (Updated April 2019)*. Cwmbran: Office of the Police and Crime Commissioner, https://www.apccs.police.uk/media/5369/police_and_crime_plan_update_final.pdf (accessed 7 October 2020).

O'Leary, Chris (2013). 'The Role of Stable Accommodation in Reducing Recidivism: What Does the Evidence Tell Us?' *Safer Communities*, 12(1): 5–12.

O'Mahony, David (2012), 'Criminal Justice Reform in a Transitional Context: Restorative Youth Conferencing in Northern Ireland'. *International Criminal Law Review*, 12(3): 549–71.

O'Neil, Megan (2014), 'Ripe for the chop or the public face of policing? PCSOs and Neighbourhood Policing in austerity'. *Policing: A Journal of Policy and Practice*, 8(3): 265–73.

Otter, Daniel (2017), *Lessons from Abroad: What the United States Can Learn from European Drug Consumption Rooms*. Washington: University of Washington.

Padfield, Nicola and Shadd Maruna (2006), 'The revolving door at the prison gate: Exploring the dramatic increase in recalls to prison'. *Criminology and Criminal Justice*, 6(3): 329–52.

Percival, Richard (2017), 'How to Do Things with Jurisdictions: Wales and the Jurisdiction'. *Public Law*, 2: 249–69.

Philp, Chris (2020), *During a debate on the Commission on Justice in Wales*. Vol. 670: debated on Wednesday 22 January 2020. Column 156WH. London: House of Commons, https://hansard.parliament.uk/commons/2020-01-22/ debates/45A32F4F-4FD7-4AE5-99B6-2780FD13082B/Commission OnJusticeInWales (accessed 28 January 2020).

Pitts, John (2015), 'Youth Crime and Youth Justice 2015–2020'. *Youth & Policy (Special Edition)*, 114: 31–42.

Playfair, Giles (1971), *The Punitive Obsession: An Unvarnished History of the English Prison System*. London: Victor Gollancz.

Policing Partnership Board for Wales (2018), *Policing Partnership Board meeting: 19 November 2018*. Minutes. Cardiff: Welsh Government, https://gov.wales/policing-partnership-board-meeting-19-november-2018 (accessed 1 September 2020).

Prison Governors Association (2014), *Written evidence submitted by the Prison Governors Association to the House of Commons Welsh Affairs Committee's inquiry into Prisons in Wales and the treatment of Welsh offenders*. London: Prison Governors Association, http://data.parliament.uk/WrittenEvidence/CommitteeEvidence.svc/ EvidenceDocument/Welsh%20Affairs/Prisons%20in%20Wales%20 and%20treatment%20of%20Welsh%20offenders/written/16321.html (accessed 17 September 2019).

Prison Reform Trust (2014), *Written evidence submitted by the Prison Reform Trust to the House of Commons Welsh Affairs Committee Prisons in Wales and Treatment of Welsh Offenders Inquiry*,

http://data.parliament.uk/WrittenEvidence/CommitteeEvidence.svc/
EvidenceDocument/Welsh%20Affairs/Prisons%20in%20Wales%20
and%20treatment%20of%20Welsh%20offenders/written/11117.html
(accessed 17 September 2019).

Prison Reform Trust (2015), *Transforming Lives: Reducing Women's Imprisonment*. London: Prison Reform Trust, https://prisonreformtrust.org.uk/transforming-lives-reducing-womens-imprisonment/ (accessed 4 November 2019).

Prison Reform Trust (2017), *Why focus on reducing women's imprisonment?*. A Prison Reform Trust Briefing. London: Prison Reform Trust, http://www.prisonreformtrust.org.uk/wp-content/themes/chd/old_files/Documents/Women/whywomen.pdf (accessed 6 November 2019).

Prison Reform Trust (2019), *Written evidence submission to the National Assembly's Equality, Local Government and Communities Committee inquiry into Voting Rights for Prisoners*, https://business.senedd.wales/documents/s82614/VRP03%20-%20Prison%20Reform%20Trust.pdf (accessed 12 February 2020).

Prison Reform Trust and Women in Prison (2018), *Home truths: housing for women in the criminal justice system*. June 2018. London: Prison Reform Trust and Women in Prison, https://www.communityjusticeayrshire.org.uk/wp-content/uploads/2018/07/home-truths-june-2018.pdf (accessed 4 November 2019).

Pritchard, Huw (2016), *Justice in Wales: Principle, Progress and Next Steps*. September 2016. Cardiff: Wales Governance Centre at Cardiff University, https://www.cardiff.ac.uk/__data/assets/pdf_file/0008/1288511/Justice-in-Wales-Sept-2016.pdf (accessed 1 February 2019).

Pritchard, Huw (2017), 'Building a Welsh jurisdiction through administrative justice', in Sarah Nason (ed.), *Administrative Justice in Wales and Comparative Perspectives*. Cardiff: University of Wales Press, pp. 218–42.

Pritchard, Huw (2019), 'Revisiting Legal Wales'. *Edinburgh Law Review*, 23(1): 123–30.

Quilgars, Deborah, Anwen Jones, Mark Bevan, Roger Bowles and Nicholas Pleace (2012), *Supporting short-term prisoners leaving HMP*

*Leeds: Evaluation of the Shelter Prisoners Advocacy Release Team*. York: University of York and Centre for Housing Policy, *https://www.york.ac.uk/media/chp/documents/2012/ShelterPART Evaluation2012.pdf* (accessed 10 April 2019).

Radzinowicz, Leon and Roger Hood (1986), *A History of English Criminal Law, Volume 5: The Emergence of Penal Policy*. London: Stevens and Sons.

Ramsbottom, Lord David (2010), 'Foreword', in Mark Leech (ed.), *The Prison Handbook 2010: The Definitive Annual Guide to Prisons in England and Wales*. Prisons.Org.Uk Limited.

Rawlings, Richard (1998), 'The New Model Wales'. *Journal of Law and Society*, 25(4): 461–509.

Rawlings, Richard (2003), *Delineating Wales: Constitutional, Legal and Administrative Aspects of National Devolution*. Cardiff: University of Wales Press.

Rawlings, Richard (2018), 'The Strange Reconstitution of Wales'. *Public Law*, 1: 62–83.

Rawlings, Richard (2019), 'The Welsh Way/Y Ffordd Gymreig', in Jeffery Jowell and Colm O'Cinneide (eds), *The Changing Constitution*. Oxford: Oxford University Press, pp. 296–324.

Rees, Amy (2019), *Oral evidence to the Commission on Justice in Wales*. HMPPS in Wales. 15 February 2019, *https://gov.wales/sites/default/files/publications/2019-03/Oral%20 evidence%20to%20the%20Justice%20Commission%20from%20HMCTS %2C%20LAA%20and%20HMPPS.pdf* (accessed 12 August 2019).

Rees, Alison, Eleanor Staples and Nina Maxwell (2017), *Evaluation of Visiting Mum Scheme*. Cardiff: Cardiff University, *http://orca.cf.ac.uk/112243/1/Final-PACT-report-Final-version.- 12.7.17.pdf* (accessed 5 June 2019).

Rees, Jenny (2020), 'Courts in Wales: Calls to tackle backlog of criminal cases'. BBC Wales News, 31 July 2020, *https://www.bbc.co.uk/news/uk-wales-53594696* (accessed 10 February 2021).

Reid, Kiron (2009), 'Race Issues and Stop and Search: Looking behind the Statistics'. *The Journal of Criminal Law*, 73: 165–83.

Rhodes, R. A. W., John Wanna and Patrick Weller (2009), *Comparing Westminster*. Oxford: Oxford University Press.

Richard Commission [The Commission on the Powers and Electoral Arrangements of the National Assembly for Wales] (2004), *Report of the Richard Commission*. Cardiff: National Assembly for Wales, https://webarchive.nationalarchives.gov.uk/20100404200945/http:/www.richardcommission.gov.uk/content/finalreport/report-e.pdf (accessed 5 February 2019).

Roberts, Julian V. and Andrew Ashworth (2016), 'The Evolution of Sentencing Policy and Practice in England and Wales, 2003–2015'. *Crime and Justice*, 45: 307–58.

Robinson Gwen, Lawrence Burke and Matthew Millings (2016), 'Criminal justice identities in transition: The case of devolved probation services in England and Wales'. *British Journal of Criminology*, 56(1): 161–78.

Rodger, John (2008), *Criminalising Social Policy: Anti-Social Behaviour and Welfare in a De-Civilised Society*. Cullompton: Willan Publishing.

Roman, Caterina and Jeremy Travis (2006), 'Where will I sleep tomorrow? Housing, homelessness, and the returning prisoner'. *Housing Policy Debate*, 7(2): 389–418.

Russell, Meg and Ruxandra Serban (2021), 'The Muddle of the "Westminster Model": A Concept Stretched Beyond Repair'. *Government and Opposition*, 56: 744–64.

Rutherford, Andrew (1988), 'Boundaries of English Penal Policy'. *Oxford Journal of Legal Studies*, 8(1): 132–41.

Rycroft, Philip (2019), *Brexit, Devolution and the General Election*. Wales Governance Centre Annual Lecture 2019. December 2019. Cardiff: Wales Governance Centre at Cardiff University, https://www.cardiff.ac.uk/__data/assets/pdf_file/0003/1737624/wgc_annual_lecture_2019_transcript.pdf (accessed 18 May 2020).

Sagar, Tracey, Debbie Jones and Katrien Symons (2015), *Sex Work, Drug and Alcohol Use: Bringing the Voices of Sex Workers into the Policy and Service Development Framework in Wales*. Swansea: Swansea University, https://gov.wales/sites/default/files/publications/2019-02/sex-work-drug-and-alcohol-use-bringing-the-voices-of-sex-workers-into-the-policy-and-service-development-framework-in-wales.pdf (accessed 6 July 2020).

Sasse, Tom and Emma Norris (2019), *Moving On: The costs of high staff turnover in the civil service*. January 2019. London: Institute for Government, https://www.instituteforgovernment.org.uk/sites/default/files/publications/IfG_staff_turnover_WEB.pdf (accessed 11 May 2020).

Sasse, Tom, Tim Durrant, Emma Norris and Kataki Zodgekar (2020), *Government reshuffles: The case for keeping ministers in post longer*. January 2020. London: Institute for Government, https://www.instituteforgovernment.org.uk/sites/default/files/publications/government-reshuffles.pdf (accessed 11 May 2020).

Savage, Michael (2010), 'Labour's computer blunders cost £26b'. *The Independent*, 19 January 2010, https://www.independent.co.uk/news/uk/politics/labour-s-computer-blunders-cost-163-26bn-1871967.html (accessed 21 April 2021).

Scharpf, Fritz W. (1988), 'The Joint-Decision Trap: Lessons from German Federalism and European Integration'. *Public Administration*, 66(3): 239–78.

Schrantz, Dennis, Stephen DeBor and Marc Mauer (2018), *Decarceration Strategies: How 5 States Achieved Substantial Prison Population Reductions*. September 2018. Washington, DC: The Sentencing Project, https://www.sentencingproject.org/wp-content/uploads/2018/09/Decarceration-Strategies.pdf (accessed 17 October 2019).

Scraton, Phil (1985), *The State of the Police*. London: Pluto Press.

Scraton, Phil (2005), 'Scant respect for children's rights'. *Safer Society*, 27: 17–19.

Scraton, Phil (2007), *Power, Conflict and Criminalisation*. Oxford: Routledge.

Scraton, Phil, Joe Sim and Paula Skidmore (1991), *Prisons Under Protest*. Milton Keynes: Open University Press.

Scott, Gill and Gerry Mooney (2009), 'Poverty and social justice in the devolved Scotland: Neoliberalism meets social democracy'. *Social Policy and Society*, 8(3): 361–5.

Selous, Andrew (2015), *Prisoners' Release. Written Parliamentary Question for Ministry of Justice*. UIN 222892, tabled on 2 February 2015. London: House of Commons, https://questions-statements.parliament.uk/written-questions/detail/2015-02-02/222892 (accessed 4 March 2020).

Senedd Business Committee (2021), *'Minutes – Business Committee'.* 13 July 2021. Cardiff: Welsh Senedd Cymru. https://business.senedd.wales/documents/g12307/Printable%20minutes%20Tuesday%2013-Jul-2021%2009.00%20Business%20Committee.pdf?T=1 (accessed 8 December 2021).

Senedd Health, Social Care and Sport Committee (2021), *Health and social care provision in the adult prison estate in Wales.* March 2021. Cardiff: Senedd Cymru, https://senedd.wales/media/ct4f03nb/cr-ld14318-e.pdf (accessed 2 April 2021).

Sentencing Council for England and Wales (2018), *Written evidence submission to the House of Commons Justice Committee's Prison Population 2020: planning for the future inquiry.* February 2018. London: Sentencing Council for England and Wales, http://data.parliament.uk/writtenevidence/committeeevidence.svc/evidencedocument/justice-committee/prison-population-2022/written/78134.pdf (accessed 23 May 2019).

Shearer, Michael (2020), 'How coronavirus is spreading through UK prisons'. *New Statesman*, 2 May 2020, https://www.newstatesman.com/science-tech/2020/05/how-coronavirus-spreading-through-uk-prisons (accessed 14 May 2020).

Shelter Cymru (2004), *Homelessness: It's a Crime – The Impact and Costs of a Failing System.* September 2004. Swansea: Shelter Cymru.

Shelter Cymru (2013), *Response to the consultation on the proposal to amend the duty of a local authority to accommodate a former prisoner as a result of their priority need status.* Swansea: Shelter Cymru, https://www.google.com/url?sa=t&rct=j&q=&esrc=s&source=web&cd=&ved=2ahUKEwjDvdfE3brxAhWCtKQKH-Vn8BBkQFjABegQIAxAD&url=https%3A%2F%2Fsheltercymru.org.uk%2Fwp-content%2Fuploads%2F2015%2F02%2FFormer-prisoner-PN-response-Shelter-Cymru.doc&usg=AOvVaw0OnEdSDGoKldd OuVnhA5aO (accessed 5 November 2019).

Shelter Cymru (2017), *Written evidence to the National Assembly for Wales' Equality, Local Government and Communities Committee's inquiry into Rough Sleeping in Wales,* http://senedd.assembly.wales/documents/s71911/RS06%20-%20Shelter%20Cymru.pdf (accessed 5 November 2019).

Shelter Cymru (2021), *What is priority need?*. Swansea: Shelter Cymru, https://sheltercymru.org.uk/get-advice/homelessness/help-from-the-council/what-will-the-council-check/priority-need/ (accessed 16 June 2021).

Shiner, Michael, Zoe Carre, Rebekah Delsol and Niamh Eastwood (2013), *The Colour of Injustice: 'Race', drugs and law enforcement in England and Wales*. London: Stopwatch & Release, https://www.release.org.uk/sites/default/files/pdf/publications/The%20Colour%20of%20Injustice.pdf (accessed 11 February 2020).

Shute, Jon, Judith Aldridge and Juanjo Medina (2012), 'Loading the policy blunderbuss'. *Criminal Justice Matters*, 87: 40–1.

Silk Commission [Commission on Devolution in Wales] (2014), *Empowerment and Responsibility: Legislative Powers to Strengthen Wales*. March 2012, https://assets.publishing.service.gov.uk/government/uploads/system/uploads/attachment_data/file/310571/CDW-Wales_Report-final_Full_WEB_310114.pdf (accessed 5 February 2019).

Sim, Joe (2002), 'The future of prison health care: A critical analysis'. *Critical Social Policy*, 22: 300–23.

Simon, Jonathan (2007), *Governing Through Crime: How the War on Crime Transformed American Democracy and Created a Culture of Fear*. Oxford: Oxford University Press.

Skogan, Wesley (1977), 'Dimensions of the Dark Figure of Unreported Crime'. *Crime & Delinquency*, 23: 41–50.

Skuse, Tricia and Jonny Matthew (2015), 'The Trauma Recovery Model: Sequencing youth justice interventions for young people with complex needs'. *Prison Service Journal*, 220: 16–25.

Smith, Douglas and G. Roger Jarjoura (1988), 'Social Structure and Criminal Victimisation'. *Journal of Research in Crime and Delinquency*, 25: 27–52.

Smith, Mikey (2020), 'Coronavirus: UK Prisons and courts face worst backlogs and overcrowding ever'. *The Mirror*. 29 April 2020, https://www.mirror.co.uk/news/politics/coronavirus-uk-prisons-courts-face-21942113 (accessed 14 May 2020).

Smith, Roger and Patricia Gray (2019), 'The changing shape of youth justice: Models of practice'. *Criminology and Criminal Justice*, 19(5): 554–71.

Social Exclusion Unit (2002), *Reducing Re-offending by Ex-prisoners*. July 2002. London: Office of the Deputy Prime Minister, https://www.prisonstudies.org/sites/default/files/resources/downloads/reducing_report20pdf.pdf (accessed 18 February 2020).

Souhami, Anna (2007), *Transforming Youth Justice: Occupational Identity and Cultural Change*. Cullompton: Willan Publishing.

South Wales Police (2018), *Written evidence submission to the National Assembly's inquiry into Rough Sleeping in Wales*, https://business.senedd.wales/documents/s71913/RS08%20-%20South%20Wales%20Police.html?CT=2 (accessed 3 March 2020).

Spurr, Michael (2019), *Oral evidence to the Commission from HMCTS, LAA and HMPPS*. February 2019. Cardiff: Commission on Justice in Wales, https://gov.wales/sites/default/files/publications/2019-03/Oral%20evidence%20to%20the%20Justice%20Commission%20from%20HMCTS%2C%20LAA%20and%20HMPPS.pdf (accessed 12 August 2019).

StatsWales (2015), *Households accepted as homeless by priority need and period*. Cardiff: StatsWales, https://statswales.gov.wales/v/4bd (accessed 7 November 2019).

StatsWales (2019), *Households found to be eligible for assistance, unintentionally homeless and in priority need during the year: Categories of priority need by type of household* (section 75). Cardiff: StatsWales.

StatsWales (2020a), *Population estimates by local authority and gender*. Cardiff: StatsWales, https://statswales.gov.wales/Catalogue/Population-and-Migration/Population/Estimates/Local-Authority/populationestimates-by-local authority-gender (accessed 1 February 2021).

StatsWales (2020b), *Financing of gross revenue expenditure, by authority (£ thousand)*. Cardiff: StatsWales, https://statswales.gov.wales/Catalogue/Local-Government/Finance/Revenue/Financing/financingofgrossrevenueexpenditure-by-authority (accessed 11 June 2021).

StatsWales (2020c), *Financing of gross revenue expenditure, by source of funding (£ thousand)*. Cardiff: StatsWales, https://statswales.gov.wales/Catalogue/Local-Government/Finance/Revenue/Financing/financingofgrossrevenueexpenditure-by-source offunding (accessed 11 June 2021).

StatsWales (2020d), *Rough sleepers by local authority*. Cardiff: StatsWales, https://statswales.gov.wales/Catalogue/Housing/Homelessness/Rough-Sleepers/roughsleepers-by-localauthority (accessed 1 February 2021).

Stevens, Alex (2011), 'Telling Policy Stories: An Ethnographic Study of the Use of Evidence in Policy-making in the UK'. *Journal of Social Policy*, 40(2): 237–55.

Stirbu, Diana and Laura McAllister (2018), 'Chronicling National Assembly Committees as Markers of Institutional Change'. *Journal of Legislative Studies*, 24(3): 373–93.

Stockdale, Eric (1983), 'Short History of Prison Inspection in England'. *British Journal of Criminology*, 23(3): 209–28.

Sykes, Gresham (1958), *The Society of Captives: A Study of a Maximum Security Prison*. Princeton: Princeton University Press.

Taylor, Charlie (2016), *Review of the Youth Justice System in England and Wales*. London: Ministry of Justice, https://assets.publishing.service.gov.uk/government/uploads/system/uploads/attachment_data/file/577103/youth-justice-review-final-report.pdf (accessed 29 November 2019).

The UK's Changing Union Partnership (2013), *A Stable, Sustainable Devolution Settlement for Wales*. Cardiff: UKCU, http://www.ukchangingunion.org (accessed 30 December 2019).

Thomas, Lord (2015c), 'The Law of Wales – Looking Forward'. Legal Wales conference speech, 9 October 2015, https://www.judiciary.uk/announcements/speech-by-the-lord-chief-justice-the-law-of-wales-looking-forward/ (accessed 7 August 2019).

Thomas, Lord (2017), 'The past and future of the law in Wales'. Lecture given to the Wales Governance Centre at Cardiff University. October 2017, https://www.cardiff.ac.uk/news/view/1324746-the-past-and-future-of-the-law-in-wales (accessed 15 May 2019).

Thomas, Lord (2001) 'Legal Wales : Its Modern Origins and its Role after Devolution: National Identity, the Welsh Language and Parochialism'. *Welsh Legal History Society*, 1: 113–65.

Thomas, Robert (2015b), 'The Draft Wales Bill 2015 – Part 2', *UK Constitutional Law Group Blog*, 3 December 2015, https://ukconstitutionallaw.org/2015/12/03/robert-thomas-the-draft-wales-bill-2015-part-2/ (accessed 9 November 2021).

Thomas, Sue (2015a), 'Children First, Offenders Second: An aspiration or reality for youth justice in Wales'. Thesis submitted for Professional Doctorate in Leadership in Children and Young People's Services. Luton: University of Bedfordshire.

Thomas Commission [Commission on Justice on Wales] (2019), *Justice in Wales for the People of Wales*. Cardiff: The Commission on Justice in Wales, https://gov.wales/sites/default/files/publications/2019-10/Justice%20Commission%20ENG%20DIGITAL_2.pdf (accessed 24 October 2019).

Thompson, Louise (2014), 'Evidence taking under the microscope: How has oral evidence affected the scrutiny of legislation in House of Commons committees?' *British Politics*, 9(4): 385–400.

Thompson, Louise (2020), 'Ministerial Turnover and Why Reshuffles Matter for Parliament'. *The Political Quarterly*, 91(2): 457–60.

Tidmarsh, Matt (2021), *Professionalism in Probation: Making Sense of Marketisation*. London: Routledge.

Tonry, Michael (2004), *Punishment and Politics: Evidence and Emulation in the Making of English Crime Control Policy*. Cullompton: Willan.

Tonry, Michael (2007), 'Determinants of Penal Policies'. *Crime and Justice*, 36: 1–48.

Torrance, David and Adam Evans (2019), 'The Territorial Select Committees, 40 Years On'. *Parliamentary Affairs*, 72(4): 860–78.

Tyler, Nichola, Helen Miles, Bessey Karadag and Gemma Rogers (2019), 'An updated picture of the mental health needs of male and female prisoners in the UK: prevalence, comorbidity, and gender differences'. *Social Psychiatry and Psychiatric Epidemiology*, 54: 1143–52.

UK Department for Education and Skills and Department for Work and Pensions (2005), *Reducing Reoffending through Skills and Employment – Government Green Paper*. London: Stationary Office, https://assets.publishing.service.gov.uk/government/uploads/system/uploads/attachment_data/file/272207/6702.pdf (accessed 16 March 2020).

UK Infrastructure and Projects Authority (2018), *Annual Report on Major Projects 2017–18*. July 2018. London: Infrastructure and Projects Authority, https://assets.publishing.service.gov.uk/government/uploads/system/uploads/attachment_data/file/721978/IPA_Annual_Report_2018__2_.pdf (accessed 21 April 2021).

Vitale, Alex (2017), *The End of Policing?*. London: Verso.
Waddington, Peter, Kevin Stenson and David Don (2004), 'In Proportion: Race, and Police Stop and Search'. *British Journal of Criminology*, 44(6): 889–914.
Wales Act 2017 (c4) Explanatory Note. Section B5 – Crime, public order and policing (110). London: Stationary Office, http://www.legislation.gov.uk/ukpga/2017/4/notes/division/6/index.htm (accessed 13 February 2020).
Wales and Chester Circuit (2018), *Written evidence submission to the Commission on Justice in Wales*. May 2018, https://gov.wales/submission-justice-commission-wales-and-chester-circuit (accessed 10 January 2019).
Wales Audit Office (2016), *Community Safety in Wales*. Wales Audit Office. October 2016. Cardiff: Wales Audit Office, https://www.audit.wales/sites/default/files/Community-Safety-2016-English_6.pdf (accessed 16 October 2020).
Wales Community Rehabilitation Company (2018), *Written evidence submission to the National Assembly's inquiry into Rough Sleeping in Wales*, Cardiff: Wales CRC, https://business.senedd.wales/documents/s72466/RS10%20- %20Wales%20Community%20Rehabilitation%20Company.pdf (accessed 30 September 2020).
Wales Governance Centre and Constitution Unit (2015), *Delivering a Reserved Powers Model of Devolution for Wales*. September 2015. Cardiff: Wales Governance Centre at Cardiff University, https://www.cardiff.ac.uk/__data/assets/pdf_file/0004/1288696/Devolution-Report-ENG-V4.pdf (accessed 2 June 2021).
Wales Governance Centre and Constitution Unit (2016), *Challenge and Opportunity: The Draft Wales Bill 2015*. February 2016. Cardiff: Wales Governance Centre at Cardiff University, https://www.cardiff.ac.uk/__data/assets/pdf_file/0011/1288694/Challenge-and-Opportunity-The-Draft-Wales-Bill-2015.pdf (accessed 2 June 2021).
Wales Office (2013), *UK Government's Evidence to the Commission on Devolution in Wales Part II: The Welsh Devolution Settlement*. London: Wales Office,

*https://webarchive.nationalarchives.gov.uk/20140605075418/http:// commissionondevolutioninwales.independent.gov.uk/search/doc-type/ evidence/* (accessed 5 February 2019).

Wales Online (2013), 'Storm over government's probation privatisation plans for England and Wales'. *Wales Online,* 20 September 2013, *https://www.walesonline.co.uk/news/wales-news/storm-over-probation-privatisation-plans-6067287* (accessed 29 September 2021).

Walker, Nigel and Henri Giller (1977), *Penal Policy-Making in England*. Cambridge: Institute of Criminology, Cambridge.

Walker, Samantha, Jill Annison and Sharon Beckett (2019), 'Transforming Rehabilitation: The impact of austerity and privatisation on day-to-day cultures and working practices in "probation"'. *Probation Journal*, 66(1): 113–30.

Walmsley, Roy (2017), *World Female Imprisonment List*. Fourth Edition. London: Institute for Criminal Justice Policy Research. *https://www.prisonstudies.org/sites/default/files/resources/downloads/ world_female_prison_4th_edn_v4_web.pdf* (accessed 11 May 2022).

Watkin, Thomas Glyn (2007), *The Legal History of Wales*. Cardiff: University of Wales Press.

Watkin, Thomas (2012), 'Dadleuon dichellgar a datganoli: Hanes yr Ymgyrch dros Awdurdodaeth Gymreig/Devious Debates and Devolution: The History of the Campaign for a Welsh Jurisdiction', Institute of Welsh Affairs Annual Eisteddfod Lecture, *https://www.iwa.wales/agenda/2012/08/devious-debates-and-devolution-the-history-of-the-campaign-for-a-welsh-jurisdiction/* (accessed 4 June 2021).

Welsh Government (2000a), *Extending Entitlement: Supporting Young People in Wales, a Report by the Policy Unit*. Cardiff: National Assembly for Wales.

Welsh Government (2000b), *Tackling substance misuse in Wales: A partnership approach*. Cardiff: Welsh Government.

Welsh Government (2005a), *Tackling Domestic Abuse: The All Wales National Strategy*. March 2005. Cardiff: Welsh Government.

Welsh Government (2005b), *Raising the Standard: The Revised Adult Mental Health National Service Framework and an Action Plan for Wales*. October 2005. Cardiff: Welsh Government, *http://www.wales.nhs.uk/documents/websiteenglishnsfandactionplan.pdf* (accessed 30 May 2019).

Welsh Government (2008a), *One Wales Commitment on Devolution of Criminal Justice System – Scoping Paper*. Presented to Welsh Government Cabinet in July 2008. Document obtained from the Welsh Government via the Freedom of Information Act 2000.

Welsh Government (2008b), *Working together to reduce harm: The substance misuse strategy for Wales 2008–2018*. Cardiff: Welsh Government, https://www2.nphs.wales.nhs.uk/SubstanceMisuseDocs.nsf/($All)/6361D5806F16EEDD80257C5B005AC8AF/$File/Working%20Together%20to%20Reduce%20Harm%20-%20SM%20Strategy%202008-2018.pdf?OpenElement (accessed 14 October 2019).

Welsh Government (2010), *The Right to be Safe*. March 2010. Cardiff: Welsh Government, https://www.thewi.org.uk/__data/assets/pdf_file/0007/49885/100325besafefinalenv1.pdf (accessed 16 October 2019).

Welsh Government (2011), *Programme for Government. 2011–2016*. Cardiff: Welsh Government.

Welsh Government (2012a), *A Separate Legal Jurisdiction for Wales*. Consultation Document WG-15109. March 2012. Cardiff: Welsh Government, https://gov.wales/sites/default/files/consultations/2018-01/120326separatelegaljurisdiction.pdf (accessed 30 April 2021).

Welsh Government (2012b), *Together for Mental Health: A Strategy for Mental Health and Wellbeing in Wales*. October 2012. Cardiff: Welsh Government, https://gov.wales/sites/default/files/publications/2019-03/together-for-mental-health-a-strategy-for-mental-health-and-wellbeing-in-wales.pdf (accessed 14 October 2019).

Welsh Government (2012c), *Minutes and papers of a meeting of the Cabinet. Item 4: Attendance of the Chief Constables*. May 2012. Cardiff: Welsh Government, https://webarchive.nationalarchives.gov.uk/20180413014833/http://gov.wales/about/cabinet/meetings/previous-administration/20mar12/?lang=en (accessed 16 July 2021).

Welsh Government (2013), *The proposal to amend the duty of a local authority to accommodate a former prisoner as a result of their priority need status*. Consultation Document. September 2013. Merthyr Tydfil: Welsh Government.

Welsh Government (2015a), *Talk To Me: Suicide and Self Harm Prevention Strategy for Wales 2015–2020*. July 2015, https://gov.wales/sites/default/files/publications/2019-08/talk-to-me-2-suicide-and-self-harm-prevention-strategy-for-wales-2015-2020.pdf (accessed 14 October 2019).

Welsh Government (2015b), *The Welsh Government's Response to the UK Government's Consultation on HM Courts and Tribunals Service Reform*. Cardiff: Welsh Government, https://senedd.cymru/deposited%20papers/dp-1479-11-16/dp-1479-11-16.pdf (accessed 8 September 2020).

Welsh Government (2015c), *National Pathway for Homelessness Services to Children, Young People and Adults in the Secure Estate*. December 2015. Cardiff: Welsh Government, https://gov.wales/sites/default/files/publications/2019-03/homelessness-services-for-children-young-people-and-adults-in-the-secure-estate_0.pdf (accessed 15 January 2020).

Welsh Government (2016a), *Government and Laws in Wales Draft Bill: Explanatory Summary*. March 2016. Cardiff: Welsh Government, https://gov.wales/sites/default/files/publications/2018-09/wales-bill-draft-summary_0.pdf (accessed 5 February 2020).

Welsh Government (2016b), *Welsh Government and Partners: Mental Health Crisis Care Concordat*. November 2016. Cardiff: Welsh Government, https://gov.wales/sites/default/files/publications/2019-03/mental-health-crisis-care-concordat.pdf (accessed 14 October 2019).

Welsh Government (2016c), *The National Training Framework on Violence Against Women, Domestic Abuse and Sexual Violence*. March 2016. Cardiff: Welsh Government, https://gov.wales/sites/default/files/publications/2019-08/national-training-framework-on-violence-against-women-domestic-abuse-and-sexual-violence-statutory-guidance.pdf (accessed 18 October 2019).

Welsh Government (2016d), *National Strategy on Violence against Women, Domestic Abuse and Sexual Violence – 2016–2021*. November 2016. Cardiff: Welsh Government, https://gov.wales/sites/default/files/publications/2019-06/national-strategy-2016-to-2021.pdf (accessed 18 October 2019).

# BIBLIOGRAPHY

Welsh Government (2016e), *Government and Laws in Wales Bill.* Cardiff: Welsh Government, https://gov.wales/sites/default/files/publications/2018-09/wales-bill-draft_0.pdf (accessed 17 March 2020).

Welsh Government (2017a), *Working Together for Safer Communities: A Welsh Government review of community safety partnership working in Wales.* December 2017. Cardiff: Welsh Government, https://gov.wales/sites/default/files/publications/2019-03/working-together-for-safer-communities.pdf (accessed 21 December 2020).

Welsh Government (2017b), *Support for Streetlife project to extend outreach work.* May 2017. Cardiff: Welsh Government, https://gov.wales/support-streetlife-project-extend-outreach-work (accessed 18 October 2019).

Welsh Government (2017c), *Prosperity for All: The National Strategy.* September 2017. Cardiff: Welsh Government.

Welsh Government (2018a), *Commission on Justice in Wales: Supplementary Paper from the Welsh Government Cabinet Secretary for Local Government and Communities.* Cardiff: Welsh Government, https://gov.wales/sites/default/files/publications/2018-08/supplementary-paper-commission-justice-in-wales-welsh-government-cabinet-secretary-for-local-government-and-communities.pdf (accessed 13 November 2020).

Welsh Government (2018b), *Draft Budget 2019–20: Detailed proposals.* October 2018. Cardiff: Welsh Government, https://gov.wales/written-statement-draft-budget-2019-20-detailed-proposals (accessed 11 April 2019).

Welsh Government (2019a), *Welsh Index of Multiple Deprivation (WIMD) 2019: Results Report.* Cardiff: Welsh Government, https://gov.wales/sites/default/files/statistics-and-research/2020-06/welsh-index-multiple-deprivation-2019-results-report.pdf (accessed 10 March 2020).

Welsh Government (2019b), *Final Police Settlement 2019–2020: Key Briefing Tables.* January 2019. Cardiff: Welsh Government, https://gov.wales/police-settlement-final-2019-2020 (accessed 30 April 2020).

Welsh Government (2019c), *Final Budget 2019–2020: Main expenditure group (MEG) allocations.* January 2019. Cardiff: Welsh Government, https://gov.wales/final-budget-2019-2020 (accessed 15 April 2020).

Welsh Government (2019d), *Substance Misuse Delivery Plan 2019–2022*. October 2019. Cardiff: Welsh Government, https://gov.wales/sites/default/files/publications/2019-10/substance-misuse-delivery-plan-2019-22.pdf (accessed 14 September 2020).

Welsh Government (2020), 'Prisoner voting plans unveiled'. March 2020. Cardiff: Welsh Government, https://gov.wales/prisoner-voting-plans-unveiled (accessed 12 October 2020).

Welsh Government (2021), *Ending Physical Punishment in Wales: briefing note*. Cardiff: Welsh Government, https://gov.wales/ending-physical-punishment-wales-briefing-note (accessed 16 December 2021).

Welsh Government (2022a), *Delivering Justice for Wales*. May 2022. Cardiff: Welsh Government. https://gov.wales/sites/default/files/publications/2022-06/delivering-justice-for-wales-may-2022-v2.pdf (accessed 25 May 2022).

Welsh Government (2022b), *Violence against women, domestic abuse and sexual violence: strategy 2022 to 2026*. May 2022. Cardiff: Welsh Government. https://gov.wales/sites/default/files/pdf-versions/2022/5/2/1653392517/violence-against-women-domestic-abuse-and-sexual-violence-strategy-2022-2026.pdf (accessed 23 June 2022).

Welsh Government (2022c), *Code of Practice Guide to tackling Modern Slavery and Human Rights Abuses*. February 2022. Cardiff: Welsh Government, https://gov.wales/sites/default/files/publications/2022-04/code-of-practice-guide-to-tackling-modern-slavery-and-human-rights-abuses-2022_0.pdf (accessed 8 March 2022).

Welsh Government and HM Prison and Probation Service in Wales (2017), *A Framework to support positive change for those at risk of offending in Wales: 2018–2023*. April 2017. Cardiff: Welsh Government, https://gov.wales/sites/default/files/publications/2019-03/framework-to-support-positive-change-for-those-at-risk-of-offending.pdf (accessed 30 December 2020).

Welsh Government, HM Prison and Probation Service in Wales, Health Boards and Public Health Wales (2019), *Partnership Agreement for Prison Health in Wales*. Cardiff: Welsh Government, https://phw.nhs.wales/topics/prison-health-in-wales/partnership-agreement-english/ (accessed 16 March 2021).

Welsh Government and Ministry of Justice (2019a), *Female Offending Blueprint for Wales*. May 2019. Cardiff: Welsh Government and Public Health Wales, https://gov.wales/sites/default/files/publications/2019-05/female-offending-blueprint_3.pdf (accessed 11 January 2021).

Welsh Government and Ministry of Justice (2019b), *Youth Justice Blueprint for Wales*. May 2019. Cardiff: Welsh Government, https://gov.wales/sites/default/files/publications/2019-05/youth-justice-blueprint_0.pdf (accessed 11 January 2021).

Welsh Government and Youth Justice Board (2004), *All Wales Youth Offending Strategy*. Cardiff: Welsh Government.

Welsh Government and Youth Justice Board (2014), *Children and Young People First*. July 2014. Cardiff: Welsh Government, https://www.gov.uk/government/uploads/system/uploads/attachment_data/file/374572/Youth_Justice_Strategy_English.PDF (accessed 15 January 2020).

Welsh Labour (2021), *Moving Wales Forward*. Welsh Labour Manifesto 2021. Cardiff: Welsh Labour, https://movingforward.wales/documents/WEB-14542_21-Welsh-Labour-Manifesto_A5.pdf (accessed 26 November 2021).

Welsh Language Commissioner (2017), *Investigation under section 17 of the Welsh Language Act 1993 – National Offender Management Service*. Reference 48, June 2017. Cardiff: Welsh Language Commissioner.

Welsh Language Commissioner (2018), *The Welsh language in prisons: A review of the rights and experiences of Welsh speaking prisoners*. December 2018. Cardiff: Welsh Language Commissioner.

White, Hannah (2015), *Parliamentary Scrutiny of Government*. Institute for Government. January 2015. London: Institute for Government, https://www.instituteforgovernment.org.uk/sites/default/files/publications/Parliamentary%20scrutiny%20briefing%20note%20final.pdf (accessed 11 May 2020).

White, Mark (2020), 'Coronavirus: Govt facing court over COVID-19 with prison system facing "catastrophe"'. Sky News, 24 April 2020, *https://news.sky.com/story/coronavirus-govt-facing-court-over-covid-19-with-prison-system-facing-catastrophe-11978233* (accessed 12 May 2020).

Williams, John L. (2021), *Bloody Valentine: The story of Britain's worst miscarriage of justice*. Harpenden: No Exit Press.

Williams, Kim, Vea Papadopoulou and Natalie Booth (2012a), *Prisoners' childhood and family backgrounds: Results from the Surveying Prisoner Crime Reduction (SPCR) longitudinal cohort study of prisoners*. Ministry of Justice Research Series. 4/12 March 2012, *https://assets.publishing.service.gov.uk/government/uploads/system/uploads/attachment_data/file/278837/prisoners-childhood-family-backgrounds.pdf* (accessed 16 June 2021).

Williams, Kim, Jennifer Poyser and Kathryn Hopkins (2012b), *Accommodation, homelessness and reoffending of prisoners: Results from the Surveying Prisoner Crime Reduction (SPCR) survey*. London: Ministry of Justice, *https://assets.publishing.service.gov.uk/government/uploads/system/uploads/attachment_data/file/278806/homelessness-reoffending-prisoners.pdf* (accessed 16 June 2021).

Wooff, Andrew (2015), 'Relationships and responses: Policing anti-social behaviour in rural Scotland'. *Journal of Rural Studies*, 39: 287–95.

Woolf, Lord (1991), *Prison Disturbances April 1990*. Report of an Inquiry by The Rt Hon Lord Justice Woolf and His Honour Judge Stephen Tumin. February 1991. London: Stationary Office.

Wyn Jones, Richard (2008), 'Devolution: The Next Step'. *Planet: The Welsh Internationalist*. Published in two parts: 188 (March/April), 38–44; 'Devolution: The Long and Winding Road', 189 (June/July), 6–11.

Wyn Jones, Richard and Roger Scully (2012), *Wales Says Yes: Devolution and the 2011 Welsh Referendum*. Cardiff: University of Wales Press.

Youth Custody Service (2020), *Youth Custody Data*. Table 2.10: Region of YOT. London: Youth Custody Service, *https://www.gov.uk/government/statistics/youth-custody-data* (accessed 15 December 2021).

Youth Justice Board for England and Wales (2011), *Youth justice annual statistics: 2009 to 2010* [workload tables]. Average under 18 custody population by region of origin and establishment, 2009/10. London: Youth Justice Board, *https://www.gov.uk/government/statistics/youth-justice-annual-statistics-2009-2010* (accessed 15 December 2021).

Youth Justice Board for England and Wales (2019a), *Written evidence submission to the National Assembly for Wales' Children, Young People and Education Committee: Inquiry into Children's rights in Wales.* London: Youth Justice Board, *https://business.senedd.wales/documents/s94640/CRW%2003%20 Youth%20Justice%20Board.pdf* (accessed 10 December 2021).

Youth Justice Board for England and Wales (2019b), *Written evidence submission to the Senedd's Equality, Local Government and Communities Committee inquiry into Voting Rights for Prisoners.* London: Youth Justice Board, *https://business.senedd.wales/documents/s82663/VRP04%20-%20 Youth%20Justice%20Board.pdf* (accessed 16 September 2020).

Youth Justice Board for England and Wales (2021a), *Youth justice annual statistics: 2018 to 2019* [supplementary tables]. Table 7.19: Average monthly youth custody population by region of home YOT and sex (under 18s only), year ending March 2020. London: Youth Justice Board, *https://www.gov.uk/government/statistics/youth-justice-statistics-2019-to-2020* (accessed 10 December 2021).

Youth Justice Board for England and Wales (2021b), *Youth justice annual statistics: 2018 to 2019* [supplementary tables]. Table 7.20: Average monthly youth custody population by region of home YOT and ethnicity (under 18s only), years ending March 2012 to 2019. London: Youth Justice Board, *https://www.gov.uk/government/statistics/youth-justice-statistics-2019-to-2020* (accessed 10 December 2021).

Zellick, Graham (1975), 'Prisoners and the Law', in Seán McConville (ed.), *The Use of Imprisonment: Essays in the Changing State of English Penal Policy.* London: Routledge and Kegan Paul, pp. 1–16.

# INDEX

Aberystwyth 21, 194f
Academics 2, 53, 103, 155, 182–3, 187–8
Accountability (including democratic accountability) 3, 10–11, 15–16, 141–66, 170–1, 184, 201f, 206, 209
Acts of Union 183
Administrative devolution 8, 58, 64–7, 70–1, 81, 179, 199f
Administrative justice (Wales) 192f, 203f
Adverse Childhood Experiences (ACEs) 49, 100, 106–7, 133, 198f, 202f
Advisory Board on Justices of the Peace 58
Advisory Panel on Substance Misuse 67
All Wales Anti-social Behaviour Co-ordinators Group 67
*All Wales Youth Offending Strategy* 67, 96, 106
Andrews, Leighton 203f
Anglesey *see* Ynys Môn

Anti-social behaviour 23–4, 67
Apprenticeship Levy 128, 136–9
Arrests 22, 28–9, 43, 47, 49, 52
Asian individuals (treatment of in justice system) 29, 36, 52, 196f, 197f
Assembly Member(s) *see* Member(s) of the Senedd
Auditor General for Wales 144
Austerity 25–7, 57, 130, 203f, 205f
Average custodial sentence length (ACSL) 35–7, 197f, 198f

Bangor 194f
Beaumaris 1
Betsi Cadwaladr University Health Board 202f
Bevan, Aneurin 15, 85, 103, 112, 114
Bingham, (Lord) Thomas 194f
Birmingham 75, 78–9, 147
Black, Asian and minority ethnic (BAME) individuals (treatment of in justice system) 29–30, 34–6, 50, 52, 196f

Black individuals (treatment of in justice system) 29, 36, 52, 196f, 197f
Blair, Tony 193f
Body corporate 5
Boughrood (Powys) 194f
Brewster, David 111
Bristol 122
British Crime Survey 195f
British Transport Police 26
Brookman, Fiona 2
Brown, Gordon 209f
Bryant, Chris 177
Business Rates *see* National Non-Domestic Rates

Cabinet Secretary for Communities and Children (Welsh Government) 75, 104
Cairns, Alun 88
Cambridgeshire 45
Cardiff 128, 137, 139, 164, 181, 200f
Cardiff Bay 140, 155
Cardiff Crown Court 196f
Cardiff Metropolitan University 194f
Cardiff Probation Service 196f
Cardiff University 194f
*see also* Wales Governance Centre
Care Inspectorate Wales 145
Caro, Robert 14, 55, 81, 84
Cathays Park 161, 183
Centralisation of England and Wales criminal justice institutions 14, 57–65, 168
*see also* London
Centre for Justice Innovation 41
Chief Crown Prosecutor 30
Chief Fire and Rescue Adviser and Inspector for Wales 144

Children (in criminal justice system) T2.1, 25, 46, 48–52, F2.13, F2.14, 67–8, 88, 96, T4.1, 104–7, T6.1, 158, 195f, 198f
Age of criminal responsibility 52
*see also* Youth Justice
*Children and Young People First* 67
Civil Nuclear Constabulary 26–7
Civil service 12, 103, 201f
Churn among 70, 76–7, 168
Concentration of senior grades in London 63–4, 80, 200f
Clarke, Peter 50
College of Policing 145
Commission on Justice in Wales *see* Thomas Commission
Committee for Administrative Justice and Tribunals Wales 203f
Community Justice Cymru 67
Community Rehabilitation Companies (CRCs) 123, 125, 146
*see also* Wales CRC
Community safety partnerships 87
Community sentences (non-custodial) 34, 41–3, F2.10
*see also* Sentencing
Conducted Energy Device (TASER) 30, 196f
Conferred powers (model of legislative devolution) 180
Conservative Party, The 172, 177, 186
Constitution and Legislative Affairs Committee *see* Legislation, Justice and Constitution Committee
Constitution Unit (University College of London) 183, 193f
Convictions 30–2, F2.5, 53
Corston, Jean (Baroness), including Corston report 46–7

County Durham 45
Courts 2, M2.1, 32, 24, 41–2, 53, T3.1, 90–1, T4.1, 177, 189, 191f, 196f
  closure of 32, 90, 104, 177, 203f
  Court of Great Session 191f
Covid (COVID-19) pandemic, including coronavirus regulations 14, 85, 102, 126, 147, 150, 202f, 209f
Crime F2.1, T2.1, 22–6, 33–4, 71, 78–81, 86–90, T4.1, 110, 192f, 193f, 195f, 201–2f, 206f
Crime and Disorder Act (1998) 87, 192f
Crime Survey of England and Wales (CSEW) 23–4, 28, 30
Criminal Injuries Compensation Authority 58, T3.1, 200f
Criminal Justice Act (1982) 144
Criminal Justice Act (1991) 144
Criminal Justice Act (2003) 87
Criminal Justice Board for Wales, including Wales Criminal Justice Board 67–8
Criminal Justice Joint Inspection 144
Crown Dependencies 4
Crown Prosecution Service (CPS) 30, T3.1, 64, 206f
  CPS Cymru-Wales 30, T3.1, 64
  CPS Direct 200f
Custodial sentences *see* Sentencing

Dehaghani, Roxanna 17
Delineating Wales 9
  *see also* Rawlings, Richard
Democratic accountability
  *see* Accountability
Department of Work and Pensions 58, T3.1
de Smith, S. A. 18

Devolution of justice 16–18, 172–88
  Arguments against (for Wales) 172–9
  To English Mayors 173
  *see also* Northern Ireland (devolution of justice to)
Devolved institutions (Welsh) *see* Senedd and Welsh Government
Dick, Cressida 25
Distances (as issue in the Welsh criminal justice system) 32, 38, 45–6, 51, 108–9, 197–8f122, 177
  For female prisoners 45–6, 197–8f
Draft Wales Bill 181
'Dragonisation' 74, 105, 118, 169
Drakeford, Mark 48, 108
Drug consumption rooms *see* Safe injecting rooms
Dyfed-Powys Police 26, 205f

*Emergence of Penal Policy, The* 20
*Encyclopaedia Britannica* 21
England (priority given to crime in its urban areas) 56, 71, 78–80
England and Wales judiciary 90, 182
England and Wales legal jurisdiction 3, 6, 8, 10, 19, 90, 113, 165, 167, 181, 183, 192f
English model (of sentencing) 20
English parole scheme 20
English penal policy 20
English policing practices 20
English prison system 20
English probation service 20
English values 20
Estyn 144–5
Ethnicity 29–30, 34–6, 50, 52, 196f
Evans, Chris 177–8
Equality Act (2006) 196f

Equality Act 2010 (Statutory Duties) (Wales) Regulations 2011, The 35
Equality and Human Rights Commission (Welsh Committee) 196f
Executive devolution 4–5, 8–9

Feilzer, Martina 2
*Female Offender Strategy* 72–3
Female Prison(s) 37, 44–7
Finnane, Mark 20
Flintshire Youth Services 135
Frazer, Lucy QC 47
Freedom of Information (requests) 13, 21, 41, 155–6
Freedom of Information Act (2000) 36, 53, 194f, 195f

G4S Care and Justice Ltd 37, 91, 93, 198f
Gardner, David 192
Garland, David 193f
Gauke, David 149
George, Manon 194f
Goddard, (Lord) Rayner 193f
Goldson, Barry 57
Government and Laws of Wales Bill (2016) 183–4
Government of Wales Act (1998) 11
Government of Wales Act (2006) 5–6, 157, 180, 199f, 202f
Gramsci, Antonio 186
Grayling, Chris 41, 65, 203f
Greater Manchester Combined Authority 173
*see also* Manchester
Guernsey 178
Gwent Police 26, 150, 205–6f, 207f
Gwynedd and Ynys Môn Youth Justice Services 135

Hanson, David 93, T4.1
Hardwick, Nick 39
Harwich 2
Hayward, Will 208f
Health and Safety Executive 58, T3.1
Health Board(s) 91–2, 192f, 202f
*see also* Betsi Cadwaladr University Health Board and Hywel Dda University Health Board
Health Inspectorate Wales 206f
Her Majesty's Courts and Tribunals Service (HMCTS), including HMCTS Wales 64, 91, 173, 203f
Her Majesty's Crown Prosecution Service Inspectorate (HMCPSI) 206f
Her Majesty's Inspectorate of Constabulary 144
Her Majesty's Inspectorate of Constabulary and Fire and Rescue Services (HMICFRS) 28, T3.1, 144
Hillside Secure Children's Home 50, 198f
Housing (Wales) Act (2014) 119
HM Chief Inspector of Prisons 39, 50, 75, 144, 148
HM Inspectorate of Prisons 40, 50–1, T3.1, 118, 121, 143, 145, 148–9, 152, 165, 171, 204f, 206–7
HM Inspectorate of Probation 41, T3.1, 143–7, 152, 165, 171, 204f
HM Prison and Probation Service (HMPPS) 37, 58, 66, 72, 88, 91
HMPPS Wales 64, 66, 67–9, 88, 92
HMP Altcourse 38, 118, 124, 204–5f
HMP Berwyn 37, T2.3, 38, 40, 47, 93, 102, 202f, 203f, 204f

# INDEX

HMP Cardiff  37, T2.3, 93, 148, 194f, 196f, 207f
HMP Eastwood Park  44, 95
HMP Low Newton  45
HMP Parc  37–8, T2.3, 38, 91, 93, 147, 198f, 207f
  *see also* HMYOI Parc
HMP Peterborough  45
HMP Send  45
HMP Stoke Heath  40
HMP Styal  58, 60
HMP Usk and Prescoed  37, T2.3, 93, T4.1
HMYOI Hindley  198f
HMYOI Parc  T2.3, 50–1, 198f
HMYOI Werrington  198f
Holloway, Katy  2
Holyhead  2
Holyrood (Scottish Parliament)  160
Home Affairs Committee *see* House of Commons Home Affairs Committee
Home Office  6, 27, 57–8, T3.1, 63–4, 69, 71, 73, 76, 78, 88–91, 111, 129, 131–2, 136–8, 144–5, 149, 158, 163–4, 171, 173, 192f, 197–8f, 199f, 200f, 201f, 204f, 206f
  Home Office Team in Wales  64
  Police Grant  129–30
  Regional Crime Reduction Director in Wales  195f
  *see also* Wales Home Office Advisory Group
Home Secretary  57, 130
Homeless Persons (Priority Need) (Wales) Order (2001)  117, 121
Hood, Roger  20
House of Commons Home Affairs Committee  25, 149–50, 157, 207f

House of Commons Justice Committee  14, 41, 149
House of Commons Public Administration and Constitution Affairs Committee  76
House of Commons Welsh Affairs Committee  38–9, 151, 157, 165, 182, 197–8f, 207f, 206f
Housing Act (Wales) (2014)  94, 119–20
Housing provision for prison leavers  95, 115–39, 148, 175, 178, 203f, 207f
Howard, Michael  65
Howard League of Penal Reform  143, 160
Howard League Scotland  160
Humphreys, Caroline  122
Hywel Dda University Health Board  205f

Imprisonment rates  F2.7, 36, F2.9, 42, F2.12, 197f
Independent Advisory Panel on Deaths in Custody  T3.1, 206f
Independent Office for Police Conduct  T3.1, 145, 199f, 206f
Integrated Drug Treatment System (IDTS)  204f, 206–7f
Integrated Offender Management (IOM) Cymru Board  67–9
Integrated Offender Management Cymru Women's Pathfinder project  47
Intergovernmental Relations (IGR)  66, 139
Institute for Government  63, 76

Johnston, Ian  207f
*Joining Together in Wales*  68

Jones, Carwyn 184, 203f
Jones, David 40, 174, 176
Jones, Robert 12, 111
Joseph Rowntree Foundation 117
Judicial Appointments Commission T3.1, 199f
*Justice at the Jagged Edge in Wales* 13
Justice Devolution Team (Ministry of Justice) 64
Justice in Wales Strategy Group 67
*Justice in Wales Working Group* 155
Justice Policy Division (Welsh Government) 97, T4.1, 203f
Justice Secretary, including Secretary of State for Justice 41, 57, 76–7, 148–9, 203f

King, Roy 2

Labour Party 93, 172, 180, 185–6
   Election Manifesto (2017) 184
   Election Manifesto (2019) 185
   *see also* New Labour, Welsh Labour and Welsh Labour MPs
Lammy, David, including Lammy Review 34–5, 196f
Law Commission T3.1
   Law Commission Wales Advisory Committee 199f
Laws in Wales Acts (1536 and 1542) 183
Leeds 201f
Legal aid 32, T3.1, 90, 196f
Legal industry (Wales) 76
Legislation, Justice and Constitution Committee T6.1, 154, 163, 208f, 209f
Legislative devolution 5, 9–10, 180
Levi, Michael 2
Lewis, Brandon 76

Licensing Act 112
Liverpool 38, T3.1, 78, 118, 125
Local Authorities 87, T4.1, 117–27, 132, 135, 158, 192
London 14, 56, T3.1, 63–5, 72–5, 78–81, 111, 116, 128, 131, 137, 139, 142, 160, 168, 173, 176, 179, 181, 184, 200f, 201f
Lord Chancellor 57, 199f, 203f
Lord Chief Justice of England (and Wales) 19, 184, 186, 192f, 193f, 209f

Madoc-Jones, Iolo 124
Magistrates courts M2.1, 32, 34, 196f
Maguire, Michael 2
Malthouse, Kit 204f
Manchester 56, T3.1, 75, 78–9, 131, 173, 198f
Marijuana 110
May, Theresa 65
Member(s) of the Senedd (MS), including Assembly Member(s) (AM) 155–6, 158, 160–2
Mental Health Act (1983) 87
*Mental Health Crisis Care Concordat* 87
Merseyside 78
Metropolitan Police 25
MI5 58
Middlesbrough 2
Milford Haven 2
Ministry of Defence Police 26
Ministry of Justice 12, 32–6, 41, 46–7, 49, 58, T3.1, 63–4, 67–88, 94–6, T4.1, 105–6, 117, 126, 135–6, 149, 155–6, 163, 171, 174, 177, 181, 193f, 194f, 196f, 197f, 199f, 200f, 201f, 205f, 209f
   Justice Devolution Team 64

Mixed ethnic background individuals (treatment of in justice system) 29, 36, 196f
Modern Slavery, including Modern Slavery Act (2015) 89, T.4.1
Montesquieu (Charles Louis de Secondat) 4
Morgan, Barry 199f

Napier, Carmel 207f
Nason, Sarah 192f
National Assembly for Wales, The 4–5, 8, 86, 146, 157, 161, 180–2, 192f, 202f, 208f
  *see also* Senedd, Welsh legislature and Welsh parliament
National Association of Probation Officers (NAPO) 161
National Crime Agency 26–7, T3.1, 89, 195f
National Non-Domestic Rates (or 'Business Rates') 86, 129
National Offender Management Service (NOMS) 64–5, 197f
  NOMS Cymru 64–5, 68, 108
National Police Chiefs' Council 89, 111
National Probation Service (NPS) 123, 158
National Probation Service Wales 89, 94
*National Rough Sleeper Count Survey* 126
Neath 50
'Necessity Tests' 181–2
New Labour 22, 57, 71, 113, 193f, 199f
  *see also* Labour Party, Welsh Labour and Welsh Labour MPs

New Public Management 57, 81
Newman, Daniel 17
North Wales Police 26, 206f
North Wales Resettlement Unit 204–5f
North-east England 201f
North-west England 201f
  Devolution of justice to 191–2f, 209f
Northern Ireland 4, 8, T3.1, 80, 133, 151, 154, 173, 180, 191–2f, 200f, 202f
Northern Ireland Justice Minister 153
Novus Cambria 93, 203f

Office of National Statistics 24
Ofsted 74
Open University 194f
Operation TARIAN 134, 206f

Parliamentary Constituency Act (2020) 207f
Patel, Priti 65
Petty France 73, 201f
Philp, Chris 174–6, 178, 209f
Plaid Cymru 172
Police Allocation Formula 130
Police and Crime Commissioner(s) 86, 88–9, T.4.1, 110, 129–36, 150, 173, 207f
Police and Justice Act 2006 144
Police Community Support Officers (PCSOs) 27–8, F2.3, 87, 104, 131–2
Police dog(s) 30
Police Force(s) 15, 22, 25, T2.2, 30, 78, 87–9, 92, 115, 127–39, 145–6, 202, 205–6f
  Funding arrangements for Welsh forces 127–39

Impact of mental health crisis on work of 92, 132, 205–6f
Police Officers F2.2, 27–28, 195f
  *see also* Police Community Support Officers (PCSOs)
Police Precept 86, 129–31, 134
Police Settlement 86
*Policing for the future* 150
Policing Partnership Board for Wales (also Policing Board for Wales) 67, 88, 97
Policy-making 17, 44, 56, 65–6, 71–2, 76, 81, 84, 98, 103, 110, 116, 127–9, 140–1, 148, 150, 163, 187
  Evidence based 15, 57, 65, 75, 80, 84, 94–5, 103–4, 106, 109, 112–16, 118, 168–9, 187
  Joined-up 9, 15
Portugal 197f
Possession of Weapons (offences) T2.2, 33, 40, 43
Poverty T4.1, 187, 195f
Pre-sentencing reports 41–2
'Preventative duty' 123–7
'Priority need' 117–26, 205f
Pritchard, Huw 192f
Prison(s) 32–40, 43–7, 49, 71–2, 91–3, 149–50, 194f, 196f, 197f, 198f, 205f, 206–7f
  Education in 92–3, 102–3
  Healthcare in Wales 92–3, T4.1, 102–3, 202f, 209f
  Mental health crisis in 44–6, 92
  Prison estate T2.3, M2.2
  Prison population rates F2.6, F2.7, F2.8, F2.9, F1.12
  Prisoner voting policy 105, T6.1, 161
  Through the Gate services for 93–5

Welsh prisons T2.3
Prison and Probation Ombudsman T3.1, 206f
Prison Health and Social Care Oversight Group 92
Prison Link Cymru 205f
Prison Reform Trust 160
*Prison Safety and Reform White Paper* 72
Prisons Act (1952) 92
*Prisons Under Protest* 20
Probation 41–3, T3.1, T4.1, 144, 146–8
  Rates F2.9, F2.11
  UK Government's privatisation of 123–5
Prosecutions 30–1
Public Health England 74
Public Health Wales 91, 150
Public Health (Minimum Price for Alcohol) Wales Act (2018) 204f
Public order offences 22, T2.2, 43
Public service board (PSBs) 87–8
Public transport 32

Race 29–30, 34–6, 50, 52, 196f
Radzinowicz, Leon 20
*Raising the Standard* (mental health strategy) 92
Rawlings, Richard 8–9, 11
Raynor, Peter 2
Reducing Re-offending by Ex-prisoners 117
Reducing Re-offending National Action Plan 192–3f
Rees, Jenny 208f
Regulation of Drugs and Alcohol 109
Reoffending, including reoffending rates 41–3, 117–18, 175, 197f, 205f

Resettlement and Rehabilitation T2.3, 38, 40, 44, T4.1, 108, 124–5, 193f, 205f
Resettlement Prison(s) 125, 205f
Reserved powers (model of legislative devolution) 5–6, 9, 80, 180–1
Revenue Support Grant 86, 129
Rhyl 146
Richard Commission 10, 193f
Ruthin 1

S4C 207f
Safe injecting rooms, including Drug consumption rooms, Safe drug injecting facility 109–20, 204f
Safer Communities Fund 96
Sasse, Tom 201f
Scraton, Phil 20
Scotland 4, 6, 8, T3.1, 63, 80, 105, 133, 160, 173, 180, 191–2f, 200f, 204f
Scotland Act (1998) 6
Scottish Cabinet Secretary for Justice 153
Scottish Law Commission 180
Scottish Parliament *see* Holyrood
Scrutiny 141–66, 171, 206f, 209f
Secondary legislation 5, T4.1
Secretary of State for Justice *see* Justice Secretary
Secretary of State for Wales 40, 88, 152, 174
Secure Schools (Welsh Government objection to) 75–6, 104–5
Select Committee on Welsh Affairs *see* House of Commons Committee on Welsh Affairs
Self-rule 6
*see also* Shared rule

Senedd 4–6, 90, T4.1, 102, 110, 152–66, 171, 175, 180, 183–4, 192f, 196f, 201f, 202f, 208f
  Business Committee 208f
  Health, Social Care and Sport Committee T6.1, 194f
  Petitions Committee 208f
  Senedd/National Assembly Committees 153, T6.1, 156–9, 161–3, 171, 208f
  *see also* National Assembly for Wales
Sentences, including Custodial sentences 32–49, F2.6, F2.10, 101, 106, 109, 125, 197f, 198f
Sentencing guidelines 106, 109
*Serious and Organised Crime* (strategy) 73, 201f
Serious Fraud Office T3.1, 206f
*Serious Violence Strategy* 73, 78–9
Separate legal jurisdiction for Wales 176, 179–85
  *see also* Distinct justice jurisdiction for Wales
Shared rule 6
  *see also* Self-rule
Shelter Cymru 120, 126, 205f
Silk Commission 174–5, 181
Social Exclusion Unit (UK Government) 46, 117
Social policy 55, 66, 84, 97, 103, 108, 184, 192f
Social Services and Wellbeing Act 75
South Wales Police 26, 92
South-west England 122
Spain 197f
Speaker's Conference (1919–20) 179
Sport (Welsh) 1
Spurr, Michael 178
*Statistics on Ethnicity and the Criminal Justice System* 35

Stirling, Tamsin 122
Straw, Jack 65
Substance Misuse 67, 85, 88–90, 93, 95, 104, 109, 175
Supreme Court (UK) T3.1, 180, 182, 199–200f
Surrey 45
Swansea 1, T3.1, 93, T4.1, 148–9, 194f, 207f

*Tackling drugs to build a better Britain strategy* 90
*Tackling Substance Misuse in Wales* 90
'Tartanisation' 105
Taylor, Charlie 75
Taylormade Medical Services 202f
Thames, River 155
Theft T2.2, 43
Thomas, (Lord) John, of Cwmgiedd 184
Thomas Commission (including Commission on Justice in Wales) 3, 13, 185
'Through the Gate' Services 85–6, 93–5, 108, 123–6
*Times, The* (London) 20
Tonry, Michael 193f
Toughness (performative) 32, 57, 81, 84, 106, 164, 168, 193f
*Transforming Rehabilitation* 94, 124–5, 147
Trinity Saint David (University of Wales) 194f

UK Government, including Whitehall 4, 6–8, 21, 55–82, 90, 129–30, 140–1, 149, 157–9, 168, 180–3, 186
    Department of Communities and Local Government 134, 136
    Department of Education 134
    Department of Health and Social Care 134–5, 145
    UK Government's privatisation of 123–5
UK Parliament, including Westminster 6, 52, 88–9, 110, 141, 149–52, 165, 176
United Nations Convention on the Rights of the Child 48, 105
United Nations Convention on the Rights of the Child Monitoring Group 52
Universities (Wales) 2, 21, 187, 194f

Vara, Shailesh 203f
*Victim Strategy* 73
Victim Support Cymru 91
Violence against Women, Domestic Abuse and Sexual Violence (Wales) Act (2015) 89, 95, T4.1, 107–8, 150
    *National Training Framework* 89, 95, 107
Violent Crime/Offences 22, 53, 79, 168

Wales Act (2017) 5–6, 16, 86, 181, 183, 192f
Wales and Berwick Act (1746) 194f
Wales Anti-slavery Leadership Group 67, 89
Wales Association of Community Safety Officers 67
Wales CRC (Community Rehabilitation Company) 123–4
    *see also* Community Rehabilitation Company (CRC) and Working Links

# INDEX

Wales Criminal Justice Board *see* Criminal Justice Board for Wales
Wales Extremism and Counter Terrorism Unity 67, T4.1
Wales Home Office Advisory Group 67
Wales Governance Centre (Cardiff University) 13, 183, 192f
Wales Office, including Welsh Office and Office of the Secretary of State for Wales 152, 179
Wales Police Schools Programme 88, 134
Wales Youth Justice Advisory Panel 67, 96
Webb, Adrian 203f
Well-being of Future Generations (Wales) Act (2015) 87, 96
Welsh Ambulance Service 87
Welsh Assembly Government see Welsh Government
Welsh Centre for Crime and Social Justice 194f
Welsh Custodial Public Health Advisory Board (WCPHAB) 91
Welsh Government 83–114, T4.1, 116–27, 131–40, 179–87
   As policy taker in criminal justice 84–5, 116, 127–8, 140–2
   Cabinet Secretary for Communities and Children 75, 208f
   Community Safety Unit Research Team 195f
   Drug detoxification policy 148, 207f
   Health Minister T4.1, 134
   Housing services for prison leavers 117–27
   Location of criminal justice functions within 208f
   Objection to Secure Schools 75–6, 104–5
   Role in funding Welsh police forces 127–38
   Role in provision of education services in prisons 92–3, 102–3
   Role in provision of health care in prisons 92–3, T4.1, 102–3, 202f, 209f
   Substance Misuse Action Plan 89
   *Substance Misuse Delivery Plan* 95, 109
   Youth Justice 48–52, 68, 96–106, 135–6, 198f, 200–2f
Welsh Index of Deprivation 195f
Welsh judiciary 184
Welsh Labour MPs 11, 172, 177–8, 185–6
Welsh Labour Party 113, 184–5
Welsh language 2, T3.1, 91, 147, 150, 192f, 197f, 207f
   Welsh-speaking children in custody 51
   In prisons 38–40
Welsh Language Act (1967) 194f
Welsh Language Board 38
Welsh Language Commissioner 40, 91, 197f
Welsh legal jurisdiction 16, 175–6, 179–85
Welsh Local Government Association (WLGA) 119–23
Welsh Office *see* Wales Office
Welsh Parliament *see* Senedd
Welsh Safer Communities programme 87
Welsh Secretary *see* Secretary of State for Wales
West Midlands 78

Westminster *see* UK Parliament
Westminster model, including
   Westminster family 3–18, 116,
   140, 142, 170–6, 186, 191f, 206f,
   209f
White individuals (treatment of by
   justice system) 29, 35–6, 52, 196f,
   197f
Whitehall *see* UK Government
Women (in criminal justice system)
   43–7, 68, 89, 95–6, T.41, 107,
   145–6, 197–8f, 205f
   Growth of female prison
      population 47
   Imprisonment rate F2.12
   Proposed women's residential
      centre in Wales 47
   Self-harm among female prisoners
      46
   Self-inflicted deaths among female
      prisoners 46
   Separation of children from female
      prisoners 46
   Violence against Women,
      Domestic Abuse and Sexual
      Violence (Wales) Act (2015)
      89, 95, T4.1, 107–8, 150

Women's Turnaround Project 46
Woolf, (Lord) Harry 194f
Working Links 123–4
World Prison Population List 196f
Wrexham 37, 47, T3.1, 146, 162, 178,
   204f
   Site of super-prison 47, 162, 178,
      204f
   Wrexham Glyndŵr University 194f

Ynys Môn 178
Youth Custody Service 200–1f
Youth Justice 48–52, 57, T3.1, 67–8,
   75–6, 78, 96, T4.1, 104–6, 142,
   158, 198f, 200–1f, 206f
   Distinctive Welsh approach to
      48–52, 67–8, 75–6, 104–5,
      198f, 200–1f
   Treatment of children from
      BAME background at
      HMYOI Parc 50
*Youth Justice Blueprint* T4.1, 105, 106
Youth Justice Board 58, 68, 74, 96,
   104, 198f
   Youth Justice Board (YJB) Cymru
      T3.1, 64, 108, 200f
Youth Justice Service 135